TRAWNIKI GUARDS

FOOT SOLDIERS OF THE HOLOCAUST

JOSH BALDWIN

SCHIFFER MILITARY
4880 Lower Valley Road   Atglen, PA 19310

Designed by Justin Watkinson
Cover design by Jack Chappell
All images are in the public domain and are courtesy of the US Department of
Justice via the Freedom of Information Act.
Type set in Stoneburg Condensed / Minion Pro / Univers LT Std

ISBN: 978-0-7643-6069-5
Printed in India

Published by Schiffer Publishing, Ltd.
4880 Lower Valley Road
Atglen, PA 19310
Phone: (610) 593-1777; Fax: (610) 593-2002
E-mail: Info@schifferbooks.com
Web: www.schifferbooks.com

For our complete selection of fine books on this and related subjects, please visit
our website at www.schifferbooks.com. You may also write for a free catalog.

Schiffer Publishing's titles are available at special discounts for bulk purchases
for sales promotions or premiums. Special editions, including personalized
covers, corporate imprints, and excerpts, can be created in large quantities for
special needs. For more information, contact the publisher.

We are always looking for people to write books on new and related subjects. If
you have an idea for a book, please contact us at proposals@schifferbooks.com.

CONTENTS

Acknowledgments

When I first embarked on this research in the first decade of this century, it seemed like the amount of information available on the topic was fairly scant. It wasn't until I discovered the Archive of the US Holocaust Memorial Museum in Washington, DC, and the Freedom of Information Act through the US Department of Justice that I began to hit "pay dirt." This led me to other academic sources, and the rest, as they say, is history. My knowledge on the subject of the Trawniki guards has gone up exponentially as a result of intense scrutinization of the source materials now available.

I would like to thank the following people for their kind assistance in aiding me in completing this project: Dr. Peter Black, chair of the Office of the Senior Historian, Center for Advanced Holocaust Studies, US Holocaust Memorial Museum, Washington, DC; Dr. David Alan Rich, a lecturer in European history and visiting researcher at the Catholic University; Dr. Steven Coe, also a historian; the late Robert Kuwalek, who passed away in 2014 and had been the former director of the Memorial Museum at Belzec and a curator at the Majdanek State Museum; Dr. Dieter Pohl, former researcher at the Institute of Contemporary History in Munich, and currently a modern history professor at the University of Klagenfurt, Austria; Vadim Altskan, chief archivist at the US Holocaust Memorial Museum in Washington, DC; Agata Witkowska, who guided me through the city of Lublin and the sites of the former camps at Majdanek, Sobibor, and Belzec and translated several documents during my visit with her to the IPN Archive in Lublin; Lucais Sewell, who has translated many German documents into English for me; Michael James Melnyk, author of the book *The History of the Galician Division of the Waffen-SS*, for his ongoing support; Stuart Emmett, author of the book *Strafvollzugslager der SS und Polizei*, for his continuous encouragement; Wojtek Mazurek, an archeologist who corresponded with me and spoke with me in person as he worked at the site of the archeological excavation of the former site of the Sobibor death camp; and last and most of all, I want to give special thanks to my wife, Peggie, who has been patient with me; accompanied me on my trips to Poland, Germany, and Washington, DC; and initially gave me the idea of writing a book on this subject matter, never stopped encouraging me to complete it, and also helped me see it through to the end.

To my knowledge, there has never been a book-length treatment of this subject in the English language, and all of the above people have made it possible to now make that a reality.

Josh Baldwin, July 2018

Introduction

In the conclusion to his book *Belzec: Stepping Stone to Genocide*, author Robin O' Neal made the following comment:

> The history of the *Trawnikimänner* has yet to be told. The lack of resources by the archives has inhibited important indexing and filing of this material. So far we have only scratched the surface of this important aspect of Holocaust research. David Alan Rich's *Reinhardt's Footsoldiers* points the way but it is a chapter of history just waiting to be explored and written.

I hope that this study will close that gap in research that O'Neal spoke of over a decade ago when he wrote that statement. In the meantime, other researchers such as Dr. Peter Black as well as the aforementioned Dr. David Rich, who has since published additional articles, have facilitated a deeper look at this subject, and their research, occurring prior to or at the same time as my own, is part of what made the current volume possible. Please note, however, that this may not be the final word on the Trawniki guards, since that notion will not be possible until all remaining documents on the subject come into the public domain. No doubt scores of documents are still held in archives and have not yet been released. All such original materials are held in archives in the former Soviet Union.

This study intends to be a snapshot of the Trawniki guards, including biographical information on their nationalities, examples of what some of these men did in their civilian lives before the war (and, in some cases, after the war), and what ranks and duties some of them had while serving in the Red Army prior to being captured and going into service for the Germans. We shall also take a look at where and in what capacity these men served the Germans, examples of those who got into trouble while in German service, those who were injured or died while in German service, those who ran away for one reason or another during their German service, and some of those who were rewarded for a job well done in German service. The primary objective of this study is to achieve a better overall understanding of some of the men who carried out Hitler's "Final Solution"—the Trawniki Guards. "The Trawnikis were undoubtedly among the 'most notorious offenders of World War II.'"[1]

CHAPTER I

DUTIES, ASSIGNMENTS, AND CRIMES

As Holocaust scholar Dieter Pohl stated, "the Trawniki guards provided an unusual auxiliary force in that they generally did not possess a unified ideological or nationalist impetus to serve the Germans in this highly ideological function." Unlike other auxiliary units used by the Germans to kill Jews, the Trawniki guards were not always made up of local recruits, nor were the units always ethnically homogeneous.[1] In official German wartime documents, the Trawniki guards were referred to most often as *Wachmänner* (guards), *Trawniki Männer* (Trawniki men), *Fremdevolkische Wachmannschaften* (Foreign Guard Force), and *Hiwis* (volunteers).[2]

SS-Gruppenführer Odilo Globocnik had probably originally intended that the Trawniki guards be used as an auxiliary police force to support German occupation forces in the eastern territories (i.e., the Soviet Union).[3] Actually, this is part of the function that they served in eastern Poland. Globocnik's initial intention had probably been to use the Trawniki guard force to support German rule from the SS and police bases in the area. However, unexpected Soviet resistance on the Eastern Front and the changing priorities of the Nazi government with regard to occupied Poland caused the Trawniki guards to become linked with Operation "Reinhard." Sometime in 1941, members of Globocnik's staff had conceived a "total planning" for the SS and police bases in the Lublin District that had assumed that the Jews in the region would be cleared out.[4]

In late 1940, Himmler had ordered Globocnik to establish SS and police bases (SS und Polizei Stutzpunkte) in the conquered eastern territories in eastern Poland, and eventually the Soviet Union. Himmler had intended these bases to be "armed and industrialized agricultural complexes" in the "maintenance of order and the stabilization of political power" as the "extended arm of the German leadership."[5] In July 1941, to this end, Himmler appointed Globocnik as his "commissioner for the establishment of SS and police bases in the New Eastern Territory."[6] Therefore, from late 1941 to March 1942 (the duration of the time for which Globocnik held this position), the Trawniki guards were collectively referred to in German wartime documentation as "guard forces of the commissioner of the Reichsführer-SS and chief of the German police for the establishment of SS and police bases in the New Eastern Territory."[7] After March 1942, when Globocnik was simply referred to as the SS and police commander of the Lublin District, they were accordingly known as "guard forces of the SS and police commander of the Lublin District."[8]

The first recruits for Trawniki guard service arrived at the Trawniki training camp in September 1941.

SS-Hauptsturmführer Hofle was tasked by Globocnik to supervise all "foreign auxiliary units" in the Lublin District, and this would have included the Trawniki guards. Additionally, in October 1941, Globocnik appointed SS-Hauptsturmführer (later promoted to SS-Sturmbannführer) Karl Streibel to be commandant of the Trawniki training camp.[9]

Historian Dieter Pohl commented that it is in dispute whether the Soviet POWs actually volunteered for Trawniki service or were coerced into it. Regardless, most POWs were anxious enough to agree to anything in order to get released from their respective POW camps in order to survive.[10] Peter Black, chief historian at the US Holocaust Memorial Museum in Washington, DC, says that one cannot conclude that the Trawniki guards volunteered to commit mass murder. The conditions in the Soviet POW camps were so horrific that the men "had limited options." If they refused to cooperate, "they could be shot on the spot," at least until spring 1943. Helge Grabitz, the late Hamburg criminal prosecutor, also believed that the Trawnikis were "coerced." They volunteered in order "to escape certain death from starvation, freezing to death, or epidemics in the POW camps."

For the Soviet POWs recruited for Trawniki service in the spring of 1942 from among prisoners taken during the German campaign at Kerch in the Crimean region, they arrived in Trawniki via the POW transit camp (Dulag 123) in Dzhankoj, Crimea, and the POW camp in Rovno (Stalag 360). By this time, Soviet POWs were not in as much danger of dying from disease or starvation in POW camps as their fellow brethren had been in 1941 and earlier in 1942.[11] Thus, their motives for joining Trawniki service are not as clear as those of the earlier POW recruits.

Postwar testimonies of former Trawniki guards cannot reconcile whether or not the recruits understood exactly what type of duties they would be undertaking in Trawniki service at the time of their recruitment. Some said they had a vague idea that they would be guards for the SS or the German armed forces, while others said they were given no description at all, and still others had been given quite specific information: "We would serve in the struggle against partisans, to drive the Jews out of Polish cities and imprison them in German camps, and capture escapees from German camps."[12]

It is also unclear whether the later civilian recruits for Trawniki service were committed to the Nazi cause ideologically, or whether, like the earlier Soviet POWs, they were simply trying to survive the war. Some were enlisted into Trawniki service by their parents, who sought the potential benefits of working for the Germans—a paid salary for their sons and exemption from deportation to Germany for forced labor. Some were clearly recruited whether they liked it or not. In certain parts of the Galicia District, the Germans put out conscription calls via local town and village mayors that all men born between 1919 and 1923 (ages 20–24) were expected to sign up for Trawniki service.[13]

The Germans wrote up or typed up a personnel file (*Personalbogen*) for each Trawniki recruit. On it, the recruits provided personal biographical information, including name; birthplace; nationality; civilian occupation; prior military rank and branch of service (usually in the Red Army, although some had also served in the Polish army, the Romanian army, or the armies of the Baltic States); names of parents, wives, and children; and distinguishing marks or scars on the body (including tattoos). The file also included a thumbprint of the recruit, as well as a photograph of the recruit with his Trawniki service identification number (sometimes in his German-provided Trawniki service uniform, and sometimes still in his Red Army overcoat if the Trawniki service uniform had not yet been issued at the time the photograph was taken). The second page of the file contained information on the guard's assigned posts and any authorized leave or punishments while in service. A third page was signed and dated by the guard, swearing that he had no Jewish ancestry, that he had not been a member of the Communist Party or any of its affiliate organizations (especially the Communist Youth Organization, known as the "Komsomol"), and that he would remain loyal to Germany and his German service for the duration of the war. A fourth page was added to the file in May 1943, attesting to the fact that all Trawniki guards were to come under the jurisdiction of the German Orpo (abbreviated form of Ordnungspolizei) for all matters of discipline, and that for any crimes or disobedience committed in the line of duty that they would be tried before SS and police courts.[14]

In May 1943, German authorities increased the salary of the Trawniki guards, bringing their pay in line with that of the Wehrmacht and Waffen-SS. They were paid in Polish zloty. They received free rations, medical care, shelter, and uniforms, allowing them to spend all of their salary, if they wanted to, on leisure goods and services—alcohol, prostitutes, cigarettes, additional food, and local entertainment. They also received home leave of one to three weeks at a time (until no further leave was permitted as of January 1944). They were also provided family support by the Germans.[15]

Recruits at Trawniki training camp received anywhere from six weeks to six months of training depending on an individual's level of ability, their capacity to understand commands in German, and the need for manpower. Training included military drills and weapons handling with rifles, submachine guns, machine guns, and grenades, and the type of functions that the guards would conduct in ghettos and camps—police escort and guard duty.[16] All training was conducted in German, and the *Volksdeutsche* among the recruits translated those commands and instructions into the language that the recruits spoke, most often Ukrainian and Russian.

After the war, some former Trawniki guards described their training at Trawniki camp to Soviet authorities interrogating them. Examples include Eduard Chrupovich, who said that he was trained to "conduct roundups in population centers, how to perform arrests and searches, and the rules for escorting and guarding prisoners." Philip Babenko recalled "anti-Soviet training," "how to carry out roundups of partisans and Jews," and that guards such as himself were to be trained to become "executioners and punishers" in death camps. Ivan

Kondratenko recounted that he and other guards "were trained in the rules for guarding and escorting prisoners who were held in German concentration camps. The Germans instructed us that we were not to give the slightest quarter while guarding and escorting prisoners. For the slightest infractions, we were to shoot them without any warning."[17] In 1942, Trawniki guards still in training were deployed for deportation operations and shooting operations against Jewish communities in the rural areas south and east of Lublin.

"The arrival of new recruits paralleled the need for manpower as Operation 'Reinhard' developed and evolved." The fall 1941 recruitment coincided with the initial construction of the Belzec, Sobibor, and Treblinka death camps. The winter 1942 Soviet POW recruits arrived concurrently with preparations for the first major deportations from Lublin and Lvov. The summer 1942 recruits were deployed for the major Warsaw deportations of July–September 1942 and the Radom deportations in September–November 1942. The winter and spring 1943 civilian-recruiting drive was consistent with the need for manpower to guard Jewish laborers in the Operation Reinhard labor camps of Trawniki, Poniatowa, Budzyn, Krasnik, Radom, Janowska, Plaszow, and Treblinka I. The summer 1943 recruitment drive coincided with the peak period of operation of the Lublin labor camps associated with Operation Reinhard. The transfer of over 600 Trawniki guards to the concentration camp system in Germany in fall 1943 and the decision to liquidate the Jewish laborers at Majdanek, Trawniki, and Poniatowa in Operation "Harvest Festival" coincided with the liquidation or transfer of the Reinhard labor camps to the SS-WVHA.[18]

In January 1942, Globocnik recommended Streibel for the War Merit Cross 2nd Class with Swords for having successfully achieved the training of over 1,200 foreign guards at Trawniki training camp by early 1942. In March 1942, Streibel recommended, and Globocnik approved, that same award for another SS officer and twenty-one SS noncommissioned officers (NCOs) and enlistees for having participated in establishing the Trawniki training camp.[19]

In addition to Hofle's small administration office and Wirth's Inspectorate for SS Special Detachments, the Trawniki training camp was the third main center for managing and coordinating Operation Reinhard. The camp had three administrative offices. The camp administration was run by Streibel's deputy, a police NCO, Albert Drechsel, until 1943. Drechsel and his staff, along with some especially competent Trawniki guards, served as the main unit for the Trawniki guards at Trawniki Camp itself. Drechsel's office, known until 1942 as the "Staff company of the commissioner for the establishment of SS and police bases," processed the Trawniki recruits upon arrival at Trawniki camp, issued them their service identification numbers, maintained their personnel files, and kept track of each Trawniki guard's rank, leave, salary, and deployment to assignments. It probably also processed the paperwork for promotions and the awarding of medals and may have helped make decisions on deployments of the guards.[20]

Trawniki guard ranks were as follows:[21] *Wachmann*, private; *Oberwachmann*, private 1st class; *Rottenwachmann*, corporal; *Gruppenwachmann*, sergeant; *Zugwachmann*, sergeant major; and *Oberzugwachmann*, master sergeant.

As Operation Reinhard entered its busiest phase of mass murder in the summer of 1942, about 1,000 men served in Trawniki service in two battalions each, and as many as 1,500 more served at various other assignments throughout southern and eastern Poland. Thirty to fifty members of the SS and police led the Trawniki guards at Trawniki training camp. The commanders of the two battalions were SS-Untersturmführer Johann Schwarzenbacher and SS-Untersturmführer Willi Franz. SS officials from Globocnik's staff or police NCOs from the Orpo Lublin served as Trawniki company commanders. Trawniki guards who were promoted to the rank of *Gruppenwachmann* or *Zugwachmann*, especially the *Volksdeutsche*, served as squad and platoon commanders.[22] At least one and possibly two battalion administrative staffs existed. They probably were responsible for writing up duties for the individual Trawniki guard companies, maintaining status reports on training, obtaining supplies and weapons for Trawniki units, and making personnel deployment recommendations. Trawniki training camp also had a branch office of the Waffen-SS Garrison Administration Lublin, which financed Trawniki and all of its staff and personnel, including the guards themselves, managed construction contracts, and evaluated and shipped looted Jewish property and valuables.[23]

AN INTRODUCTION TO AKTION REINHARD

Most authors are in agreement that Globocnik received the authorization to initiate Operation Reinhard between late September and mid-October 1941.[24] The SS could not have implemented the "Final Solution" without assistance from the Trawniki guards, who provided needed manpower. The phase of the Final Solution carried out in the Lublin District and partly in the Warsaw District (in the case of Treblinka II) was known as Operation Reinhard (a.k.a. Aktion Reinhard, in German). The operation was managed by SS-Gruppenführer Odilo Globocnik, the senior SS and police commander of the Lublin District, and his staff. Deportations from the local ghettos to the death camps were managed by the Operation Reinhard HQ in Lublin, which was under the administration of one of Globocnik's deputies, SS-Hauptsturmführer Hermann Hofle.[25] The actual supervision of the three death camps, Belzec, Sobibor, and Treblinka II, was undertaken by SS-Hauptsturmführer Christian Wirth (later promoted to *SS-Sturmbannführer*), a Kripo (abbreviation for Kriminalpolizei) officer.

Scholars are still not sure exactly when and under what circumstances Operation Reinhard was implemented by the SS, but the first of the Reinhard death camps, Belzec, became functional in March 1942, and the other two camps, Sobibor and Treblinka II, by summer 1942. What is known is that Globocnik had put together his staff members for the operation after meeting with Reichsführer-SS Himmler on October 13, 1941.[26] Although "Reinhard" is best known for the deportation and mass murder of Jews, it had more-detailed objectives, as stated by its primary overseer, Globocnik: "resettlement" of Jewish populations (a euphemism for mass murder), the use of some Jews for slave labor to contribute to the German war effort, and the exploitation of material assets and property confiscated from the Jews who were "resettled." Globocnik and his staff, including the accountant, SS-Obersturmführer Georg Wippern, took possession of, and did an accounting of, the assets and valuables confiscated from the Jews deported to the camps, in cooperation with the SS-WVHA, which was headed by SS-Obergruppenführer Oswald Pohl. Wippern was head of the SS Garrison Administration in Lublin.[27]

Majdanek, also known as Lublin concentration camp, was part of Operation Reinhard. It served as a death camp in November and December 1942 to eliminate 24,000 Jews who might otherwise have been sent to Belzec to be killed; however, that camp had since ceased use of its gas chambers. Initially, the prisoners at Majdanek were to consist primarily of Soviet POWs, but by January 1942, about 80 percent of the prisoners were Jewish. The camp fulfilled one of the Operation Reinhard goals—that of exploiting Jewish forced labor.[28] Himmler had considered the idea of putting Majdanek under Globocnik's authority; however, by late 1941, he decided to give it to the jurisdiction of the SS-WVHA. An SS-Totenkopf guard battalion composed of Germans and *Volksdeutsche* from southeastern Europe guarded the camp's perimeter. While the Trawniki guards provided the bulk of the manpower guarding the Reinhard death camps of Sobibor, Belzec, and Treblinka II, as well as other camps in the Lublin and Warsaw Districts, they served at Majdanek only sporadically prior to late 1942. Two Trawniki guard companies served there with the SS-Totenkopf guard battalion from mid-November 1942 to early March 1943. An additional Trawniki guard squad of twenty-six men was also added on February 15, 1943. The Trawniki guard units at Majdanek participated in the late 1942 killing operation of Jews there.[29]

In a monthly report to the RSHA in January 1943, SS-Hauptsturmführer Hofle stated that 12,761 Jews had been admitted into Lublin in December 1942. Simultaneously, the number admitted to the death camps that month were

Belzec   0
Sobibor   515
Treblinka II 10,335

The 24,000 Jews sent to Majdanek at this time were to be killed on arrival.[30] Although Majdanek had gas chambers, the SS did not plan to use them for mass murder on the same scale as at Auschwitz-Birkenau or the Operation Reinhard death camps.[31]

At any given time, this was the arrangement of the Trawniki guard company, divided into three platoons, assigned to each of the Reinhard death camps: one platoon manned guard posts around the camp, one platoon handled incoming transports, and one platoon was on rest/off-duty. During a six-day period, each Trawniki guard rotated through three days of guard duty or killing duty.[32] The Trawniki guards formed a single or double cordon by the train-unloading ramp during the arrival of incoming transports. They also accompanied Jews from the undressing rooms to the gas chambers, digging up trees for the cremation of bodies and supervising the work Jews at the sorting barracks. The *Volksdeutsche* NCOs were very close to the SS in the Reinhard camps and were essentially deputized by them to carry out the extermination process. These overseers were given wide discretion by the camp leadership in their daily duties, including executions.[33] Throughout the entire period of genocide in all three Reinhard death camps, it was the *Volksdeutsche* Trawniki NCOs and the Trawniki guards, assisted by Jewish forced laborers, who carried out the extermination process from start to finish. The small group of German SS and police present in the camps acted only as supervisors.[34] Once the victims left the undressing barracks and entered the "tube," the Trawniki guards, supported by the Jewish work group, took over and were able to complete the whole extermination process with very little SS assistance.[35]

The Operation Reinhard death camps were torn down and trees were planted in their place to eliminate any evidence of the mass murder that had taken place. Trawniki guards guarded each site to keep away locals who came looking for Jewish valuables that they believed were buried in the ground at the former camps.[36] In an "after-action" report to Himmler once Operation Reinhard had been concluded, Globocnik had made reference to the Trawniki guards as "an auxiliary force known as the SS-*Wachmannschaften* [SS guard units]" that had been established to "exploit Jewish labor." Globocnik went on to mention their participation at each major deportation operation, during many local shooting operations, and as guards at the three Reinhard death camps.[37]

On the basis of a number of sources, Dr. Peter Black was able to identify approximately 777 Trawniki guards who had served at the Operation Reinhard death camps of Sobibor, Belzec, and Treblinka II (not including sixteen assigned to Sobibor in late 1943–early 1944 after it had already closed down). This accounted for about 16 percent of all Trawniki guards in German service at the time. The number, however, does not include two companies assigned to Majdanek in late 1942, when 24,000 Jews were murdered there, nor does it include the Trawniki guards who helped liquidate the remaining Jewish prisoners at Treblinka I and

Janowska, or those that brutally took part in clearing ghettos during deportation operations.[38] The breakdown of where those Jews were killed is as follows:[39]

Belzec: 434, 500
Sobibor: at least 167,000
Treblinka II: about 925,000
Majdanek: 24,000
Mass shooting operations (including Operation Harvest Festival): 200,000

On July 19, 1942, Himmler issued an order to the senior SS and police commander in Krakow, SS-Obergruppenführer Friedrich Wilhelm Kruger, that the resettlement of the entire Jewish population in central and eastern Poland was to be completed by the end of the year. Those unable to work were to be eliminated, and the rest were to be deported to camps. Operation Reinhard had claimed the lives of an estimated 1.7 million Jews (roughly one in four of all Holocaust victims during the war). In addition, the property and valuables confiscated from the murdered Jews were tallied up by the SS to a value of about 179 million reichsmarks (about $70 million in US money at the time, and roughly $750 million in US money in 2017).[40] In February 1944, Himmler told Pohl, head of the SS-WVHA, to clear Globocnik of responsibility for any wrongdoing that might have occurred during Operation Reinhard. This was in reference to all the Jewish property looted, some of which was not turned over to the proper German authorities in Berlin, but instead was personally pocketed by SS officials such as Globocnik, in Lublin, and by camp staff, including the Trawniki guards. The value of that which never reached the authorities in an official capacity will never be known.[41]

OTHER DUTIES

The Lublin POW camp of the Waffen-SS, though not formally converted into a concentration camp until February 23, 1943, came under the jurisdiction of the SS-WVHA when it was first established in November 1941, and functioned more or less as a concentration camp. The camp became known as Majdanek because it was located in the Lublin suburb of Majdan.[42] The last Trawniki guards left Majdanek no later than March 4, 1943.[43] In early 1943, the Majdanek camp staff experienced serious disciplinary problems with some of its Trawniki guards. As a result, in late February or March 1943, the entire Trawniki contingent was removed from the camp. There is no evidence of Trawniki guards serving there after that.[44]

Hofle deployed Trawniki guard detachments for ghetto-clearing operations throughout eastern Poland. His staff coordinated with the railway office, which provided the trains, and German Orpo units provided the manpower along with the Trawniki guards under the supervision of the security police and SD and local SS and police commanders (SSPFs). In such operations, Trawniki guards would provide cordon security and augment teams of Orpo and Jewish police who forced the Jews from their homes to the waiting trains for deportation.[45]

Trawniki guards helped carry out a major deportation from Lublin in March 1942. They also participated in at least one mass shooting of Jews in the woods outside Lublin in April 1942. Trawniki guards from Trawniki itself and from Treblinka I participated in deportations from the Warsaw Ghetto to Treblinka II from July to September 1942. This resulted in the deportation of 265,000 Jews and shooting of 25,000 within the ghetto. On April 19, 1943, a Trawniki guard battalion of about 350 men was deployed to help suppress the Warsaw Ghetto uprising.[46]

In September 1942, a Trawniki guard detachment deployed to Czestochowa in Radom District to aid the Schutzpolizei there in deporting 40,000 Jews to Treblinka II. They also took part in local shooting operations in the area. At least two Trawniki guard companies deployed to help suppress the Bialystok Ghetto uprising in August 1943. Trawniki guards helped liquidate the Lublin Ghetto and also deployed to several smaller ghettos and towns in the nearby countryside.[47] Trawniki guards helped liquidate the Lublin Ghetto in November 1942.[48]

Trawniki guards were essential in implementing the Operation Reinhard goal of exploiting Jewish labor. Globocnik wanted to improve the chaotic efforts to mobilize Jewish labor for his border fortification project along the German-Soviet border.[49] After July 1941, the SS company "DAW" (German Equipment Works) began investing funds in the construction site at Majdanek and in Globocnik's staff as commissioner for the establishment of SS and police bases. In the fall of 1941, funding was extended to the Trawniki camp to a special account for Operation Reinhard. Construction at the time began on Majdanek, with it initially intended to be a massive labor site to produce construction materials for the SS and police bases following the expected defeat of the Soviet Union.[50]

Determined to solve the "Jewish Question" in central and eastern Poland by the end of 1942, in October 1942 Himmler ordered the imprisonment of all Jewish laborers in concentration camps, to be assigned to the armaments industry. Globocnik's staff expanded the number of labor camps in the Lublin District and assigned Trawniki guards to them. Globocnik ordered that all Jews in the district be transferred to Majdanek.[51]

Globocnik intended four benefits to come out of the Reinhard labor camps:[52] compensation for the increased burden the war had imposed on German industry, reduction in the acute labor shortage in Germany and the release of German workers to focus on other purposes, the relocation of key industries damaged by or vulnerable to Allied bombing, and an increase in production in the war industry through tighter supervision.

In the fall of 1942, the SS and police formalized and expanded the Trawniki labor camp and established new labor camps at Poniatowa, Budzyn, and Krasnik. Jewish laborers working under Globocnik's Operation Reinhard were put under the auspices of the "GmbH" (Eastern Industry, Inc., a.k.a. Osti), which was established by Globocnik and the SS-WVHA in Lublin in March 1943.[53] By June 1943, GmbH had branch offices in Trawniki, Poniatowa, Budzyn, Majdanek, the Lipowa Street camp, and the Old Airfield camp in Lublin.[54] Jewish laborers in Trawniki worked at a storage depot that housed the clothing of Jews who had been deported to the Reinhard camps. Forty Jewish women sorted, washed, and mended the clothing. When Warsaw Ghetto Jews were deported to Trawniki camp in 1943, Jewish labor expanded. The Schultz Company, one of the two largest employers of Jews from the Warsaw Ghetto, signed a contract with Globocnik to relocate its fur-clothing plant to Trawniki camp, along with its 4,000 Jewish workers, as well as a brush-making plant and its 1,500 Jewish workers. In Trawniki, the company would produce winter uniforms and other items for the German armed forces.[55]

In late 1943, Streibel established a satellite training facility for Trawniki guards at Poniatowa camp. This included three or four Trawniki guard companies that included new recruits. The camp, located about 20 miles from Lublin, had been a camp for Soviet POWs, most of whom had died of starvation or were shot in 1941–1942. During an inspection of the site in summer 1942, SS-Obersturmführer Amon Goth, from Globocnik's staff, recommended the location for the construction of a Jewish labor camp. In late 1942, Globocnik selected Poniatowa as the location for the Warsaw Ghetto branch of the company W. C. Tobbens, which produced military uniforms and accoutrements. In January 1943, Globocnik signed a contract with Tobbens and 11,000 Jews from Warsaw to Poniatowa from February to May 1943. The Trawniki guard contingent at Poniatowa had been part of the unit sent to help suppress the Warsaw Ghetto uprising. Some Trawniki guards at Poniatowa had also been part of the last guard detachment at Belzec before it had closed.[56] Following several serious disciplinary problems, the initial Trawniki guard detachment at Poniatowa was rotated out and replaced by another one in December 1942. In February 1943, a number of the guards deserted, which resulted in the detachment being replaced by another one yet again. By summer 1943, a 500-man Trawniki battalion guarded the 12,000–16,000 Jews held in Poniatowa.[57]

Schutzpolizei Oberwachtmeister Karl Basener commanded the Lublin Detachment. Basener took his orders from Globocnik but was under the administrative and personnel jurisdiction of Streibel. In Lublin, the detachment guarded the Lipowa Street labor camp and the storage depots where the looted property of Reinhard victims was held, including the Old Airfield camp. By 1943, the Lublin Detachment had become a field headquarters of the Trawniki training camp, similar to Poniatowa, and housed three or four Trawniki companies.

The detachment also guarded local sawmills and estates and assisted the German police in maintaining law and order in the surrounding areas. A small contingent was also assigned to guard Jewish laborers at the Waffen-SS Troop Supply Depot in Lublin (TWL).[58] The Trawniki training camp had three training centers: Trawniki itself, Poniatowa, and the Lublin Detachment.[59]

In 1942, SS-Untersturmführer Amon Goth, from Globocnik's staff, established a camp of 2,000 workers near a "Heinkl" Aviation factory that was under construction. The factory was never completed; however, Jewish prisoners from Budzyn labor camp worked on the repair and production of aircraft wings for Heinkl. Trawniki guards were assigned to guard them.[60]

Fearful of further uprisings in eastern Poland following those in the Warsaw Ghetto, the Bialystok Ghetto, Treblinka II, and Sobibor, Himmler ordered Operation Harvest Festival, the liquidation of the Jewish laborers in Trawniki, Poniatowa, and Majdanek. On November 3–4, 1943, SS and police units shot up to 18,000 Jews at Majdanek, 12,000–14,000 at Poniatowa, and 4,000–6,000 at Trawniki. No Trawniki guards had been assigned to Majdanek by that time, the ones at Trawniki itself were confined to their barracks during the killings, but some of the ones at Poniatowa may have been assigned to guard the perimeter of the camp during the shootings.[61] Following the killings in Trawniki, the SS brought in a small Jewish labor force from Milejow to burn the bodies. Once the work was completed, the SS, assisted by Trawniki guards, shot them.[62]

Trawniki guards were assigned to the SS and police commander in Lvov District starting in January 1942, to serve as the guard force at the Janowska labor camp for Jews.[63] Some of these guards transferred to Sobibor when that camp opened up in May 1942.[64] Another Trawniki guard unit was sent there in May 1943 and was reinforced with another unit on September 25, 1943.[65] Unlike the Trawniki guards assigned to Trawniki itself and Poniatowa, the ones posted to Janowska actually participated in several mass killings at the camp. On May 25, 1943, 2,000 Jewish prisoners were shot into a pit.[66] The guard Nikolaj Skorokhod watched as his Trawniki superior Sergej Malov selected an attractive young Jewish girl from among the prisoners who were to be shot, took her to the bathroom, where he apparently raped her, then brought her out and shot her.[67] About 200–250 Jews had been assigned to dip the pits at the "piaski" ravine and were then shot.[68] Under the security police and SD Lvov, the Trawniki guards shot an additional 1,000 Jews in Janowska on October 25–26 1943, and up to another 3,000 on November 19, 1943, in the ravine behind the camp. The October and November 1943 killings were considered part of Operation Harvest Festival.[69] However, Dr. David Rich suggests that the killings were more likely linked to the fact that members of the Sonderkommando 1005 body-burning group at the camp had killed some of their police guards and escaped. This later apparently sparked a riot among camp prisoners in which a number of them escaped as well. The Trawniki guards in the five watchtowers reportedly opened fire with machine guns on the mass of running prisoners.[70] About eighty Jewish men were spared in order to exhume and burn bodies. Eight Trawniki guards watched over them, and the work lasted about three weeks. Then the guards shot them.[71]

A Trawniki guard company was assigned to Treblinka I starting in November 1941. About eighty guards remained at the camp until the advance of the Red Army into the area in July 1944, when the 300–700 Jewish prisoners held there were taken into the nearby forest and shot. The Trawniki guards carried out the killings under German SS supervision, then abandoned the camp.[72] The "Main Commission for the Investigation of Nazi Crimes in Poland" indicated that at least forty mass graves containing 6,500 bodies were found within a quarter mile of Treblinka I. During the camp's history, at least 10,000 people had been imprisoned there.[73]

In early 1942, two Trawniki guard detachments were assigned as auxiliaries to the commander of the security police and SD in Warsaw.[74] In September 1942, a Trawniki guard detachment was assigned to the Rozwadow labor camp for Jews who worked at a steel plant and construction sites under the jurisdiction of the SS and police commander in Krakow. In March 1943, about 200 Trawniki guards were assigned to the SSPF Krakow and served as guards at the Plaszow labor camp. In March and April 1943, this unit shot a large number of Jews who were considered no longer capable of work.[75]

On March 29, 1943, a 150-man Trawniki guard company was assigned to Auschwitz-Birkenau.[76]

In late 1941 and early 1942, Globocnik's staff organized a clothing depot near the Old Airfield Camp in Lublin. It was to receive, repair, and ship clothing and other personal property confiscated from Jews deported to the Reinhard death camps. Trawniki guards from the Lublin Detachment guarded the Jewish laborers from the Lipowa Street labor camp and Majdanek who worked at the depot. The SS transported currency, jewelry, and other valuables from the death camps to a storage cellar at the SS Garrison Administration Headquarters, next to the SSPF HQ Lublin, at Chopin Street #27. There was also a storage facility for such valuables at Trawniki itself and in Chelm.[77]

In 1942, the SS Garrison Administration Lublin established additional storage depots in Poniatowa, Zamosc, Rejowiec, and Lubartow. Trawniki guard detachments guarded each one.[78] On March 3, 1943, Globocnik sent a detailed report to Himmler with the total value of cash, precious stones, and other valuables confiscated from Jews during Operation Reinhard.[79] In September 1942, the SS-WVHA issued regulations regarding the shipping of property and valuables confiscated from the Jews in death camps.[80]

In his recommendation that Streibel be promoted to *SS-Sturmbannführer*, Globocnik pointed out that the Trawniki guard units had proven themselves in antipartisan operations and also "especially within the framework of the Jewish resettlement" operations.[81] In late summer 1943, Globocnik was transferred to another assignment: that of senior SS and police commander of the Adriatic Coast in Italy/Yugoslavia. Seventy Trawniki guards transferred with him. Before he left Lublin District, he transferred jurisdiction of the district's labor camps to the SS-WVHA, and the Trawniki guards would be integrated into the SS-Totenkopf guard battalion assigned to Majdanek.[82]

The SS-WVHA ordered the transfer of nearly 1,000 Trawniki guards to duty in concentration camps in Germany, where they served in the SS-Totenkopf guard battalions at each of the main concentration camps.[83]

An estimated 700 or so Trawniki guards were assigned to concentration camps in Germany and Austria, starting in fall 1943 as Operation Reinhard was nearing completion. About 130 of them were assigned to Flossenbürg and about 550 to Sachsenhausen. Others went to Stutthof, Buchenwald, Mauthausen, Ravensbrück, and other camps.[84] (Through wartime documentation, Trawniki guards are known to have served at Sachsenhausen, Mauthausen, Stutthof, Ravensbrück, Neuengamme, Natzweiler, and Dachau subcamp Landsberg.) Those guards not transferred with Globocnik or to the concentration camps in Germany remained behind in the Lublin District to guard the now-empty camps at Poniatowa and Trawniki, and the still-functioning Budzyn labor camp.[85]

The guard Ivan Bogdanow stated after the war that he and his Trawniki guard unit, along with a Ukrainian SS unit and a German police unit, searched for partisans in the area of Hrubieszow in March 1944. After the partisans killed two Trawniki guards and wounded two others, the unit burned down several settlements, consisting of fifty houses. The residents were in their houses as they burned. Those who attempted to escape were shot as they came out.[86]

In late July 1944, the Red Army advanced on the Lublin District and overran Trawniki camp. The Trawniki guards and their German superiors had retreated westward toward Kielce, Jedrzejow, Pinczow, and Zlota, west of the Vistula River. They formed a unit named after their commander—the "Streibel Battalion." The unit carried out antipartisan operations, guarded bridges and buildings, and rounded up local Polish civilians, who were forced to dig fortifications and trenches along the Nida River to try to slow down the advance of the Red Army.[87] By February 1945, the battalion had withdrawn to Dresden, where it was used to help clear bodies and rubble from recent mass air raids. By April 1945, the unit had fled into western Bohemia, and the remaining members burned their identification papers, changed into civilian clothing if they could, and went their separate ways. Most disappeared into the civilian population.[88]

Dr. Peter Black put it best when he remarked of the Trawniki guards: "For all their indiscipline, for all the harsh treatment they received from their German trainers, and for all the desertions, the Trawniki men helped make it possible for Globocnik, with his tiny staff of fewer than 200 men, to carry out the physical elimination of 1.7 million people." Also, "As entrepreneurs in the business of grand larceny, enslavement, and mass murder, Globocnik and his staff developed a force bound not to territory or future nationalist aims, but solely to commanders and missions." Finally, "The Trawniki men not only served as foot soldiers of the Final Solution; they also represented prototypes for the enforcers of the world that the Nazis intended to construct."[89]

AT AUSCHWITZ-BIRKENAU

At least three SS-Totenkopf companies were already guarding Auschwitz-Birkenau by the time that the Trawniki guard company arrived there on March 29, 1943. Those companies consisted of Germans or *Volksdeutsche* from southeastern Europe and included older SS men and others no longer fit for combat duty. The SS-Totenkopf battalion commander incorporated the Trawniki guards into his unit and designated them as the 8th Ukrainian Company, under the command of SS-Untersturmführer Theodore Lange and a staff of nine SS NCOs and enlistees, some of whom were bilingual,[90] and were assigned to the unit as training personnel, including Max Schmidt, Alexander Wirth, Jochann Wojciechowski, Mitte Filop, Ruzicic, Fuchsberger, Rutschke, Wieczorek, and Sudarewitch.[91] Regardless of the company's identification as a Ukrainian unit, the unit did not consist of just Ukrainians. At least eighteen were Russian, at least four were *Volksdeutsche*, one is known to have been Belorussian, and one identified himself as Bulgarian. Nevertheless, the national self-identity of some of these men was ambiguous. For example, some Russians were born and raised in central Ukraine, and some of the Ukrainians in Russia. The *Volksdeutsche* came from various regions of the Soviet Union. All were Soviet citizens, and most had previously served in at least one of the Reinhard death camps (at least 123 of the 150).

Within two weeks or so of their arrival, the Trawniki guards began standing guard duty at Auschwitz-Birkenau. The SS guard battalion commander, SS-Sturmbannführer Hartjenstein, handled them carefully. He ordered that their company commander monitor their performance on every guard post to which they were assigned. The commander was concerned about their discipline and reliability. The other SS guard companies were allowed to move about freely in their off-duty hours, but not so for the Trawniki guards. They may very well have resented this, considering their relative freedom of movement while they had been serving at the Reinhard camps, going into the local towns to look for alcohol and women.[92]

The Trawniki guard unit at Birkenau lived and mostly served guard duty separate from the other SS guard companies at the camp. The German SS staff found them difficult to discipline and distrusted their reliability:

Several guard towers were located along the perimeter of the Birkenau camp. Guarding was organized so that if one tower were occupied by a Trawniki guard on duty, the tower next to it had a German standing guard.[93]

The German camp administration did not trust the *Wachmänner* and had German guards shadow the Ukrainians when on guard duty.[94]

This stringent regime that the SS authorities implemented to manage the Trawniki guard company at Birkenau—"unique among security regulations at the Auschwitz" camp—"violated a central premise of the concentration camp system: uniformity of training and operations for all guards." Apparently, the Trawniki guards didn't fit in.[95]

The SS guard companies at Birkenau had four types of guard duty: prisoner escort, the large sentry chain around the camp perimeter, the small sentry chain, and "alert duty." The companies rotated in twenty-four-hour duty cycles; the shifts began at noon every day. The intent of the guard companies was to prevent the escape of the camp's roughly 60,000 prisoners. Prisoner escort duties entailed taking prisoners from the camp's main gate to labor sites. The two sentry chains established tight cordons through which no unauthorized person could pass through. During the day, the large sentry chain enclosed the entire area of the camp and its labor sites. At sundown, the guards formed the small sentry chain around the immediate compound of the camp in watchtowers and on foot patrols.[96]

There were three types of "alert duty" (*Bereitschaft*) for the guards: general alert duty—which provided cordon around incoming trains bringing new prisoners to the camp, or formed search detachments in the event of prisoner escapes; nighttime alert duty—which provided reinforcements to those on daytime general alert duty when incoming trains with prisoners arrived in camp after sundown; and operational duty (*Einsatzkompanie*)—which "provided manpower for undefined extraordinary actions."[97]

The garrison-type system of guard company rotation was familiar to Trawniki guards who had previously served in the Reinhard death camps. The *Volksdeutsche* Trawniki NCOs understood their role in this system, since they were the bilingual intermediaries between the German SS cadre and the rank-and-file non-German Trawniki guards.[98] Apparently, the SS commanders at Birkenau did not make use of the Trawniki guard company in the standard rotation of duties with the other SS guard companies. They seemed to have stood in the sentry chain and escorted prisoners but never guarded the unloading of trains.[99] However, by early July 1943, the Trawniki guard company was considered suitable for weeklong "alert duty" by the SS at Birkenau.

Following a mass desertion of Trawniki guards from the camp on July 4, 1943, Auschwitz commandant Rudolf Hoss sent a message to Berlin:

Due to the situation in Auschwitz concentration camp, it is impossible to assign duty to the Ukrainian guards in such a manner that they would not have any contact with prisoners or civilians. Thus, prevention of another escape attempt by individual Ukrainians cannot be guaranteed. Furthermore, on the basis of statements by prisoners, it was noted that individual prisoners planned to attempt their escapes during details that were guarded by Ukrainians because they expected to have a better chance for successful escape with them. . . . The security of the camp is jeopardized by this and can be ensured only by having an active and powerful guard force available.[100]

After the war, Pery Broad, a *Volksdeutsche* who had served as an SS NCO in the political section at Auschwitz, stated that while serving at Auschwitz, the Trawniki guards had "kept to themselves" and had a low profile within the SS at the camp. Following the mass desertion, the remaining Trawniki contingent was removed from Birkenau and reassigned to Buchenwald for the duration of the war. No other Trawniki guard unit would ever serve at Auschwitz again. Additionally, after the desertion incident, the SS-WVHA heeded Hoss's report and issued an order to all concentration camps that from then on, all non-German camp guards were to be integrated into German SS guard companies rather than have their own companies, as had been the practice up until then. This would enable the Germans to supervise their activities better and cause them to feel less isolated from the rest of the camp garrison. In this way it was hoped that future desertions could be discouraged and prevented.[101]

THE ZAMOSC PLAN

Globocnik's planned project to repopulate/colonize the Zamosc region of eastern Poland with Germans in 1942 had failed. With the assistance of Trawniki guard detachments, the Polish population of this region had been deported elsewhere, so the area could be taken over by Germans. However, partisan units fighting the Germans in the area made it impossible for the newly settled Germans there to live in peace.[102] In two pacification actions, November 1942–March 1943, involving 116 villages, and June–July 1943, involving 171 villages, 110,000 Poles were expelled from the Zamosc area by the SS, Gestapo, Wehrmacht, and Ukrainian auxiliaries. The SS Ukrainian Guard Force (i.e., Trawniki guards) participated in these actions. Among those expelled were 30,000 children, 4,450 of whom were sent to Germany for "Germanization" because they had blond hair and blue eyes.[103]

In November 1941, on Globocnik's orders, German forces carried out a trial displacement of the population of seven villages near Zamosc. The Zamosc region was to be the "first settlement area" of occupied Poland. The mass deportation of the population of the Zamosc region was initiated on November 27, 1942. The first stage of this operation included the villages in the Zamosc and Tomaszow Lubelski areas. The second stage began on January 13, 1943, and by March 6, 1943, the villages in the Hrubieszow area had been emptied. The final stage reached as far as the Bilgoraj area and took place in the summer of 1943, and during this time, the Germans carried out large-scale pacification actions.

To conduct the deportations, SS and police units were used. Those removed from their villages were sent to displaced persons' camps in Zamosc, Zwierzyniec, and Bilgoraj. Following selections, they were then sent on either as forced laborers to Germany, to Auschwitz or Majdanek, or to villages in the Warsaw District. Of the 30,000 children deported out of the Zamosc region, some were chosen for "Germanization" and were sent to special centers and adopted by German families, while about 10,000 died.[104] By August 1943, 110,000 Poles had been deported/displaced from nearly 300 villages. As it turned out, the Zamosc region was the first and only territory where the Germans attempted to implement the so-called "General Plan Ost" (General Plan East)—the plan to "Germanize" eastern Europe and the Soviet Union.[105]

The deportations from the Zamosc region resulted in military actions by the Polish resistance. Well-organized units of the AK (Home Army) and Bch (Peasant Battalions) were active in the region. These military actions included evacuating populations in danger of being deported, retaliatory actions against German settlers and the German occupation authorities (including the police), and sabotage of communication lines. In total, partisan units conducted about 300 armed actions against the Germans.[106] Simultaneous to all this, there was a conflict taking place between Poles and Ukrainians that in 1943 turned into violent combat in the Hrubieszow and Tomaszow Lubelski areas. Many people died, villages were destroyed, and the territory became a zone of divided loyalties—with some villages on the side of the Poles (the AK) and some on the side of the Ukrainians (the UPA). Such an extensive network of partisan units that fought in the Lublin District would not have been possible without the help of civilians, especially the peasants from the villages in the Zamosc region who supported partisan units in the forest.[107]

By the time the Germans were about to retreat from the Eastern Front in 1944, future plans for General Plan Ost were terminated, especially considering that so far it had not brought about the expected results. The Germans had planned to expel 140,000 people from nearly 700 villages, but they had cleared out only 110,000 from about 300 villages.[108] As the Red Army approached the Bug River in summer 1944, the Germans undertook antipartisan operations in the Zamosc region. The operations were known as Sturmwind I and Sturmwind

II and included the participation of police units and three Wehrmacht divisions totaling 30,000 troops. Combat actions took place in Lasy Janowskie, Lasy Lipskie, and the Solska Wilderness. The most-severe skirmishes took place near Gorecko Koscielne and Osuchy, and the partisan units that took part, including AK, Bch, and Soviet partisans, suffered heavy losses.[109] In August 1944, Operation "Burza" (Tempest) was initiated and elements of the AK 9th Infantry Regiment were deployed to Lasy Janowskie, Lasy Zwierzynieckie, Las Szostowiecki, Las Strzelecki, and the Solska Wilderness. During the operation, the regiment's troops, commanded by Major Stanislaw Prus "Adam," helped expel German units from many villages in the Zamosc region. Unfortunately for the AK, its commanders were arrested upon arrival of Soviet units in the area, and the Zamosc region came under the authority of a pro-Soviet puppet government known as the Polish National Committee of Liberation (PKWN).[110]

Prepared by Konrad Meyer, a professor at Berlin University, General Plan Ost became a reference point for the plan to resettle the population of the Zamosc region. It was to be a continuation of the displacement-colonization action that was taking place in the part of western Poland that had been annexed to Germany. In July 1941, Himmler issued an edict in which the Zamosc region was designated as a resettlement area. It was to be a "bastion of German nationhood," organized in so-called bases, from which further colonization of the east was to take place. The plan was to be implemented by the SS and police commander of the Lublin District, Odilo Globocnik. "Cleansed" of Poles, the Zamosc region was to be colonized with Germans from Bessarabia, Ukraine, Bosnia, Serbia, Slovenia, and other places.[111] The entity responsible for preparing the removal of Polish citizens and the resettlement of the Ukrainian population was the SS-Forschungsstelle für Ostunterkunfte (SS Office for the Planning and Study of Eastern Issues). Studies were conducted in order to demonstrate that Germans had begun colonizing the Zamosc region as far back as the eighteenth century.[112] A trial operation took place, on November 6–25, 1941, in which the populations of seven villages near Zamosc were deported. Those villages were Huszczka Mala, Huszczka Duza, Wysokie, Dulnik, Bialobrzegi, Bortatycze, and Zawada, totaling over 2,000 people. Initially, the Polish and Ukrainian inhabitants were held in the old Zamosc castle, and from there they were to be sent to Wolyn. Instead, they were sent to the Hrubieszow area. In the emptied villages, *Volksdeutscher* from the Radom district were settled.[113]

The mass resettlement of the population of the Zamosc region began on November 27, 1942, in the village of Skierbieszow. The operation lasted, with a few months interruption, until August 1943. Those deported were sent to displaced persons' camps in Zamosc, Zwierzyniec, and Budzyn. A total of 110,000 Poles and 18,000 Ukrainians were relocated from a total of 293 villages. The emptied villages were colonized by 13,000 German settlers. The deportations from the villages were conducted by the police, SS, Wehrmacht, and Ukrainian police in German service.[114]

The implementation of the Zamosc resettlement operation became a source of conflict between Governor Hans Frank and Reichsführer-SS Heinrich Himmler. Frank was against conducting such an operation until after the war and recommended postponing it. Himmler, however, got his wish with Hitler's approval and ordered the operation initiated while the war was in progress. It was the opportunity to establish the bases that would ensure full implementation of General Plan Ost.[115]

On January 13, 1943, the Germans initiated the "Ukraineraktion." The goal was to deport the population of Polish villages in the Hrubieszow area and resettle them with Ukrainians relocated from the Zamosc region. The operation was carried out in sixty-four villages in the districts of Bialopole, Dubienka, Grabowiec, Krylow, and Moniatycze. Over 12,000 Poles were deported, and by May 1943, over 7,000 Ukrainians were deported.[116] In the summer of 1943, as the threat of Polish partisan attacks on German settlers increased, the resettlement of the Ukrainian population from the Hrubieszow area to the Bilgoraj area was initiated, establishing a security belt that was supposed to prevent attacks on German settlers from the direction of the Solska Wilderness.[117] On June 23, 1943, Globocnik began the operation code-named "Wehrwolf." It was a deportation operation in the Bilgoraj area as well as in the Tomaszow Lubelski and Zamosc areas, and also a small part of the Hrubieszow area. By August 15, 1943, 171 villages had been emptied and about 60,000 people were resettled. Over 36,000 people expelled from their homes were initially sent to displaced persons' camps in Zamosc, Zwierzyniec, Budzyn, Bilgoraj, and other smaller ones. Some were sent directly to Germany as forced laborers; however, most were first sent to Majdanek concentration camp or the Lublin labor camp. Simultaneously, the Germans conducted a series of pacification operations, destroying villages and killing at least 1,000 people. Nearby forests were searched for fugitives who hid there to avoid deportation.[118]

As armed resistance in the Zamosc region grew, German military and police units, supported by the Ukrainian police, conducted large-scale pacification operations against partisan units, who hindered the resettlement efforts. During Operation Wehrwolf, June 23–August 15, 1943, the Germans carried out executions in 163 villages, and about 1,000 people were killed. Some fugitives, when captured, were sent to Zamosc, which had a Gestapo prison and execution site. By July 1944, about 8,000 Poles had been executed there.[119]

During the last stage of the deportations in the Zamosc region, carried out mostly in the Bilgoraj area but also in parts of Zamosc and Tomaszow Lubelski, a few transports were sent to Majdanek. Some were sent there directly, but most had first been held in the displaced persons' camps in Zamosc and Zwierzyniec. The first transport was sent to Majdanek on June 30, 1943. The total number sent there from the Zamosc region deportations is estimated at about 9,000. Most of these people were later forwarded to Germany as forced laborers.

Others were released in early August 1943 and sent by a resettlement center to special areas in the Lublin District.[120] During the deportation actions carried out in the Zamosc region, over 33,000 people were sent to Germany for forced labor, mostly to work on German farms, and the rest to work in industry. Some Poles were to remain in their home villages as forced laborers on farms taken over by German settlers.

By the end of 1944, about one million Polish citizens from the territory known as the "Generalgouvernement" and the Bialystok region had been deported to Germany as forced laborers. After the war, many of them were placed in special "Polish camps" and then were repatriated to their homeland.[121]

THE TRAWNIKI GUARDS AT TREBLINKA

In Treblinka, when a transport arrived, the *Zugwachmann* on duty called the *Wachmänner* into formation. This meant about forty to sixty guards. They joined the ten to fifteen SS men on duty in Camp I and Camp II. "Our entire service in Treblinka consisted only of exterminating people."[122] In August 1942, "a Polish partisan, named Trzcinski, from a nearby village, had reached the railway station after being forced to flee across the Bug River. He was on his way south, armed, in search of another partisan group, and intended to travel south on the train to Sokolow. At a nearby platform were train cars waiting to be taken to Treblinka II. Trzcinski went up to one of the train cars, reached into his coat, and gave a young Jew a grenade, asking him to throw it among some Germans."[123] Zabecki learned later that the Jew had thrown the grenade at a group of Trawniki guards at the ramp in Treblinka II. One of them was seriously wounded. The Jew was shot. The guard Nikolaj Malagon was on duty at the ramp and witnessed the incident.[124] "When one of the prisoners on the unloading area threw a grenade, one of the guards was killed. The other guards standing in cordon formation immediately shot the prisoner on the spot."[125]

During the first five weeks of operations in Treblinka, July 23–August 28, 1942, about 312,000 Jews, about 5,000–7,000 per day, were transported there. So many transports had arrived that they could no longer be handled. The gas chambers had frequent technical breakdowns, and the surplus from each transport had to be shot in the reception area of the camp. Many prisoners and more pits were required for burying the thousands of bodies. The problem of digging more pits was partly solved by bringing in a scoop shovel from the quarry at Treblinka I.

In September 1942, SS-Oberscharführer Lorenz Hackenholt and a small detachment of SS men and Trawniki guards were transferred from Belzec to Treblinka by Wirth. Treblinka had been in operation for only a few weeks, but already it was in chaos. Thousand of decomposing bodies littered the camp, and long lines of railway wagons filled with Jews waited on the sidings for their turn to enter the camp to be gassed. The first task, however, was to clean up the mess and bury the rotting corpses. The worst mess was in Camp II, the extermination area, where a large pile of bodies had accumulated near the gas chambers, under which, according to SS-Scharführer Franz Suchomel, there was "a cesspool 3 centimeters deep, full of blood, maggots, and excrement." No one person—not German SS men, Trawniki guards, or Jews—wanted to touch this mess, not even after dire threats from Wirth. The Jews preferred to be shot rather than perform this clean-up. SS-Scharführer Erwin Kainer was assigned by Wirth to supervise the task of cleaning up this mess. Reportedly, Kainer was so distressed at the sight in front of him, and so in fear of Wirth should he refuse, that he shot himself in desperation. In the end, Wirth himself and his detachment from Belzec had to carry out the gruesome task.[126]

Wirth came to Treblinka for a three-to-four-week period accompanied by Oberhauser, Franz, and Stangl in order to clean up and reorganize the camp. Commandant Eberl was dismissed for his inability to maintain order in the camp, and was replaced by Stangl and Franz. The bodies lying around the camp were bloated. The work of clearing them up was done by 500 Jewish prisoners, under the supervision of a Capo Galewski, who buried them. They were overseen by Trawniki guards and the SS. They were then killed. After reorganization in Treblinka, Hackenholt returned to Belzec where exhumations and cremations were to begin. For a few weeks, he operated an excavator opening the mass graves and removing the decomposing contents. According to local villagers who met Hackenholt in a bar when he was off-duty, "he stank of corpses." SS-Scharführer Herbert Floss was brought in to give instructions on the cremations.

GASSINGS AND BODY BURNING AT TREBLINKA

"After summer 1942, a new, bigger gas chamber building was constructed with six chambers."[127] "The gassings lasted 20–30 minutes, after which the chambers were unloaded by a Jewish work group."[128] "When I came to Treblinka, the man who was in charge of the gassings was Schmidt. He used to sit in the excavator and dig the pits. He would start the gassing process and then give the order to open the doors when everyone was dead. Then Marchenko arrived in the camp and took over this duty."[129] "Schmidt was in charge of the gas chamber engine."[130] "Schmidt supervised the gassings. Two Ukrainians worked under him. One of them operated the gassing engine; the other supervised the prisoner work detail that removed the bodies from the gas chambers and carried them to the burial or cremation pits. Other Ukrainians in the camp rotated their duties, but these two were assigned to the gas chambers permanently. The engine operator's name was Ivan."[131]

Whips, clubs, and iron bars were used on people who hesitated to enter the gas chambers.[132] Wachmann Prokofij Ryabtsev, who stood near the entrance to the gas chamber building, stated that he saw the Zugwachmänner Jager and Pilman go into the gas chamber corridor: "I personally did not herd people into the gas chambers but stood at my post near the entrance, and from there I could see what was happening inside the chambers."[133] "People were chased along the 'tube' by a group of SS men, very often including SS-Untersturmführer Kurt Franz and his dog, Barry."[134]

At the three Reinhard death camps, only a few Trawniki guards worked in the area between the gas chambers and the burial pits. The number of Jews who belonged to the labor detachment that did the work of disposing of the bodies fluctuated between 150 and 250. These Jews were overseen by a *Capo*. There were also a few SS men, including the excavator operators, the gas chamber supervisor, and a few *Volksdeutsche* Trawniki NCOs who worked in this area. At all three death camps, one or two Trawniki guards also operated or assisted in operating the gas chambers. The Jewish labor detachment that had to bury and later burn the victims survived on food taken from Jews who had been gassed and on small rations issued to them by the camp office.[135]

In Treblinka II, there were two mass excavators to dig the burial pits. "These pits were constantly being dug deeper and wider by one of the excavators operated by a German."[136] According to another guard, "Pit digging was an almost full-time occupation for that German, a man named Willi, who operated the heavy equipment."[137]

A *Wachmann* who assisted the German who operated the mechanical excavator told KGB interrogators after the war that he worked with the excavator except when trains arrived with new Jews to bring to the gas chambers. When such trains arrived, he had to assist in the killing process.[138] On occasion, some victims survived the gas chamber and were determined to be semiconscious following the gassing process. Such individuals were taken to the burial pits nearby and immediately shot:[139]

Large pits were dug throughout the northern area of the camp (Treblinka II). Corpses from the gas chambers were placed in these pits. As soon as a pit was full, it was lightly covered with soil. A pit could hold 15,000–17,000 bodies.[140]

The cremation process at Treblinka II was similar to that used at Sobibor and Belzec. A Jewish labor detachment burned and then reburned the remains and then sifted through the ashes.[141] A cremation "expert" arrived in Treblinka II to organize the burnings. He had also organized the burnings in Sobibor. He was SS-Unterscharführer Herbert Floss. With such body-burning going on in Treblinka II, it became difficult, if not impossible, to disguise the murderous nature of the camp from further incoming transports of Jews:

> The problem was that at the beginning of 1943, upon orders from the Germans, the Jewish labor detachment began to burn the corpses of the murdered people over fires, and the smell of the bodies was a sign that the camp was designed for the extermination of people. Henceforth, the people who arrived did not want to leave the train cars.[142]

Treblinka II had at least two cremation pyres in use. One former guard described that the bodies "were stacked on the rails of the two pyres. The pyres consisted of foundations about 2 meters high and 20 meters long, built very narrowly. Two rows of rails were secured on top of the foundation. Each pyre could burn more than 1,000 corpses in four to five hours. The ashes were then sifted through a sieve and mixed with sand in the pits."[143] Also, "The population in the surrounding villages knew that the extermination of the Jewish population was being carried out in the Treblinka camp because of the stench. The smell drifted from the camp. I do not know why the corpses were burned, but I believe that it might have been to conceal the traces of extermination of thousands of people."[144]

IVAN MARCHENKO: GAS CHAMBER OPERATOR AT TREBLINKA

Occupation: Coal miner in Kryvy Rog (in Ukrainian-Kryvy Rih), a big steel-producing city in central Ukraine. Other statements say he was a supervisor on riverboat barges floating lumber on the Dnieper River.

Although most statements claim he was not a member of the Communist Party, there is a reference to him being considered in 1941 as a candidate for the NKVD.[145] According to his Trawniki personnel file (TPF), he was a farmer, but he may have told the Germans this in order to avoid being assigned to hard manual labor, as he might have been if he had admitted that he was really a miner. Married, at the start of the war he had a five-year-old son, a nine-year-old daughter, and a third child, a daughter, who was born in May 1941, a few months before his capture by the Germans in the summer of 1941. Reportedly he carried a photo of his family while serving at Treblinka.[146] He was drafted into the Red Army at the start of the German invasion in 1941. He was captured near Belaya Tserkov, about 50 miles south of Kiev; in battle, his unit had been surrounded. He was taken to the POW camp in Chelm—Stalag 319. In October 1941, he was selected for Trawniki service, serving at Treblinka II from summer 1942 to fall 1943. He was assigned Trawniki ID #476:[147]

Marchenko wore a black uniform, similar to a German SS uniform.[148] Marchenko often wore a leather jacket."[149] "Marchenko was armed with a pistol.[150] He always roamed around the camp carrying a 2-meter-long water pipe. He was an expert at killing people with the water pipe. I personally saw how he killed a man with one blow from the pipe.[151]

From the very beginning, Marchenko became friends with SS-Untersturmführer Kurt Franz and was "always hanging around the Germans."[152] Marchenko especially spent time with SS-Scharführer Fritz Schmidt, who was in charge of the SS garage and metalwork shop. Marchenko and Schmidt repaired cars together, and when transports arrived in the camp, they were together on the ramp.[153] Marchenko's main task as a mechanic included making sure the gas chamber engine was functioning properly.[154] In September 1942, Nikolai Shalayev arrived in Treblinka and was assigned to work with Marchenko as a mechanic in the gas chamber engine room.[155] Shalayev became friends with SS-Scharführer Erich Schultz, who often visited Shalayev in his barracks.[156] Marchenko and Shalayev turned on the gassing engine. They were assisted by two Jews who refueled and sometimes turned on the engine.[157] Because of their responsibility at the gas chambers, Marchenko and Shalayev "had the greatest prestige" in the camp.[158] They were on duty for twelve hours and off duty for twelve hours.[159]

Marchenko and Shalayev considered themselves among the elite in the camp. They preferred fraternizing with the Germans when off duty, and they very rarely visited the barracks where the other Trawniki men resided.[160]

Marchenko earned the nickname "Ivan Grozny" (Ivan the Terrible) by the work Jews.[161] Marchenko took part in herding people into the gas chambers, standing at the entrance and hurrying the people to get inside.

Marchenko and Shalayev would shout at people to hurry up and get in the gas chambers.[162] Marchenko had a cavalry sword with which he mutilated people outside the gas chambers. He cut off women's breasts and cut off noses and ears both of men and women.[163] In addition to Marchenko and Shalayev, five or six SS men armed with clubs and whips also drove the Jews into the gas chambers. In this activity, the Germans competed with Marchenko and Shalayev in brutality toward the Jews.[164] SS-Scharführer Erich Schultz also had a dog, trained by Nikolai Shalayev. He set the dog on people running to the gas chambers.[165] Marchenko made sure that once the chamber was full, the door was closed and locked.[166] "Marchenko and Shalayev went together to the engine room and started the engine."[167] "Marchenko checked the progress of the gassings through observation slits in the doors."[168] Another guard, Pavel Leleko, also looked through the observation slit on one occasion, although he claims he couldn't see anything inside:[169]

> There were two Ukrainians in Camp II on a permanent basis. One was Nikolai; the other, I don't remember his name. These two took care of the engine room at the gas chambers when Fritz Schmidt was absent. Usually Schmidt was in charge of the engine room. In Camp II, in the area of the gas chambers, were stationed about six to eight Ukrainians.[170] Ivan [Marchenko] took great pride in his position as Schmidt's assistant and felt that this status placed him a few rungs above the other Ukrainians, who acted merely as guards. Ivan would appear only after a trainload of victims arrived, and would leave as soon as he accomplished his assigned task, leaving the removal of the bodies to the other Ukrainian and his Jewish work crew.[171] Marchenko worked in Treblinka as the operator of the motor of the gas chambers. I was also appointed to the post of operator of the motor. Marchenko had the rank of guard (*Wachmann*). His job as operator included ensuring that the motor was functional, that it gave off fumes; he had to open the valves of the gas pipes and helped the guards put victims in the chamber when they displayed resistance. I, Marchenko, two Germans, and two Jews worked at the motor in the engine room of the gas chambers.[172] The Jews refueled and turned on the motor that fed the gas into the chambers.[173]

Shalayev claimed during interrogation in 1951 that he had worked as a supervisor in the engine room for only three weeks. He says he then became supervisor of the electric generator, which was also located in the engine room. The generator provided electricity to the whole camp and was run by two Jews working under Shalayev.[174]

In addition to running the gas chambers, whenever firing-squad executions were carried out in the camp, Marchenko always took part.[175] On one occasion, Oberwachmann David Robertus was cut on the neck by a Jew, in self-defense. As punishment, practically the whole Jewish work group was shot by firing squad.[176] A total of ten to fifteen work Jews were shot next to one of the excavators in Camp II, on the orders of Franz. The firing squad reportedly consisted of Marchenko, Levchishin, Kuzminsky, Zugwachmann Emanuel Schultz, and other *Wachmänner*.[177] When Trawniki guards were attacked and injured by Jews, it was characteristic of them to seek revenge on the Jews at every opportunity.[178]

By all accounts, Marchenko was an alcoholic, always drunk, both on and off duty.[179] On one occasion, "I was off duty in the nearby village of Wolka. I ran into Marchenko and he punched me. He was very drunk. The next day he said he didn't remember why he did it."[180]

On September 20, 1943, a convoy of SS men and about 100 Trawniki guards left Lublin for Trieste on the Adriatic coast. Marchenko and Shalayev were among them. The convoy was led by SS-Gruppenführer Odilo Globocnik, accompanied by SS-Sturmbannführer Christian Wirth and SS-Hauptsturmführer Franz Stangl.[181] In Trieste, Marchenko was assigned to the San Sabba rice mill, which was Wirth's HQ for the roundup and deportation of local Jews to Auschwitz and other camps. "Marchenko guarded German warehouses at the port, guarded the San Sabba HQ, and took part in rounding up local citizens for forced labor in Germany."[182]

In the spring of 1945, Marchenko and a man named Grigorij, who had been a mechanic in the gas chambers at Sobibor, seized an armored personnel carrier in Fiume (Rijeka) and fled to the partisans over the border in Yugoslavia.[183] Shalayev last saw Marchenko in Fiume (Rijeka) in late March 1945:

> I saw him coming out of a brothel. He invited me to a nearby restaurant, where he told me about deserting the Germans and joining the partisans. He said that he had no intention of returning home to Ukraine after the war and that he wanted to remain in Fiume, where he met a Yugoslav girl whom he wanted to marry. She was involved with the partisans too.[184]

Shalayev also stated that a Trawniki *Volksdeutsche* named Alexander Schultz, twenty-seven years old, from the Povolzhye region of the Volga, married a Yugoslav woman and remained in Udine. The fate of Ivan Marchenko remains unknown. In April 1945, Shalayev retreated with the Germans over the border into Carinthia (Austria). In late May 1945, he was handed over to the Soviets as a POW and was redrafted into the Red Army. After demobilization, he returned to the Soviet Union.

THE FATE OF IVAN MARCHENKO?

There was a community of White Russians, Ukrainians, and Cossacks living in Serbia both before and during World War II (1920–1945). They all sided with the Germans during the war, and many served in pro-Nazi militias and killed thousands of Serbs. After the war, as a reprisal, they were hunted down and killed. If Marchenko really had remained in postwar Yugoslavia, he wouldn't have lasted five minutes. Tito's postwar regime was a police state where everyone spied on everyone. Marchenko couldn't read or speak the local language; he would have stuck out like a sore thumb.[185] According to several statements by Slovenian partisans, Marchenko was captured with some SS/Gestapo-SD men, and they were all executed shortly thereafter. Marchenko's identity was reportedly determined by his personal papers and descriptions provided by Tito's secret field police. At the time, Tito's units were executing anyone and everyone. This story, however, seems to contradict Shalayev's postwar statement that Marchenko had deserted the Germans and had joined Tito's partisans. Captured German documents containing Marchenko's name, including a roster for the San Sabba camp, are part of the holdings at the Museum of National Liberation in Ljubljana, Slovenia:

> In early August 1990, I flew to Zagreb with Ed Nishnik, John Demjanjuk's son-in-law, where we rented a car and drove to Ljubljana. The director of the Resistance Museum there made several boxes of records available to us for our examination. The files and documents were all from the *SS-Vernichtungslager* in Trieste, usually referred to as the "Rice Factory." The records contained numerous rosters, duty assignment lists, camp journal entries, etc. that noted Marchenko's name, date of birth, and, most importantly, his Trawniki ID number. There were also several photos of him.
>
> Ed Nishnic, John Demjanjuk's son-in-law, engaged me to help research some of the background of the charges [author's note: against Demjanjuk]. I was the one who investigated the fact that Ivan Marchenko was the real Ivan the Terrible from Treblinka and that he transferred from Poland to Trieste with many of the other Reinhard people in fall 1943. The records are in a museum in Ljubljana, and we flew there and spent several days going through them.[186]

In 1992, Ed Nishnic, the son-in-law of John Demjanjuk, incorrectly convicted by an Israeli court of being the gas chamber operator at Treblinka, went to visit the Marchenko family in Ukraine. Court testimony given in the 1950s and 1960s by a number of former Trawniki guards that served at Treblinka demonstrated that Ivan Marchenko had been the gas chamber operator and not Demjanjuk, and Demjanjuk would be freed on appeal. Nishnic found the family in Marchenko's hometown of Seryovka, in the Dnepropetrovsk region. Marchenko's wife had just died that year, 1992. Marchenko's youngest daughter, Katarina, told Nishnic that she had never known her father because she had been too young and that he had never returned home after the war.[187] Katarina was shocked when she heard what crimes her father was accused of, and that it was a good thing her mother was not still alive to hear these things. She also revealed that in the late 1940s and early 1950s, KGB personnel had often come to the Marchenko home and confiscated several photos of Ivan Marchenko. The KGB had never told the family why they had come to their home and taken these photos, or what Ivan had been wanted for or suspected of.[188] Responsible for running the gas chambers at a camp where it is estimated that at least 750,000 people were murdered, Marchenko could be on record as the most prolific killer in recorded history.

THE TRAWNIKI GUARDS DURING THE TREBLINKA UPRISING AND END PHASE OF THE CAMP

The SS personnel were to be attacked and eliminated at the beginning of the plan, one at a time. The Trawniki guards would be handled differently. Those at guard posts had to be killed and their weapons taken. The others, who would be in their barracks, would be taken alive, their weapons taken, and they would be held under guard for the duration of the uprising. In Camp II, the extermination area, a problem was how to deal with the Trawniki guards in the two watchtowers: one in the center of the compound, and the other near the southeastern corner of the camp. Particularly threatening was the one in the center of the compound. It had unimpeded observation and control over all activity at the prisoners' barracks and near the cremation grills. The camp underground decided that a prisoner would approach the tower and entice the guard to come down by offering him money and gold in exchange for food. In view of the guards' eagerness for money and valuables, the guard could be expected to take the bait, so when the uprising broke out, he would be on the ground and could be eliminated.[189]

In Treblinka, in preparation for an uprising, attempts were made to procure weapons from outside the camp through the Trawniki guards. Some of the *capos* and other Jewish prisoners cultivated ties with Trawnikis who were prepared, for suitable compensation, to bring food into the camp from the outside. Several attempts were made to obtain weapons in this way. The guards, however, while prepared to take the money, did not produce guns; still, they refrained from informing on these activities. All they were interested in was keeping the money.[190]

The Trawniki guard posted in the watchtower at the camp's eastern fence realized what was going on when he heard gunshots and explosions. He then jumped down from the tower. A prisoner ran up to him and said, "Hey, the Russians are coming." The prisoner grabbed his rifle and the guard offered no resistance. The prisoner told him to "get out of here," and the guard ran off. However, the guards in the other watchtowers opened fire on the prisoners. Some prisoners ran into lone Trawniki guards and took their rifles.[191] During the Treblinka Uprising: "I was standing guard at the first gate, fires started and shots were fired all around, but I didn't know who was shooting or where the shots were coming from. The commandant ran out and we dropped to the ground and lay there, and then we saw people running away. We were ordered to shoot, but this was far away from us."[192] The exact number of SS and Trawniki guards killed during the Treblinka Uprising is not known because there are no known German-documented reports on it. One German, Kuttner, was wounded, and perhaps five or six Trawniki guards were killed or wounded.[193]

The remaining work Jews in Treblinka II were guarded by SS-Scharführer Franz Rum and a detachment of Trawniki guards from Treblinka I. SS-Scharführer Paul Bredow took those remaining work Jews and shot them. He was assisted by SS-Scharführer Willi Mentz and an *SS-Scharführer* from Treblinka I. The shooting was overseen by SS-Untersturmführer Kurt Franz. The bodies were cremated by the Trawniki guards.[194] After helping to suppress the prisoner revolt in Treblinka II in August 1943, a Trawniki guard detachment there escorted surviving work Jews to Sobibor, and those prisoners were killed there on October 21, 1943, one week after Sobibor itself had experienced a prisoner uprising. Sobibor was closed down in November 1943, but a small Trawniki guard detachment remained behind to guard the possessions of the last murdered Jews there and to guard an ammunition warehouse.[195]

At the former site of the camp, a small farm was built using bricks from the demolished gas chambers. It consisted of a wooden peasant-style hut on a brick foundation, a farmyard with a wooden barn, a wooden cellar, and a barracks hut. There were horses, cows, pigs, and a vegetable garden. The area around the farm was fenced off to keep away local villagers who wanted to scavenge the site for money and jewelry left behind by the camp's victims. According to Franciszek Zabecki and the local villagers, Eugeniusz Goska and Waclaw Niemgowski, the farm was inhabited by two Trawniki guards and their families: a *Volksdeutsche*, Oswald Strebel, and another known only as Sashka. Both had served at Treblinka II. They were probably both armed to guard against local intruders. Their only visitor was said to be a fellow Trawniki guard from Treblinka I.[196] In July 1944, the Red Army advanced on the area. The Trawniki guards at the former site of Treblinka II burned the farm and fled with their families.[197] It was evident that once the Trawniki guards had fled, local Poles had thoroughly dug up the ground in search of Jewish loot.

From 1944 to 1950, various investigation commissions inspected the former site of the camp to collect evidence of the crimes committed there:[198] in 1944, the "Extraordinary Soviet-Polish Investigation Commission," in Warsaw; 1947, the area is fenced off and a Polish army unit is ordered to guard the site from further intrusion by so-called treasure hunters; also in 1947 was the founding of the "Committee for Honoring the Victims of Treblinka." In the fall of 1945, the "Main Commission for the Investigation of Nazi Crimes," based at the Ministry of Justice in Warsaw, carried out an investigation of Treblinka. The investigators were Polish and Soviet and were under the supervision of the Polish judge, Zdzislaw Lukaszkiewicz. Zabecki turned over the railway transport documents for Treblinka to the investigators.[199] Since 1983, the former site of Treblinka II has been the responsibility of the "Museum of Fighting and Martyrdom in Treblinka," a branch of the regional museum in Siedlce. The site includes both Treblinka I and II.[200]

Franciszek Zabecki, the Treblinka Railway station master, claims he kept a careful account of all arriving transports, which he passed on to the AK, and insists that the total was 1.2 million people sent to Treblinka II.[201] Another source gives the number of people deported to Treblinka II as 886,000, with the largest number being sent there from the Radom District

(348,000), the Warsaw Ghetto (310,000), the Warsaw District (92,000), the Bialystok District (50,000), and the Lublin District (38,000).[202]

THE TRAWNIKI GUARDS AT BELZEC

The *Volksdeutsche* Trawniki NCOs "were considered a 'special breed,' and they were relied on by the SS to 'work the camps.'"[203] The bilingual *Volksdeutsche* Trawniki NCOs were the backbone of the camp operation. Working immediately below the SS men, these platoon commanders held complete power over life and death. They were the principal supervisors who handled the Trawniki guards and managed their discipline.[204] The *Volksdeutsche* Trawniki NCOs were reportedly the most undisciplined element in Belzec. They abused the power given to them, usually under the influence of alcohol:[205]

> The guards were always intoxicated when they came to the bakery to get bread. I asked them why they drank so much, and they told me, "if you worked in this camp (Belzec) you'd drink too."[206] Schneider, Sievert, and Kostenkow were members of the guard unit. I believe Kostenkow was Russian. He probably worked at the gas chambers. Schneider worked in Camp II. Without doubt, the worst of them was the guard Schmidt. He liked killing. Later in Italy, he committed suicide.[207]

It first appears that oversight of the Trawniki guards fell to SS-Untersturmführer Johann Niemann. Later, SS-Oberscharführer Kurt Franz took over this position before he transferred to Treblinka II. In late summer 1942, he was replaced by SS-Scharführer Reinhold Feix. Apparently, SS-Oberscharführer Fritz Jirmann was also in charge of the Trawniki guards in Belzec, but after he was accidentally shot by SS-Oberscharführer Gley, SS-Scharführer Werner Dubois succeeded him as the *Spiess* (supervisory NCO) of the Trawnikis.[208] Subjected to weekly inspections, if even the smallest irregularity was discovered, twenty-five lashes with a whip was given as punishment. The punishment was usually carried out by the *Volksdeutsche* Christian Schmidt, or by SS men responsible for overseeing the Trawniki guards.[209]

Despite the threat of punishment for smuggling Jewish valuables and money, for trading such items, or for visiting Polish and Ukrainian homes in the neighboring village, all of these things took place during the existence of Belzec. The residents of Belzec and the surrounding villages who sold alcohol and food to the Trawniki guards took advantage of the fact that the guards did not know the true price of the goods they had pilfered in the camp. A Belzec villager stated after the war that he had sold bottles of vodka to the guards for 200 zloty each, while he had originally paid sixty zloty for each.[210]

GASSINGS AND BODY BURNING AT BELZEC

"The gas chamber motor was delivered by train from Rejowiec to Belzec. It was packed in three wooden boxes. Wachmann Szaszka and Waszka told me the motor would be used to kill people."[211] At Belzec, once Wirth had thoroughly worked out the extermination process, the German SS would have little actual participation in the gassings apart from supervision. "We didn't have to do anything; we just had to be there."[212] Hackenholt, with the help of Trawniki guards, operated the gassing engine in Belzec. He was assisted by two Trawniki guards and two Jews:

> I think the actual work was carried out by the Ukrainians (Trawnikis) and Jews, and Hackenholt only supervised them.[213] After the Jews entered the gas chambers, the doors were shut by Hackenholt himself or by one of the Ukrainians assigned to him. Then Hackenholt started the engine.[214] The gassing engine was started by a mechanic from among the Ukrainian guards.[215]

One of Hackenholt's Jewish assistant mechanics was a cab driver from Krakow named Moniek. He was in charge of starting the gassing engine when Hackenholt was absent or drunk:

> The gassing engine was manned by two Ukrainians. Always the same two. Ukrainians also opened the doors when the gassing was over. Hackenholt supervised the gassing engine. The engine was sometimes switched on and off by Moniek.[216]

A small team of Jewish mechanics helped operate the gassing engine. A man known as Moniek is said to have assisted. Rudolf Reder allegedly serviced the gassing engine when it had technical difficulties, and delivered benzene to the engine room:

> The work of the motor was watched over by Moniek. The motor was always run for twenty minutes, after which Moniek gave one of the machinists the signal to turn it off. On Moniek's order, prisoners opened the doors and pulled out the dead.[217]

SS men supervised the gas chambers, including Schwarz, Niemann, Dubois, and Schluch. Ukrainians forced the victims into the chambers and closed the doors. With a signal from an *SS-Scharführer*, the engine was started. When the gassing stopped, the Jewish workforce led by Moniek went to work removing the bodies from the chamber. Postwar testimony makes particular reference to Zugwachmann Christian Schmidt, a twenty-five-year-old *Volksdeutsche* from Latvia. He worked in the gas chamber area and led the Jewish work detail that had to remove the bodies from the chambers to the mass graves or cremation pits. He had a reputation for brutality and for killing members of the work detail when they were no longer fit for work. Also implicated in brutality were other Trawniki *Volksdeutsche*; Reinhard Siebert from Volhynia and Friedrich Schneider from the Volga region, both twenty-two years old at the time, were said to have killed people near the gas chambers and elsewhere in the camp. Zugwachmänner Samuel Kunz and Heinrich Schutz were likewise heavily implicated according to witness testimonies.[218] According to one *Wachmann*, all the dirty work done in the area of the gas chambers was done by a Jewish labor detail. They dug the burial pits, pulled the bodies out of the gas chambers, threw them into the pits, and buried them, and starting in summer 1942 they burned them.[219] "In Belzec, the pace of killing almost immediately outstripped the preparation of burial pits." In the summer of 1942, the Belzec commandant ordered 120 Jews be chosen from among new arrivals in the camp and assigned them to dig a new burial pit. When they finished digging the pit, guards and SS men shot them at the pit.[220]

Newly arrived Jews who were too sick or weak to walk to the gas chambers were taken to the burial pits and shot:[221]

Mass shooting of prisoners was carried out in the camp [Belzec]. While I served there, the Germans forced prisoners to exhume pits full of corpses and to burn them. I do not know how many people were shot there, but there were very many pits that held corpses.[222]

In Belzec, a grave overflowed and a cesspool seeped out in front of the SS dining hall. It stank in front of the dining hall and the barracks. Wirth, Oberhauser, Hackenholt, and Franz had to clean up the mess and put the bodies back into the mass grave. Franz and Hackenholt refused at first, but Wirth threatened them if they did not participate.[223] The exhumation and burning of the bodies in Belzec is generally said to have begun in late 1942.[224] Burning of bodies went on around the clock, day and night.[225] One *Wachmann* who transferred from Belzec to Sobibor stated that the body-burning process was identical at both camps.[226] In Belzec, a Jewish labor detachment exhumed the bodies from the mass graves apparently by hand, just using shovels. No former guards from the camp mention the use of mechanical excavators like those used at the other two Reinhard death camps: Treblinka II and Sobibor. The bodies in Belzec were burned in special trenches on the campgrounds.[227] Train rails were constructed in the shape of a scaffold, and large stacks of bodies of the murdered people were placed on top and burned. The burning went on around the clock.[228] In Belzec, the burning of bodies went on until at least March 1943. "There were two Jewish labor detachments at the camp, and one of them worked exclusively at the trenches. They were engaged in the burning of bodies."[229] From the entire period during which Belzec existed, the residents of the village remembered the "burning phase" most clearly. They had to endure the sight and smell of fire and smoke coming from the camp on a daily basis:

In late fall 1942, no more transports with Jews arrived. Large mechanized cranes arrived in the camp in order to exhume the murdered Jews from the pits. The bodies that were exhumed were stacked onto piles and doused with some sort of liquid. Two or three fires burned simultaneously. At this time, a horrible smell of rotting corpses and burned bones permeated the area. This awful stench could even be smelled 10 miles from Belzec. The burning of bodies went on without interruption for three months.[230]

Once Belzec was closed down and cremations there had been completed, the Trawniki guard detachment there accompanied the surviving work Jews in the camp to Sobibor, where the prisoners were killed on arrival in June 1943.[231]

EDWARD WLASIUK: GAS CHAMBER OPERATOR AT BELZEC

"Wlasiuk was from the village of Slawuta [Ukraine] in the Soviet Union. He was a driver. He drove lorries and cars. He delivered food and supplies to Belzec. He was a chauffeur for one of the Germans. In Austria, he joined the Red Army and died in a car accident. I then went back to Belzec with our child. We had married in July 1943. I have since remarried."[232] "Wlasiuk and I went to Austria, and he died there in May 1945. I then went back to live in Belzec."[233] "Wlasiuk was caught by the Red Army in Vienna."[234]

One of the men responsible for overseeing the motor was Edward Wlasiuk. Polish residents in Belzec recalled him, including Edward Luczynski: "As I was told by the guard Wlasiuk, who is no longer alive, it was he who operated the gasoline motor located next to the gas chamber when the chamber was full of people." The name of the second motor operator can no longer be determined with certainty, but it possibly could have been Stefan Jadziol, since a witness at Belzec described him as the "mechanic of death."[235] Edward Luczynski was the uncle of Maria Wlasiuk, the wife of Edward Wlasiuk, who lived in Belzec. Maria Wlasiuk claimed not to know that her husband had operated the gassing motor. She claimed she had not wanted to hear anything about the camp from him.[236] "Grisza and Stefan were responsible for running the engine. My ex-husband [Edward Wlasiuk] had told me that the engine killed people."[237]

THE FATE OF EDWARD WLASIUK?

According to available documentation, after departing his assignment at Belzec, Wlasiuk, whose Trawniki ID number was 218, returned to Trawniki and deployed with the unit that was sent to help suppress the Warsaw Ghetto uprising on April 17, 1943,[238] and was then assigned to the Lublin Detachment on May 17, 1943.[239] Any trace of him seems to have been lost after that. If he rejoined the Red Army in Austria around the end of the war, as his ex-wife claimed, he may have ended up there after having departed either from the SS "Streibel" Battalion, which ended the war around the German-Czech border region, or after having retreated from the jurisdiction of the HSSPF Adriatic Coast into Austria, as other Germans and Trawniki guards seem to have done in that region.

Contrary to what Maria Warzocha stated about her ex-husband and his fate, Robin O'Neal has stated that "Wlasiuk was killed in Lublin just before the liberation in a 'hit-and-run accident' by the Lublin AK. They knew he had been a guard at Belzec."[240]

THE TRAWNIKI GUARDS AT SOBIBOR

When a transport arrived in Sobibor, Trawniki guards acted as helpers to the work Jews who unloaded the trains (*Bahnhofskommando*) and assisted them with emptying the cattle cars, overseeing the forced undressing of the victims, and then moving them toward the gas chambers. They also guarded the work Jews who emptied the gas chambers and buried and later burned the bodies. The Trawnikis were armed with whips and Russian rifles. They were on guard at the entrances to the different parts of the camp and at the main gate. They patrolled day and night around the camp, between the double barbed-wire fence, and they manned the watchtowers. Within the camp, they guarded Camp III, the extermination area. On the arrival of new transports, they cordoned off the surroundings of the camp to prevent possible escapes:

Some of the German and Ukrainians appear drunk when the transports arrive. Their speech becomes slurred and they stagger when they walk. Alcohol makes them even more savage.[241] A certain Ukrainian guard barters with prisoners. He routinely enters the sorting shed and asks for money in exchange for food and alcohol. He asks for gold and promises to bring salami and vodka in exchange. He makes good on his promise and asks for diamonds in exchange for more food and drink. A willing Ukrainian guard can always be found.[242]

GASSINGS AND BODY BURNING AT SOBIBOR

"The victims were led to the gas chambers by Ukrainian guards. Once the chambers were full, the Ukrainians closed the doors. The motor was then started by a Ukrainian named Emil and a German named Bauer."[243] "The Jews were escorted to the gas chambers by one SS man and five or six Ukrainian guards. The motor was turned on by one of the Ukrainian guards whose name I don't remember and the German, Gotringer."[244]

For cremations in the Reinhard death camps, steel railroad tracks were put on top of masonry blocks above a pit. The Jewish laborers stacked bodies onto the scaffold, or grill, and the bodies were burned. The ashes that remained after the burning process fell through the grill into the pit below. In Sobibor the exhumation process was said to have been completed by late March 1943.[245] The pits had been emptied of their buried victims by that time. Goncharenko described the Sobibor cremation apparatus as "cast-iron posts" that extended "out of a reinforced concrete base, and on top were iron rails assembled to form a grate." It measured "about 10 meters long and about 6 meters wide. The corpses were laid on the steel grate in four rows, and stacked a meter high." They were doused with some type of white substance and then burned. Once all the bodies were burned, the Jewish labor detail collected the ashes and searched for gold, including teeth.[246] The burning of the bodies in Sobibor continued until the camp closed in late fall 1943.[247] "The corpses of the people who had been killed were loaded onto carts, carried over to specially built pyres, and burned. The bones that remained were ground into powder and put on a pile."[248] At least one guard in Sobibor admitted to personally guarding the Jewish workers who burned the bodies at the pits.[249] "The mass burnings resulted in huge fires. The guards in the watchtowers could see the flames whenever the wind blew in their direction, making it hard for them to breathe."[250]

WHO WAS THE TRAWNIKI GUARD WHO OPERATED THE GAS CHAMBERS AT SOBIBOR?

Less is apparently known about the Trawniki guard or guards who operated the gassing engine at Sobibor than either of the other two Reinhard camps. The names Emil and Grigorij have been referred to in association with that function, by different sources. According to the site deathcamps.org, there were two men with the name Emil who had served at Sobibor: Emil Zischer and Emil Kostenkow/Kostenko.[251] Zischer deserted from Sobibor in December 1942. An SS-*Zugwachmann*, Emil Kostenko, is listed as having been killed in Trieste on May

15, 1944.[252] There were also at least two Grigorijs that had been assigned to Sobibor: Grigorij Lyachov and Grigorij Sergienko.[253] A Grigorij who had worked at the Sobibor gassing engine is said to have deserted along with his Treblinka counterpart, Ivan Marchenko, while assigned to the HSSPF Adriatic Coast in 1945.[254]

THE TRAWNIKI GUARDS DURING THE SOBIBOR UPRISING AND END PHASE OF THE CAMP

In addition to killing the Germans, the revolt's success also hinges on stealing enough guns to fend off possible resistance from most of the 100 or so Ukrainian guards. Rifles and ammunition would have to be taken from the SS armory.[255]

According to an earlier plan for an uprising, around August 1943, after killing the SS, the Trawniki guards were supposed to join the prisoners and escape with them to the forest and join the partisans:[256]

Knowing that some Ukrainian guards have deserted the German cause in the past, if they do not open the front gate, Pechersky and his men will tell them in Russian that the Red Army is closing in and the Germans are losing the war. They will implore the Ukrainians to lay down their arms and join us in defeating the Germans.[257] Ukrainian guards shoot at us from the watchtowers. The main gate is well covered by these Ukrainians.[258]

When the last work Jews finished dismantling Sobibor, they were shot in Camp III by SS-Oberscharführer Gustav Wagner and two Trawniki Volksdeutsche NCOs, Alexander Kaiser and Franz Podessa.

THE ADRIATIC COASTAL REGION

The Trawniki guard company that was deployed to the Adriatic coast region from Poland in fall 1943 was commanded by SS-Obersturmführer Johann Schwarzenbacher. At least initially, it was integrated into the SS-Wachmannschaften battalion in Trieste and was known as Wachmannschaft I: Ostvolker (Guard Force I: Eastern Peoples). The strength of this company is believed to have been seventy men; however, according to Oberhauser, it was a reinforced company of about 200 men.[259] Its tasks included providing guards for German headquarters and offices in Trieste, and escorts during deployments into the operational areas where there were partisans.[260] Wachmannschaft I (Ostvolker) was the Trawniki guard company. Its strength had been reduced to fewer than 100 men after others of the company were dispersed among the other companies of the SS-Wachmannschaft battalion. By early 1944, the Trawniki guard company had about eighty-five men, of whom six were Germans, and a few were locally recruited men.[261] Schwarzenbacher handed over command of the Trawniki company to Schupo lieutenant Kurt Eibisch a few weeks after arriving in Trieste, so that he could focus on taking command of the entire SS-Wachmannschaft battalion.[262] On May 4, 1944, Himmler ordered that an additional fifty Trawniki guards be sent to Trieste to be assigned as cadres for the formation of local units in the Adriatic coast region.[263]

The SS-Wachmannschaften battalion (SS Guard Battalion) in the Adriatic coast region was formed mainly from locally recruited men, but its cadres also consisted of Germans from the Aktion Reinhard staff and Trawniki guards. Among the Reinhard staff of the battalion were Kurt Franz, Josef Oberhauser, Gottfried Schwarz, and Kurt Bolender. They were all members of the Waffen-SS.[264] The SS-Wachmannshaft battalion had six companies as of summer 1944, and Oberhauser's 6th Company is the one that guarded the Risiera complex in Trieste. Some elements of the company relocated in May 1944 to the outpost of Castelnuovo d'Istria, and later to the outpost of Mattuglie, both of which were located along the Trieste-Fiume road, side by side with Aktion Reinhard staff taking part in antipartisan operations.[265]

An organizational chart from February 1944 showed the SS-Wachmannschaft battalion as being composed of the following units in the following locations:[266] Wachmannschaft I (Ostvolker), with one company in Trieste, and Wachmannschaft II, with three companies: 1st Company in Trieste, 2nd Company in Trieste, and 3rd Company in Fiume and Pola.

According to Oberhauser, about thirty Trawniki guards were also transferred to the "Aussenstelle HSSPF in Pola."[267] This was probably the Sipo/SD branch office in Pola, which had a company that deployed for antipartisan operations in Istria. The unit consisted of Germans, Italians, and Belorussians and was commanded by SS-Obersturmführer Helmut Prasch. "In post-war interrogations, Prasch claimed that his company in Pola had had nothing to do with the Gestapo or the SD, but action reports signed by him in May 1944 referred to his unit as BdS-Aussenkommando Pola, or as SD-Einsatzkommando Pola."[268] Additionally, documents from March 1944 and January 1945 were signed by Prasch on letterhead that read "Befehlshaber der Sipo und SD i.d. OZAK Triest-Aussendienststelle Pola" (Commander of Sipo and SD of the Adriatic coast region, Trieste branch office in Pola). Of note is that another company formed by Belorussians serving in the SD was assigned to the Adriatic coast region in 1944. It was part of the 13th Belorussian Schuma battalion of the SD. In September 1944, it was stationed in San Daniele del Friuli, where there was a Sipo/SD headquarters, and the following month it was transferred to Pola, where it was subordinate to Prasch. The transfer order stated that the unit was to be used to fight partisans.[269]

The names of at least seven Trawniki guards who served in Wachmannschaft II are known:[270] Christian/Heinz Schmidt, SS-*Zugwachmann*, *Volksdeutsche*, committed suicide in Trieste, April 9, 1944; Emil Kostenko, SS-*Zugwachmann*, from 6th Company, killed in Trieste, May 15, 1944; Mychailow Sawka, SS-*Oberwachmann*, from 5th Company, killed on the Senosecchia-Storie road, June 2, 1944; Petro Nahorniak, SS-*Wachmann*, from 5th Company, reported missing, probably captured by partisans near Castelnuovo, May 24, 1944; Arnold Rosenke, SS-*Zugwachmann*, *Volksdeutsche*, quartermaster of 6th Company in 1945; Helmut/Heinrich Dahlke, *Volksdeutsche*, 6th Company, San Sabba (as of April 1945); and Siebert, *Volksdeutsche*, 6th Company, San Sabba (as of April 1945).

Apart from the Trawniki guards, the rest of Wachmannschaft II consisted of locally recruited men in the Adriatic coast region—Italians, Slovenes, and Croats.[271]

The 6th Company / SS-Wachmannschaft battalion: Formed around May 1944 at the Risiera di San Sabba complex, using Italian soldiers. The company initially numbered about eighty-five men, all Italians, plus Germans and Trawniki guards as cadre. Its commander was SS-Untersturmführer Josef Oberhauser, and his deputy was SS-Unterscharführer Kurt Bolender.[272] The company remained at the Risiera until the end of the war. Its men guarded the entrance to the complex, the courtyard, and the external perimeter. The unit also provided security along the Trieste-Fiume road under the command of security commander Christian Wirth, and then Dietrich Allers. This included guarding outposts and taking part in antipartisan operations. The main outpost (*Stutzpunkt*) manned by the unit was Castelnuovo d'Istria, and later Mattuglie. The unit bolstered Aktion Reinhard staff also assigned to these outposts.[273]

In early 1944, some elements of the SS-Wachmannschaft battalion were transferred to Gorizia and put under the command of SS-Untersturmführer Kurt Franz. Franz took part in recruitment for the Landschutz, targeting the villages in Gorizia Province. According to Franz, after six to eight weeks of training, the recruits were assigned to units. Most were probably assigned to the SNVZ (Slovenian Landschutz), but some may have also been integrated into the SS-Wachmannschaft battalion. Also according to Franz, his company was used "to protect the building sites of the defensive lines around Gorizia, and later also to patrol a section of the Gorizia-Trieste railway line. It was also certainly used in antipartisan operations." As a sector security commander, Franz was tasked with the protection of the road and railway line between Gorizia, San Daniele del Carso, and Opicina. As of June 1944, he had at his disposal only Italian RSI units but not units from the SS-Wachmannschaft battalion.[274]

The Trieste-Fiume road was one of the main communication lines in the Adriatic coastal region and so had great importance. It stretched through an area that was heavily infested by partisans, and ambushes against German vehicles became a daily occurrence, so it became a necessity to drive along in convoys with escorts of armored cars or other armored vehicles. Franz

Reichleitner, commander of the Reinhard section in Fiume, was killed on January 3, 1944, while driving by car on this road toward Trieste, in a partisan ambush, about 2 miles from Castelnuovo d'Istria.[275] The following day, probably in response to this ambush, German forces carried out a sweep operation in the area just north of Castelnuovo and killed five partisans.[276]

Aktion Reinhard staff who transferred from Poland to the Adriatic coast region were divided into three sections, which were located in Trieste, Fiume (Rijeka), and Udine. The section in Trieste was initially commanded by Gottlieb Hering, the one in Fiume by Franz Reichleitner, and the one in Udine by Franz Stangl. The section in Trieste was the one with the most staff, probably fifty in number. It was based in Risiera di San Sabba, a former rice mill. Part of this complex became a prison for Jews, political opponents of the Nazis, and partisans captured during sweep operations. For the management of the complex, including security, the staff included about twenty-to thirty Germans and about twelve to fifteen Trawniki guards.[277] In July 1944, Hering was replaced as the section commandant in Trieste by Josef Oberhauser. The section commandant in Fiume, Reichleitner, was killed by partisans on January 3, 1944. His successor was Stangl. The section based in Udine was commanded by Stangl and then by Fritz Kuttner, and then Arthur Walther starting in March 1944. This section helped provide security along the Trieste-Fiume road.[278]

Christian Wirth was killed on May 26, 1944, in an ambush on his car, by Slovenian partisans of the "Istrski Odred" (Istria Detachment), near the village of Erpelle, along the Trieste-Fiume road. "The exact place is indicated as near the village of Nazire di San Dorligo della Valle or near the so-called Vetta di Erpelle hill, around 1 kilometer northwest of the twin villages of Cosina-Erpelle, according to a Yugoslav reconstruction."[279] Wirth, who a few weeks earlier had been appointed German security commander of the Trieste-Fiume road, was traveling from Fiume to discuss an antipartisan operation when he was killed. After his death, Wirth's body was sent to the Risiera. A few days later he was buried in the German military cemetery of Opicina with military honors, in the presence of Globocnik and Aktion Reinhard staff. Immediately, rumors began to circulate that he had been killed by his own men, who feared and hated him. However, no concrete evidence has ever been shown to support this. Wirth was replaced in his position by Dietrich Allers.[280]

The Aktion Reinhard staff carried out various tasks in the Adriatic region, including tracking down and arresting Jews and seizing their property, managing of the Risiera San Sabba prison complex, training and commanding locally formed military/paramilitary units, providing security on the Trieste-Fiume road, conducting search operations and antipartisan actions, and helping in the construction of defensive lines in the region.[281]

The Risiera di San Sabba, often referred to as an extermination camp, was actually a police prison, used to hold detainees in transit to concentration camps and labor camps in

Germany. Nevertheless, many prisoners were killed in the prison, and their bodies were burned in a crematorium on the site.[282] The crematorium was built by Erwin Lambert, who had also helped build the gas chambers in the Aktion Reinhard death camps in Poland.[283]

According to the most-recent estimates, around 1,450 Jews, from the Adriatic coastal region, Veneto, and Croatia, passed through the Risiera on their way mainly to Auschwitz and Ravensbrück. "At least twenty-eight of them are confirmed" as having been killed in San Sabba.[284] Several thousand people passed through the Risiera, on their way to camps in Germany. An estimated 2,000–5,000 were killed in the San Sabba complex.[285] About thirty Jewish prisoners remained at the complex on a permanent basis working as tailors, shoemakers, cleaners, etc., just as the Reinhard staff had kept prisoners alive in the death camps in Poland to service their personal and administrative needs.[286] What criteria were used as the basis to kill prisoners at the complex is not known. "It seems likely that in most cases the killings were arbitrary," without a court decision. These killings were carried out in different ways—according to accounts of former prisoners, bludgeoning, hangings, and shootings were done.[287] Josef Oberhauser stated that prisoners were also gassed by using exhaust fumes.[288] The peak of the executions was August–November 1944 but continued through as late as March 1945. Apparently, the executioners were generally, but not always, Trawniki guards (indicated as "Ukrainians" in depositions). They also burned the bodies afterward. These Trawniki guards—there were apparently twelve to fifteen of them—also guarded the Risiera complex.[289]

The senior NCO at the prison, called the *Spiess*, was Heinrich Gley, who had previously served at Belzec and had overseen cremations there. He was later replaced by Werner Dubois, and then Otto Stadie.[290] The Risiera was not only a prisoner transit facility; it also served as a warehouse for seized goods, contained a barracks that housed a unit that fought against partisans and provided security for the Trieste-Fiume road, and was considered the main base for the Aktion Reinhard staff in the Adriatic coastal region.[291] Lorenz Hackenholt, who had designed the gas chambers in the Aktion Reinhard camps in Poland, worked at the complex. He was apparently in charge of the vehicle garage. In April 1944, he was awarded the Iron Cross 2nd Class by Globocnik.[292] The Risiera complex was closed on April 29, 1945. On that day, the Jewish prisoners who worked there were freed. "Oberhauser even shook their hands." Most of the personnel headed for the city center as partisans entered the area. During the night, the crematorium was blown up in an attempt to hide what had happened at the site.[293]

Johann Schwarzenbacher was born in 1909, in Munich. He had served in the SS-Totenkopfverbande in 1941 and was then assigned to the SSPF Lublin, Globocnik. He became a company commander in the Trawniki training camp. In January 1942, he was promoted to SS-*Untersturmführer* and became a Trawniki guard battalion commander. He led this battalion during the suppression of the Warsaw Ghetto uprising in spring 1943. For the remainder of his time in Poland, he commanded the three Trawniki guard companies guarding Poniatowa labor camp. He was then assigned to the HSSPF Adriatic Coast, Globocnik, for the rest of the war. Formally, he was assigned to the staff company of HSSPF "East" until November 20, 1943, then to the staff company of the Waffen-SS in the service of the RSHA, and finally, from May 1, 1944, to the staff company of the Waffen-SS in the service of the HSSPF Adriatic Coast.[294] Schwarzenbacher was killed by Slovenian partisans in an ambush on June 2, 1944, on the road between Senosecchia and Storie, east of Trieste. "According to a partisan account, the ambush targeted a convoy formed by a truck, a car, and three motorcycles, and took place near the village of Sinadole; the vehicles were returning to Trieste from Senosecchia, after a raid in the village of Villabassa, during which two partisans and four civilians had been killed."[295] In the report on Schwarzenbacher's death, it was indicated that he had been shot in the head and legs. It was also noted that the partisans had confiscated his identity tag. In addition to Schwarzenbacher, ten troops from the SS-Wachmannschaft battalion were killed, four had been wounded, and eleven others were reported as missing.[296] After Schwarzenbacher's death, command of the SS-Wachmannschaft battalion was temporarily taken over by *SS-Hauptsturmführer* and Schupo (abbreviation for "Schutzpolizei") captain Guido Hornof, an operations officer for antipartisan operations.[297] Command was then taken over either by Dietrich Allers or Kurt Eibisch.[298]

Kurt Franz had been a trainer and commander of the Trawniki guard company in Belzec. Later, he was deputy commandant of Treblinka II, and once Franz Stangl departed for the Adriatic coast, he became commandant of Treblinka II. Franz claimed to have been assigned to Trieste starting in November or December 1943. He was reportedly assigned to the school where the SS-Wachmannschaft battalion was being formed and trained, as trainer and commander of a platoon of Italian recruits. In January 1944, with his platoon, which later expanded to company size and was known as Kommando"G," he transferred to Gorizia. In Gorizia, he formed and led a school for Landschutz troops, where Slovene recruits were trained. On March 17, 1944, he was awarded the Iron Cross 2nd Class. In mid-1944, he was appointed security commander of the San Daniele del Carso sector. He was wounded in combat against partisans probably in October 1944. He returned to duty in Gorizia in February 1945 as a security commander and as a trainer for a Republican Fascist militia unit.[299]

Josef Oberhauser had been commander of a Trawniki guard platoon at Belzec and was then an assistant to Christian Wirth. Like Franz, as the SS-Wachmannschaft battalion was being formed he was assigned to the school as a company commander and possibly also as a trainer. Later, his position in the guard battalion was taken over by Gottfried Schwarz, and he went back to being Wirth's right-hand man. However, in May 1944, he took command of the 6th Company of the SS-Wachmannschaft battalion and retained that assignment until the end of the war. The company was housed at the Risiera San Sabba. He also became commandant of the Risiera complex, replacing Gottlieb Hering. He remained there until the German retreat from the area on April 29, 1945.[300]

Gottfried Schwarz had been deputy commandant of Belzec. After that camp closed, he became commandant of the Dorohucza labor camp. In the Adriatic coast region, he was appointed commander of the 2nd Company of the SS-Wachmannschaft battalion. This unit was stationed in Udine Province, and in May 1944 he was based in Gemona, where he was probably also the security commander. He was killed in a fight with partisans on June 19, 1944, near San Pietro di Ragogna, northwest of Udine.[301]

Elements of the SS-Wachmannschaft battalion participated in the last large antipartisan operation conducted by the Germans in the Adriatic coast region, known as Operation "Winterende," which took place March 19–April 5, 1945, in the valley and plateaus north and east of Gorizia.[302] The advance of the southeastern front made it necessary to try to eliminate the threat of the partisans in the immediate rear areas. As a result, two parallel operations were conducted: Operation Winterende (Winter End); and Operation "Fruhlingsanfang" (Spring Start).

Winterende was carried out in the Chiapovano valley (Cepovanski dol), north and east of Gorizia, under the command of the HSSPF Adriatic Coast. Fruhlingsanfang was led by the HSSPF Alpenland and was conducted in the area around Circhina, also northeast of Gorizia, including mountainous areas across the border between Italy (the Adriatic coast region) and the German Reich (the Oberkrain region, part of the annexed northern Slovenia). Because all areas belonging to the Adriatic coast region, Laibach/Ljubljana Province, and the Reich were involved, the operations were conducted jointly by HSSPF Adriatic Coast, Globocnik, and HSSPF Alpenland, Rosener.[303]

Among the units deployed for Operation Winterende was Kampfgruppe "Lerch," led by SS-Sturmbannführer Ernst Lerch, a member of Globocnik's personal staff.[304] The unit consisted of elements of Globocnik's headquarters staff and elements of a Serbian-Chetnik division that had deployed to the Adriatic coast region in December 1944–January 1945.[305] In late March 1945, when Kampfgruppe "Lerch" was deployed in the area of Monte Signi (Sinji vrh), north of Aidussina, it also included a unit referred to as the "Allers" Company.[306] This unit was probably an Aktion Reinhard staff unit or one of the companies of the SS-Wachmannschaft battalion.[307]

Casualties of these operations included the following:[308]

SS-Zugwachmann Arnold Rosenke, reported as MIA, March 1945
SS-Unterscharführer Kurt Bolender, wounded and transported to a hospital in Ljubljana, March 31, 1945
SS-Obersturmführer Josef Oberhauser, lightly wounded
SS-Oberscharführer Karl Frenzel, wounded by a mortar splinter

The result of these final two antipartisan operations was to "temporarily weaken and disorganize the units of the partisan IX Corp operating in the area"; however, the partisans were not destroyed, and in a short time they regained their strength and were able to take initiative in the closing days of the war as the Germans retreated.[309]

Among Aktion Reinhard staff who were awarded the Antipartisan Badge was Karl Schiffner, who had attended a six-week antipartisan combat course at the Partisan Combat School in Duino. Gustav Munzberger (who had worked at the gas chambers in Treblinka II) had attended a similar course for about ten days, probably at the same school.[310]

In mid-March 1945, a Yugoslav offensive along the Dalmatian coast, conducted by the Yugoslav Liberation Army, began in the Knin-Gracac region. Weak German forces in Dalmatia could not counter with effective resistance and withdrew northward along the coast, reaching the Fiume/Susak area in the second half of April 1945. By April 20, the Germans had to abandon Susak and retreat, taking up positions along the fortified defensive belt around Fiume. Yugoslav units managed to penetrate German lines north of the Fiume sector and southwest of there on the Istria Peninsula and began to approach Trieste, their final and main objective. Starting on April 28, 1945, fighting against German forces took place in several areas of the Trieste external defensive belt, and by April 30 the city was surrounded.[311] Troops of the German 97th Army Corps, formerly called Generalkommando "Kubler," deployed to defend Fiume, were surrounded by the end of April, in the area of Villa del Nevoso. Fiume had to be abandoned by May 2, 1945, and the German troops surrendered on May 7, 1945.[312]

It is likely that when the Yugoslav army approached Fiume, any elements of Aktion Reinhard staff still in the city retreated to Trieste. As Yugoslav forces entered the Adriatic coast region from the southeast, from the west came British and New Zealand units advancing from the Italian front after breaking through the Gothic Line and crossing the Po River. On May 1, 1945, elements of the British 6th Armored Division reached Udine. The following day, the 2nd New Zealand Division entered Trieste. "Globocnik abandoned Trieste at the last moment." A few hours before the city was cut off, on April 28, he left the city with his SS and police staff, heading north in a motorized column toward Austria.[313] Globocnik's column drove toward the Tagliamento River valley, but near Tarcento, on April 30, it was attacked by Allied aircraft and temporarily scattered. Shortly thereafter, the column reached the Carnia region, where the Udine province borders Austria. Aktion Reinhard staff were with him. During the retreat, it is known that Franz Hodl was heavily wounded. He had for a time worked at the gas chambers in Sobibor.[314]

On May 2, 1945, British forces had advanced north, heading toward the Tagliamento River valley, leading toward Austria. The British advance was momentarily halted near Gemona by a German defensive position taken up by 200–300 Waffen-SS troops of the "Karstjager" division, supported by some tanks and artillery. Other more numerous German units were concentrated in Venzone a few miles farther north. On May 2, during their withdrawal through the area, the Germans massacred fifty-one inhabitants, including women and children, in the village of Avasinis, west of Gemona.[315] The Germans abandoned Venzone and began to retreat toward Austria on May 6, 1945. British advance elements followed after them. On May 7, 1945, the general German surrender was signed in Reims. A ceasefire was to take effect on May 9. Up to this point, the Germans feared that the British advance into the Carinthia region might become an obstacle to the retreat of Army Group "E" withdrawing from Yugoslavia. When the German surrender was signed, it became clear that elements of that army group would not be able to reach Austria and would have to surrender in Yugoslavia. British occupation was considered preferable to that of the dreaded Soviets and Yugoslavs.

On May 8, 1945, British advance units reached Klagenfurt.[316] "Globocnik went into hiding, but a few weeks later he was tracked down by the British in an Alpine hut near the Weissensee Lake, where he was hiding with Rainer and a few close collaborators [Lerch, Michalsen, Hofle]." Upon capture, on May 31, 1945, he committed suicide with poison. In early May, Aktion Reinhard staff had also entered Austria. Around May 7–8, the unit was disbanded by its commander, Allers. "The men attempted to go back to their homes in small groups. Some perhaps succeeded, but many were taken prisoner by the Allies. According to some depositions, some were captured by the British, who let them go after disarming them, since they were wearing police uniforms" as opposed to SS uniforms. Those captured by American forces were put in internment camps. Later, they were released and returned to civilian life. Some, fearing prosecution for their role in Aktion Reinhard, disappeared, such as Lorenz Hackenholt, and some fled abroad, such as Franz Stangl and Gustav Wagner.[317] Some were detained in a camp in Bad Aibling, in Bavaria. Others, mainly from the Udine section, were held in Habach (near Weilheim), in Bavaria, and in Aalen in Baden-Württemberg. Allers himself was held in a British camp near Villach, and later in the Wolfsberg camp, then in a labor camp in Weissenstein an der Donau. He was released from there in early 1947.[318]

After the war, several former Trawniki guards lived in Trieste for varying periods. Some remained temporarily and obtained residence permits from the Italian authorities until they resettled in other countries. Some also obtained Italian citizenship and remained in Trieste or Italy.[319] At least one Trawniki guard (a Ukrainian from a village near Sobibor) is known to have transferred from the SS-Wachmannschaft battalion to the 24th Waffen-Gebirgs "Karstjager" Division der SS (the 24th SS Mountain Division "Karstjager") in December 1944. He was reportedly killed in the area of Gemona, north of Udine, in the last days of the war.[320]

CHAPTER 2

PROFILES OF THE *WACHMÄNNER*

BIRTHPLACES AND NATIONALITIES

As noted by historian Dr. David Rich, the Trawniki guards were almost universally identified as "Ukrainians" in descriptions given after the war by bystanders and victims who witnessed their activities up close and personal. This, however, was a blanket generalization, since the Trawniki guard force overall consisted of numerous eastern European nationalities. Although a definitive breakdown is not possible, a rough estimate could be as follows:

Ukrainian: 50%
Russian: 30%
Volksdeutsche: 10%
Other: 10% (Balts, Tatars, Poles, et al.)

Looking at the roster of guards deployed to Auschwitz-Birkenau, for example, Dr. Rich noted the following:

The contingent of 150 men did not consist exclusively of Ukrainians. Of the sixty-two men whose ethnic origins are known from wartime records, thirty-eight were Ukrainian, eighteen were Russian, there were four *Volksdeutsche*, and one each of Belorussian and Bulgarian nationality. All were Soviet citizens.

However, also of interest was the idea that "the self-identification of nationality that the men provided to the Trawniki office staff when they entered service was ambiguous: some Russians were born and lived in parts of central Ukraine, and some Ukrainians in Russia."[1] Dr. Rich expanded on this concept when asked about the nationality of the Trawniki guards and the apparent ambiguousness in many cases of distinguishing Ukrainians from Russians and vice versa:

That is a great unresolved mystery, but I truly suspect there is no "right" or knowable answer. The whole question of self-identification is mired, even among the greatest academic specialists, in really intractable understanding of individual identification. Many of these men undoubtedly saw themselves as Soviet: no longer Russian, Ukrainian, etc. Their ethnic heritage had ceased to mean anything to them.[2]

Some Trawniki recruits even passed themselves off as being of other nationalities in order to increase their chances of being recruited. Some of the known examples of this were the following:

Emanuel Vertogradov: a Russian who passed himself off as a *Volksdeutsche* by speaking passable German and went by the last name of Schultz
Alexander Zakharov: a Russian who passed himself off as a *Volksdeutsche* by speaking passable German and went by the last name of Pruss
Vladimir Pronin: a Russian who passed himself off as Ukrainian
Emil Gutarz: Hid the fact that he was half Jewish. This fact was later discovered; however, he was allowed to remain in Trawniki service as the aide to the commandant of Treblinka I.
Petr Karnashnikow: a Russian who passed himself off as Lithuanian and went by the Lithuanian equivalent of his Russian name, Petras Karnashenkas
Jakob Zechmeister: May or may not have been a *Volksdeutsche*. After the war, when he was tried, the Soviet authorities referred to him as Yakov Tsekmistro, which would have been the Russian or Ukrainian equivalent of the German name he had used.
Mitrofan Klotz: it is unclear if this man was *Volksdeutsche* or Ukrainian; however, his last name is clearly German.

It will never be known how many Trawniki guards were actually of a nationality other than what they claimed to be. Some knew that the Germans preferred recruiting Ukrainians and Balts over Russians and Poles, and sometimes identified themselves to suit their needs of survival accordingly, as shown by the above examples. At a conference held in Trawniki in 2013, Dr. Peter Black, chief historian of the US Holocaust Memorial Museum in Washington, DC, presented his findings for a statistical analysis on the nationality of the Trawniki guards. He based his results after examining approximately 981 Trawniki *Personalbogen* (which represents nearly 20 percent of all Trawniki guards). His findings were the following:

Ukrainian: 45%
Russian: 27%
Volksdeutsche: 15%
Other: 13%

Dr. Black also found that 57 percent of the sample were nineteen to twenty-four years of age.[3]

EXAMPLES OF CIVILIAN OCCUPATIONS OF TRAWNIKI GUARDS

Vladas Amanaviczius: barber in Lithuania (prewar); miner in Belgium (postwar)
Mikhail Andrejenko: accountant (postwar)
Philip Babenko: farmworker on a collective farm
Andrej Babitsch: allegedly an NKVD officer (prewar)
Georg Backer: laborer
Wilhelm Baltschys: student
Nikolaj Belous: metalworker at the Kharkov Tractor Plant (prewar); stevedore at the Lvov Locomotive and Rail Car Repair Plant (postwar)
Eugen Binder: metalworker or locksmith
Nikolaj Bondarenko: machinist
Dimitri Borodin: completed a two-year accounting course; shop steward in road construction, with twelve commendations received on the job (postwar)
Nikolaj Boschko: mechanic
Piotr Browzew: plumber; machine fitter / metalworker in Leningrad (postwar)
Vladimir Bruchaki: cabinetmaker
Nikolaj Bukowjan: laborer
Vasili Burljajew: metalworker or locksmith
Prokofij Businnij: worker on a state farm in the Kiev region (postwar)
Alexander Byschkow: guard at a power station (postwar)
Ivan Chapajew: laborer
Nikolaj Chernyshev: machinist (prewar); tractor driver (postwar)
Vasili Chlopeckyj: butcher, Lvov region (prewar); sausage maker at a dining facility in the Lvov region (postwar)
Ivan Chornobaj: stoker in a depot at the Rava-Russka railroad station and locomotive conductor / assistant operator of steam engines in the Lvov region
Eduard Chrupowitsch: music student
Alexander Chruschew: lathe operator
Jurko Danilov: agricultural laborer
Valerian Danko: mechanic
Konstantin Demida: cartwright
Ivan Demjanjuk: tractor driver
Alexander Dukhno: student at the Sverdlovsk/Yekaterinburg Mining Institute (postwar)
Vladimir Emelyanov: barber

Alexander Fedchenko: unemployed pensioner in the Rostov region (as of 1968)
Ivan Filipow: mechanic
Myron Flunt: blacksmith
Vladimir Gadsicki: worker at a building materials combine in Rovno (postwar)
Paul Garin: driver
Stanislau Gliscinski: farmer
Josef Glista: carpenter
Alexander Golub: laborer
Anton Gontscharuk: shoemaker
Mikhail Gorbachev: plumber in Angarsk in the Irkutsk region (postwar)
Nikolaj Gordejew: farmer
Alexei Govorov: head of a collective farm, 1947–1949; farmer in an agricultural cooperative
Ivan Grigorchuk: worker at a paper factory (prewar); stable boy (postwar)
Ilmar Haage: farmworker
Bronislaw Hajda: cobbler/shoemaker
Theodor Heinrich: agronomist
Nikolai Isatschenko: driver
Ivan Ivchenko: cook
Liudas Kairys: gardener
Petr Karnashnikov: farmer
Yakov Karplyuk: worker on a collective farm; arsenal specialist in the Novograd-Volynsk Timber
    Procurement Establishment (postwar)
Andrej Keliwnik: agricultural laborer on a collective farm
Semen Kharkovskij: stoker and mechanic in a laundry facility in Kharkov (postwar)
Yakov Klimenko: strap operator for a housing construction trust in the Tula region (postwar)
Mitrofan Klotz: mechanic or metalworker on a collective farm (postwar)
Grigorij Kniga: crew member in geological exploration
Ivan Knysch: laborer (prewar); director of a collective farm (postwar); convicted in 1946 for
    illegally storing combat weapons and sentenced to one year in a collective labor camp.
Alexei Kolgushkin: craftsman's assistant at a cheese factory in the Yaroslavl region (postwar)
Ivan Kondratenko: completed courses at the Kiev Pedagogical School in 1941; trained to be a
    teacher (prewar); worker on a peat farm in the Cherkassy region (postwar)
Stefan Kopytiuk: entered Trawniki service at the age of sixteen (probably the youngest person
    ever to serve as a Trawniki guard)
Mikhail Korzhikow: engine stoker (prewar); instructor at agrarian department in the Orenburg/
    Chkalov region (postwar); assistant excavator mechanic (postwar)

Ivan Kostinow: cook or agricultural laborer on collective farms and a state farm
Nikolai Kototschilow: electric technician
Petr Koval: farmer on a collective farm
Andrei Kuchma: farmer on a collective farm
Alexei Kulinitsch: laborer
Samuel Kunz: carpenter in the German Ministry of Construction in Bonn (postwar)
Ivan Kurinnij: guard at a labor camp in Kiev, 1946; inspector at the Kiev regional labor camp; completed Kaliningrad Officer Cadet School of the MVD and assigned to Norilsk, 1951–1954; candidate member of the Soviet Communist Party, 1951–1954; excluded from party and dismissed from MVD after it had been discovered that he had served the Germans during the war; craftsman; technician in a highway department; and railway switchman at a train station
Yakov Kusmin: agricultural laborer
Ananij Kuzminsky: carpenter on a collective farm (postwar)
Stepan Kwaschuk: farmer
Mikhail Lapot/Laptev: forger on a collective farm (postwar)
Alexei Lazorenko: carpenter (prewar); timberman at a mining plant (postwar)
Nikolai Leontev: mechanic in a clock factory (postwar)
Filip Levchishin: disinfector in a regional hospital (postwar)
Grigorij Linkin: animal technician on a collective farm (postwar)
Vasili Litvinenko: storeman
Josef Loch: farmer
Nikolaj Malagon: manual laborer
Ewgen Maliart: tailor
Sergej Malov: math teacher
Nikita Mamchur: horseman on a collective farm (postwar)
Ivan Marchenko: farmer in Krivoi Rog (according to his family, he had been a miner)
Anastasij Mawrodij: construction worker (postwar)
Alexei Milutin: electromechanic
Stepan Mogilo: driver
Vladimir Morozov: student at a music conservatory in Kharkov
Grigorij Nesmejan: teacher (unemployed as of 1965)
Boris Odartschenko: painter and plasterer
Taras Olejnik: plumber / pipe handler in a repair and construction company (postwar)
Vasili Orlovskij: bookkeeper on a state farm (postwar)

Vasili Pankov: mechanical technician at the "Stalin" Machine Works in Krematorsk, Stalino/ Donetsk region (postwar)
Georg Pankratov: driver
Evdokim Parfinyuk: bricklayer on a collective farm (postwar)
Nikolaj Pavli: civil engineer in an agricultural department in the Dnepropetrovsk region
Nikolaj Petriuk: assistant conductor
Vasili Podenok: teacher
Mikhail Poleshuk: farmer
Alexander or Vasili Popov: electromechanical engineer for the "Don Power Utility" in Gorlovka; completed studies at the Novocherkassk Mining Institute
Alfred Poppe: mechanic
Yevgenij Prigoditsch: shoemaker/cobbler
Samuel Pritsch: carpenter (prewar); farmer on a collective farm (postwar)
Kiril Prochorenko: driver on a state farm (postwar)
Vladimir Pronin: mechanic
Vasili Pudenoks: farmer
Dimitri Pundik: worker in a sugar factory (postwar)
Jakob Reimer: student
Waclaw Reymann: peasant
Anatoli Rige: teacher; spoke German, Russian, and Italian
Alexander Rittich: student
Vasili Rjaboschapka: student
Valentin Rozhanskij: student
Nikolaj Rubanov: wall worker
Anatoli Rumjanzew: mechanic; telegraph: Morse code operator
Fedor Ryabeka: driver (prewar); freight handler/loader and guard at a secondary school (postwar)
Prokofij Ryabtsev: mason for a collective farm construction administration (postwar)
Boris Safronow: cooper
Rustambek Saitow: factory worker
Ivan Saplawny: electric technician
Alexei Schamordin: machinist
Heinrich Schafer: office clerk
Karl Schaubert: agricultural laborer, machine operator in the Omsk region (Siberia)
Wasyl Scheftschuk: laborer
Vasili Schishajew: tractor driver
Emanuel Schultz: engineer in Pechora forest combine in Komi ASSR (postwar)

Alexander Semigodow: metalworker or mechanic at a radio set factory in Kuznetsk, Penza region (postwar)
Mychajlo Semtschij: tailor
Vasili Shkarpovich: farmworker and apprentice tailor (prewar); machinist at a brick factory in the Moscow region (postwar)
Vasili Shuller: worker in a bread factory in Stalino/Donetsk; concreter at a reinforced-concrete construction factory (postwar)
Ivan Shvidkij: farmworker and ore miner (prewar); loader in the transport section of the Dzerzhinsk Coal Trust (postwar); as of 1952, his brother Mikhail was serving as a captain in the Soviet army
Nikolaj Skakodub: instructor in artificial animal insemination on a state farm (postwar)
Nikolaj Skorokhod: agricultural laborer
Kuzma Sokur: tractor driver
Nikolaj Soljanin: driver
Willi Stark: electrician
Alexander Sturkis: student
Trofim Sucharyba: cook/baker
Franz Swidersky: farmer (prewar); ropemaker (postwar)
Stanislau Swidrak: logger
Oleksa Tarasiuk: cobbler
Fedor Tartynskij: fire stoker at a zinc factory (postwar)
Ivan Tellmann: agricultural laborer/worker on a state farm in the Novosibirsk region
Ivan Terekhov: peasant farmer (prewar); driver and car park dispatcher at a mine in Yakut ASSR; awarded merit certificate for good work, July 1961
Vladimir Terletskij: cashier at a mill; actor at a drama theater (prewar)
Abram Thiessen: administrative clerk in Altenkirchen, Germany (postwar)
Fedor Tikhonovskij: farmer; worker at a bread factory; worker at a metallurgical factory (prewar); worker at a mechanical repair factory (postwar)
Mikhail Titov: tractor driver at a mine (postwar)
Andrej Tkatschow: railroad dispatcher
Petro Tschaplinski: salesman
Ivan Tscherkasow: farmer
Vladimir Tscherniawsky: student
Zaki Tuktarov: order placer at a village consumer office (postwar)
Andrei Vasilega: tailor
Michael Vasilenko: driver

Sergej Vasilenko: wagon boy on a collective farm; "shock worker," awarded two medals for good work (postwar)
Fedor Vilshun: strapper at a brick factory (postwar)
Ivan Voloshin: completed two years of law school; investigator at the Novo-Yarychev Prosecutor's Office in the Lvov region, 1947; milling machine operator at a factory
Philip Wergun: farmer
Alexander Wisgunow: tractor driver
Vladas Zajankauskas: agricultural laborer
Akim Zuev: stock keeper at a summer camp (postwar)
Ivan Zvezdun: driver in Tajshet, Irkutsk region (postwar)

EXAMPLES OF PRIOR RED ARMY SERVICE OF TRAWNIKI GUARDS

Vladas Amanaviczius: soldier, infantry; captured in June 1942
Mikhail Andrejenko: captured in August or September 1941, near Korsun-Shevchenko
Philip Babenko: soldier, infantry; conscripted in May 1941; captured on July 9, 1941, near Lyubar; remobilized in June–October 1945
Boris Babin: captured by Soviets in September 1944 and remobilized into Red Army, January 1945–July 1946
Georg Backer: soldier, artillery
Konstantin Balabayev: corporal, infantry; captured in May 1942
Wilhelm Baltschys: sergeant, infantry; conscripted in 1937; captured on December 28, 1941
Nikolaj Belous: soldier, infantry; conscripted in July 1941; captured in August 1941 near Mironovka railway station, near Kiev
Eugen Binder: soldier, armored; conscripted in 1940
Viktor Bogomolow: junior sergeant, armored vehicle commander; 40th Reconnaissance Battalion, 72nd Rifle Division; conscripted in November 1939; captured on July 27, 1941, near Vinnitsa
Nikolaj Bondarenko: soldier, infantry
Dimitri Borodin: sergeant, artillery; conscripted in November 1939; captured on June 26, 1941
Nikolaj Boschko: soldier, motorized; conscripted in April 1941; captured on August 10, 1941
Piotr Browzew: captured around August 1941 in the Novograd-Wolynsk region
Nikolaj Bukowjan: soldier, armored
Vasili Burljajew: soldier, artillery; captured in May 1942
Prokofij Businnij: captured in August 1941
Ivan Chapajew: soldier, signals; conscripted in 1940; captured in May 1942

Nikolaj Chernyshev: soldier, infantry; 227th Rifle Division; conscripted in May 1941; captured on July 29, 1941, near Korosten, in the Kiev region

Vasili Chlopeckyj: soldier, infantry; conscripted on June 29, 1941; captured on July 30, 1941

Ivan Chornobaj: soldier, infantry, sapper; sapper platoon, 66th Rifle Division; conscripted in July 1941; captured in May 1942 near Kharkov

Eduard Chrupowitsch: soldier, infantry and signals; conscripted in 1940; captured on July 26, 1941, in the Tarashchansk District

Alexander Chruschew: sergeant, border guards; conscripted in 1938; captured on July 14, 1941

Ignat Danilchenko: soldier, artillery; captured in May 1942; his left hand is tattooed with an airplane

Jurko Danilov: soldier, infantry

Valerian Danko: NCO, infantry (Romanian army, 1936); left Trawniki service to rejoin Romanian army

Konstantin Demida: soldier, infantry; conscripted on May 7, 1941; captured in May 1942

Ivan Demjanjuk: soldier, artillery; conscripted in 1940; captured in May 1942; shrapnel wound in the back

Wasyl Djomin: sergeant, infantry

Alexander Dukhno: captured on July 3, 1941

Fedor Duschenko: soldier, engineering; conscripted on May 30, 1941; captured on July 9, 1941

Vladimir Emelyanov: squad commander, replacement unit; conscripted in 1939; captured in May 1942 in Crimea

Jakob Engelhardt: captured in 1941, near Grodno

Alexander Fedchenko: soldier, infantry, machine gunner in an antiaircraft unit; 400th Rifle Division; conscripted on June 22, 1941; captured in May 1942 near Kerch

Fedor Fedorenko: soldier, truck driver; conscripted on June 23, 1941; captured in July 1941

Ivan Filipow: soldier, armored, motorcyclist

Myron Flunt: soldier, artillery (Polish army, 1933–34)

Paul Garin: NCO, artillery; conscripted in November 1939; captured on July 12, 1941

Stanislau Gliscinski: corporal, artillery (Polish or Red Army)

Josef Glista: German army, July–December 1942

Petro Goncharov: captured in spring 1942

Mikhail Gorbachev: conscripted on August 11, 1941; captured in May 1942; wounded in both legs

Nikolaj Gordejew: soldier, artillery; captured on July 4, 1941

Terentij Gordijenko: captured in August or September 1941, near Korsun-Shevchenko

Alexei Govorov: conscripted in 1937; captured on July 9, 1941; wounded by shrapnel in the chest; enlisted in Vlasov army, March 1945

Mikhail Gubrijenko: soldier, infantry; conscripted on July 10, 1941; captured on August 14, 1941

Ilmar Haage: soldier, artillery (served in Estonian army and Red Army)

Theodor Heinrich: corporal; conscripted in October 1939; captured on June 28, 1941

Nikolai Isatschenko: soldier, airborne assault trooper; conscripted in 1940; captured on July 2, 1941

Ivan Ivchenko: soldier, railroad combat engineer

Alexander Jager/Yeger: soldier, infantry

Pawlo Jurtschenko: soldier; captured in May 1942

Liudas Kairys: soldier, artillery; conscripted in 1940; captured on June 22, 1941

Yakov Karplyuk: conscripted in May 1941; captured on July 5, 1941

Andrej Keliwnik: heavy artillery; conscripted in October 1939; captured on July 11, 1941, in the Volhynia region

Semen Kharkovskij: captured in September 1941 in Kirovograd

Grigorij Kniga: soldier, communications; conscripted on May 28, 1941

Ivan Knysch: soldier, marine infantry; 83rd Marine Infantry Brigade; conscripted on June 10, 1941; captured in May 1942 near Kerch

Alexei Kolgushkin: conscripted in November 1939; captured in May 1942 in Crimea

Ivan Kondratenko: sergeant, infantry; conscripted in July 1941; 630th Reserve Rifle Regiment near Tbilisi, then 156th Rifle Division, 51st or 52nd Army in the Kuban region; captured in May 1942 at Kerch; remobilized into Red Army by field military commissariat in Oswiecim/ Auschwitz, June 1945, and served in an evacuation hospital until August 1946

Mikhail Korzhikow: soldier, cavalry; conscripted in 1940; captured on June 26, 1941

Grigorij Koslow: conscripted on May 10, 1941

Ivan Kostinow: soldier, infantry; 217th Guards Rifle Regiment; captured in May 1942 in Kerch

Nikolai Kototschilow: NCO, artillery

Petr Koval: soldier, mortar unit; captured in May 1942

Pavel Kozlov: captured in May 1942

Grigorij Kuchichidze: soldier, infantry

Andrei Kuchma: conscripted in June 1941; captured in August 1941 near Mironovka, Kiev region

Ivan Kurinnij: conscripted in 1940; captured in May 1942; awards: "Victory over Germany during the Great Patriotic War" medal, and "30 Years of the Soviet Armed Forces" medal

Yakov Kusmin: soldier, signals; conscripted on September 27, 1941; captured in July 1942

Ananij Kuzminskij: conscripted on July 10, 1941; captured on July 20, 1941

Stepan Kwaschuk: soldier, flak
Mikhail Lapot/Laptev: soldier, antiaircraft; conscripted in December 1939; captured in May 1942 at Kerch
Alexei Lazorenko: soldier, infantry; conscripted on June 5, 1941; captured on July 27, 1941
Nikolai Leontev: captured around November 1941
Filip Levchishin: conscripted in 1935–1937; conscripted again on July 7, 1941; captured on July 14, 1941
Grigorij Linkin: conscripted in July 1941; captured in September 1941
Josef Loch: soldier, artillery (Polish army, 1929–1931 and 1939)
Mikhail Lysak: captured on August 2, 1941, near Mironovka, Kiev region
Nikolaj Malagon: conscripted in February 1941; captured in August 1941
Sergej Malov: lieutenant, artillery
Nikita Mamchur: conscripted in June 1941; captured in October 1941
Ivan Marchenko: soldier, infantry; conscripted on May 27, 1941; captured on July 10, 1941
Eugeniusz Maytchenko: sergeant, Polish army, 1944–1945; awarded for bravery
Alexei Milutin: soldier, artillery; conscripted in 1939; captured on July 22, 1941
Stepan Mogilo: soldier, transportation section; conscripted in 1940; captured in May 1942
Alexander Moskalenko: soldier, infantry, antitank unit; captured in May 1942 near Kerch; remobilized into Red Army and served in airfield engineering battalion (1947)
Boris Odartschenko: soldier, infantry; conscripted on June 29, 1941; captured in February 1942
Taras Olejnik: conscripted in May 1941; captured in July 1941
Nikolaj Olejnikov: captured in May 1942
Georgij Ossowoy: soldier, infantry (German army at Stalingrad)
Vasili Pankov: soldier, truck driver, reconnaissance; conscripted on June 23, 1941; captured on July 29, 1941
Georg Pankratov: soldier, armored
Evdokim Parfinyuk: conscripted in 1932–1934; conscripted again on June 22, 1941; captured in late July 1941
Nikolaj Pavli: soldier, artillery; conscripted in 1940; captured on July 16, 1941; remobilized into Red Army, July 1945–May 1946
Nikolaj Petriuk: soldier, artillery; conscripted in 1940; captured on July 11, 1941
Vasili Pochwala: soldier, infantry; conscripted in 1941; captured in May 1942
Mikhail Poleshuk: soldier, artillery; conscripted in July 1941; captured in May 1942
Alfred Poppe: soldier, motorized; conscripted in 1940; captured on July 10, 1941
Vasili Pudenoks: soldier, machine gunner (eight months in Latvian army, one year in Red Army)
Yevgenij Prigoditsch: soldier, infantry; conscripted in 1940; captured in May 1942 in Kerch

Samuel Pritsch: conscripted in 1938–1940; conscripted again in May 1941; captured in August 1941

Vladimir Pronin: soldier; captured in May 1942

Jakob Reimer: lieutenant, infantry; conscripted in January 1939; captured on July 6, 1941

Nikita Rekalo: soldier, infantry

Waclaw Reymann: gendarmerie in Dubno, Ukraine

Anatolie Rige: soldier, infantry; conscripted on June 23, 1941

Vasili Rjaboschapka: soldier, infantry; conscripted in May 1941; captured on August 12, 1941

Mikhail Rosgonjajew: soldier, engineering; conscripted in 1940; captured on July 20, 1941

Valentin Rozhanskij: soldier, infantry; captured in May 1942

Nikolaj Rubanov: soldier, infantry; captured in May 1942

Anatoli Rumjanzew: soldier, infantry, telegraph; Morse code operator; conscripted in 1940; captured in May 1942

Fedor Ryabeka: captured in August or September 1941, near Zhitomir

Prokofij Ryabtsev: soldier, reconnaissance; captured in late August 1941 near Rovno

Boris Safronow: soldier, artillery; captured in May 1942

Rustambek Saitow: private first class; captured on July 30, 1941

Ivan Saplawny: soldier, infantry

Yakov Savenko: conscripted on June 24, 1941; captured in August 1941

Heinrich Schafer: NCO; conscripted in November 1939; captured on June 22, 1941

Alexei Schamordin: infantry

Karl Schaubert: conscripted in 1939; captured in 1941 or 1942; shrapnel injury to left eye

Wasyl Scheftschuk: Soviet labor army; conscripted on May 24, 1941; captured on July 8, 1941

Vasili Schishajew: junior sergeant, infantry

Emanuel Schultz: conscripted in November 1939; captured in July 1941

Ivan Shalamow: soldier, infantry

Nikolai Shalayev: soldier, infantry, sapper, 58th Rifle Division, 13th Corps, 12th Army; conscripted in 1940; captured on July 3, 1941, near Ternovka, Kiev region; remobilized into Red Army, June 1945–August 1946

Vasili Shuller: senior sergeant, artillery; conscripted in 1939; captured in July 1941

Ivan Shvidkij: soldier, replacement unit; conscripted on June 28, 1941; captured on August 2, 1941, near Mironovka, Kiev region; remobilized into Red Army, March–October 1945

Nikolaj Skakodub: captured in July 1941

Nikolaj Skorokhod: soldier, armored

Georgij Skydan: soldier, artillery; 878th Artillery Regiment; conscripted on June 24, 1941; captured in mid-August 1941, probably in the Kiev region

Kuzma Sokur: soldier, infantry; conscripted on May 29, 1941; captured on July 10, 1941
Nikolaj Soljanin: sergeant, infantry; conscripted in 1939; captured on July 25, 1941
Anton Solonina: soldier, infantry; conscripted on June 1, 1941; captured on July 12, 1941
Willi Stark: sergeant, infantry, radio operator; conscripted in 1940; captured on July 1, 1941
Trofim Sucharyba: soldier, infantry
Wasyl Stoljarow: soldier, artillery; conscripted in 1939
Alexander Sturkis: soldier; conscripted in 1939; captured in 1941
Franz Swidersky: soldier, artillery; conscripted on May 25, 1941; captured on July 14, 1941;
    shrapnel injury to right eye: eye had to be removed; wears an eye patch
Fedor Tartynskij: soldier, infantry and telephone technician/communications; 227th Rifle Division;
    conscripted in May 1941; captured on July 30, 1941, in the Kiev region
Ivan Tellmann: conscripted in 1940; captured on July 24, 1941
Ivan Terekhov: heavy artillery regiment; conscripted in 1940; captured on August 4, 1941;
    wounded in leg and head
Fedor Tikhonovskij: soldier, communications; conscripted on June 23, 1941; captured on July
    6, 1941, near Shepetovka
Mikhail Titov: company 1st sergeant, machine gunner and artillery; conscripted in November
    1941; captured in May 1942 in Crimea
Ivan Tkachuk: captured in August 1941
Andrei Tkatschow: sergeant, artillery; conscripted on June 20, 1941; captured on July 20, 1941
Alexei Tronko: captured in August 1941
Ivan Tscherkasow: soldier, artillery; conscripted in 1940
Vladimir Tscherniawskij: soldier, chemical unit; conscripted on August 18, 1941; captured in
    May 1942; awarded bravery medal in silver during Trawniki service; awarded the wound
    badge in silver during Trawniki service, September 16, 1943
Zaki Tuktarov: conscripted in July 1941; captured in May 1942
Andrei Vasilega: soldier, infantry; conscripted on June 23, 1941; captured on August 3, 1941,
    in the Kiev region
Michael Vasilenko: soldier, infantry; conscripted on June 23, 1941; captured on July 23, 1941
Sergej Vasilenko: soldier, antiaircraft artillery, 6th Army; conscripted in 1938–1940; conscripted
    again on June 25, 1941; captured on August 17, 1941
Fedor Vilshun: captured in May 1942 in Kerch
Alexander Volobuyev: captured on July 19, 1941, in the Zhitomir region, wounded (changed
    his last name to Kuris after the war)
Ivan Voloshin: captured in October 1941
Philip Wergun: soldier, infantry; conscripted in October 1939; captured on July 7, 1941

Alexander Wisgunow: soldier, artillery; captured on July 21, 1941
Grigorij Yezhov: infantry
Vladas Zajankauskas: NCO, communications; conscripted in 1939; captured on July 10, 1941
Alexander Zakharov/Pruss: captured in August 1941
Eugen Zeitler: soldier, artillery; conscripted in 1940; captured on June 22, 1941
Akim Zuev: conscripted in June 1941; captured in July 1941
Ivan Zvezdun: captured in 1941 near Dubno

RECRUITMENT SOURCES

1) #1–1,250: September 1941–early 1942, 1,250 Red Army POWs, primarily Ukrainians but also Russians, Belorussians, Tatars, Balts, and *Volksdeutsche*, captured during the initial German attack on the Eastern Front in the summer and fall of 1941, especially in western and central Ukraine[4]

2) #1,250–2,550: April–June 1942, 1,300 Red Army POWs, primarily Ukrainians but also Russians, Belorussians, Tatars, Balts, and *Volksdeutsche*, captured during German attacks in southern Ukraine and the Crimean region in spring 1942[5] (Evidence, however, indicates that Red Army POWs were still represented sporadically up to the #2,900 range. For example, the *Volksdeutsche* recruit Willi Stark, a former Red Army POW, was assigned #2910.)

3) #2,550–3,050: November 1942–January 1943, 500 Ukrainian and Polish civilians living in southeastern Poland (Lublin District), and Galicia and Volhynia-Podolia (western Ukraine), and Goralians (an ethnic people living in the Goral region of the Tatra Mountains in southern Krakow District in southern Poland)[6]

4) #3,050–3,550: February–April 1943, 500 Ukrainian civilians primarily from the Stanislavov (Ivano-Frankivsk) region of eastern Galicia (western Ukraine)[7]

5) #3,550–4,550: June–July 1943, 1,000 Ukrainian civilians from southeastern Poland (southeastern Lublin District)[8]

6) #4,550–5,082: Late 1943–early 1944, 532 civilians, Ukrainian auxiliary policemen already working for the Germans, who retreated along with German forces upon the westward advance of the Red Army in late 1943–early 1944 (some of these auxiliary policemen were also *Volksdeutsche*; for example, Waclaw Reymann, assigned #4889), and Russian volunteers originally intended for the Vlasov army[9]

Virtually all of the early Trawniki guard recruits had been selected from among Soviet POWs held in the following POW camps:[10]

1) Stalag 301 in Lublin
2) Stalag 319 in Chelm
3) Stalag 360 in Rovno
4) Stalag 334 in Belaya Tserkov
5) Stalag 307 in Biala-Podlaska
6) Stalag 316 in Bialystok
7) Stalag 358 in Zhitomir
8) Stalag 324Z in Hrodna

German SS and police recruiters dispatched from Trawniki to find recruits for Trawniki guard service were told to pick out *Volksdeutsche* (ethnic Germans) and Soviet soldiers of non-Russian nationality; however, in reality, the recruiters apparently disregarded these guidelines, at least to an extent, as is reflected in the fact that a significant minority of Trawniki recruits were, in fact, Russian. The more reliable criterion when selecting recruits was to find those who still appeared relatively healthy despite the harsh conditions that prevailed in POW camps, such as lack of adequate food and shelter.[11]

EXAMPLES OF THOSE AWARDED MEDALS

Recommendation List: Eastern Peoples Medal for Bravery, 2nd Class with Swords, in Bronze, June 7, 1944:[12]

Zugwachmann Abraham Asmus, Saratov: Courageous in frequent deployments against bandits. Deployed his squad to a threatened area and captured an antitank rifle.
Zugwachmann Michael Bilezki: proved himself excellently at the construction project at the Bug River
Gruppenwachmann Fedor Filiminov, Zaporozhe: Abducted twice by bandits, yet made his way back to his unit. Has repeatedly proven himself in deployments against bandits/partisans.
Gruppenwachmann Roman Bilan, Kolomea: Acted courageously during a partisan ambush on Poniatowa, May 16, 1944. He disabled several bandits and captured several weapons.

Gruppenwachmann Nikita Bondar, Kiev: Repeatedly distinguished himself with courage in deployments against bandits/partisans. On May 16, 1944, he finished off a Russian lieutenant decorated with the Order of Lenin, in a battle with partisans in the Hrubieszow region.

Gruppenwachmann Vasili Salnikov, Tula: Captured by two bandits in Siedliszcze, 4 miles northeast of Chelm. He managed to shoot both as they ordered him to undress. He has excelled in several deployments.

Gruppenwachmann Nikolaj Olejnikov: has proven himself well in deployments against bandits/partisans, and in Aktion Reinhard

Rottenwachmann Nikolaj Demediuk, Zhytomir: captured a machine gun and shot a bandit in combat against bandits/partisans

Wachmann Fedor Jaworow, Odessa: Distinguished himself well in Aktion Reinhard. He belonged to the Aktion Reinhard Camps *Sonderkommandos* for nearly two years and conducted himself well.

Wachmann Wasyl Procyk, Brzezany: He is a machine gunner and distinguished himself while recovering fallen comrades, March 23, 1944, near Laskow-Smolikow, in a battle with numerically superior bandits/partisans.

Wachmann Nikolaj Wisinskij, Kolomea: As a machine gunner, distinguished himself, March 23, 1944, near Laskow-Smolikow, and saved his company from more-serious losses.

Recommendation List: War Merit Service Medal, SS Special Staff "Sporrenberg," SS "Streibel" Battalion, September 26, 1944:[13]

Oberzugwachmann Eugen Adler, Terespol
Oberzugwachmann Xaver Rucinski, West Prussia
Oberzugwachmann Heinrich Ulrich, Grunfeld
Zugwachmann Konstantin Schubrich, Torun/Thorn
Zugwachmann Wilhelm Reinhardt, Dennhof
Zugwachmann Leo Bisewski, West Prussia
Zugwachmann Samuel Karl, Balzer
Zugwachmann Heinrich Schaefer, Husenbach
Zugwachmann Samuel Kunz, Volga region
Zugwachmann Fritz Seibeneicher, Volkersdorf, Germany
Zugwachmann Jakob Frost
Zugwachmann Abraham Theissen
Zugwachmann Jakob Reimer
Zugwachmann Albert Braun

Recommendation List: Award for Bravery 2nd Class in Bronze, SS Special Staff "Sporrenberg," SS"Streibel" Battalion, September 26, 1944:[14]

Zugwachmann Franz Swidersky
Zugwachmann Vladas Zajankauskas
Zugwachmann Vladimir Chlopeckyj
Zugwachmann Nikolaj Olejnikov
Zugwachmann Boris Rogosa

EXAMPLES OF DISCIPLINARY PROBLEMS

Gerhard Blendowsky: three weeks under arrest for selling a bottle of vodka to a Jew in Trawniki, shortly after returning from Sobibor[15]

Alexander Borodin: shot fellow guard Wasyl Daniljuk while assigned to SS "Streibel" Battalion; handed over to the SS and Police Court in Czestochowa, December 11, 1944[16]

Tadeusz Denkiewicz: killed on August 30, 1943, for an undisclosed reason while possibly serving with the SS Garrison Administration HQ Zamosc[17]

Fedor Duschenko: three weeks under arrest for theft in Trawniki[18]

Paul Fessler: Sent back to Trawniki from Treblinka I because of chronic drunkenness. He remained a chronic drunk after the war.[19]

Ilmar Haage: shot and killed while breaking into the Trawniki material depot, July 1942[20]

W. Hryb: Involved in a brawl after purchasing alcohol. The Criminal Police in Zamosc investigated the incident, December 1943–January 1944.[21]

Dimitri Ivanov: while assigned to the SS "Streibel" Battalion, sent to police prison in Dresden, March 4, 1945 (reason unknown)[22]

Damian Jaroschuk: while assigned to the SS "Streibel" Battalion, sent to police prison in Dresden, March 4, 1945 (reason unknown)[23]

Nikolai Kototshilow: gross insubordination and dereliction of guard duty while assigned to Poniatowa; three weeks of imprisonment and then discharged from Trawniki service and sent back to his POW camp, Stalag 319, in Chelm, March 19, 1943[24]

Nikolaj Nikitin: was supposed to have been assigned to Flossenbürg on October 1, 1943, but instead was imprisoned at SS and Police Penal Camp Danzig-Matzkau (reason unknown)[25]

Petro Ostafijczuk: shot and killed by another guard as he broke into a Waffen-SS storage facility, March 18, 1943[26]

Nikolaj Pashchenko: was supposed to have been assigned to Flossenbürg on October 1, 1943, but instead was arrested (reason unknown)[27]

Alexander Potschinok: drunk on duty; sentenced to four weeks in a penal platoon[28]
Vladimir Pronin: imprisoned for theft of Jewish valuables in Trawniki[29]
Vasili Pudenoks: shot and killed while caught looting in a Jewish camp, July 20, 1942[30]
Ivan Shalamow: theft and assaulting a German; imprisoned in Majdanek[31]
Alexander Shapirov: was supposed to have been assigned to Flossenbürg on October 1, 1943, but instead was imprisoned at SS and Police Penal Camp Danzig-Matzkau (reason unknown)[32]
Nikolai Soljanin: theft of Jewish property during deportations in the Warsaw Ghetto, summer 1942; discharged from Trawniki service and sent back to his POW camp, Stalag 319, in Chelm, October 17, 1942[33]
Alexander Wisgunow: shot and killed while assaulting Schupo *Oberwachtmeister* Philip Grimm in Poniatowa, December 14, 1942[34]
Alexei Zhukov: arrested for drunkenness while escorting Jews to their work sites in Lvov[35]

Three drunk Trawniki guards posted at Sobibor went for a joyride and opened fire on men of the SS Galicia Division who were guarding a nearby estate in March 1944.[36]

The most-common disciplinary violations for Trawniki guards:

1) desertion or absence without leave
2) drunkenness
3) theft
4) corruption
5) violating curfew
6) sleeping on guard duty

Hundreds deserted, perhaps up to 20 percent.[37] Six or seven Trawniki guards were arrested and sent back to Trawniki in August 1943 for drunkenness and disciplinary problems while assigned to Janowska labor camp.[38] A German policeman noted that the Trawniki guards stole pervasively and that they particularly liked American $20 gold coins, which circulated by the dozens.[39] Stefan Kopytyuk stole goods taken from Jews at Trawniki and Sobibor and gave them to his sister. During almost all deportations, Trawniki guards stole valuables from Jews.

In Lublin, Nikolai Shalayev stole items during the deportations in March and April 1942. Nikolaj Olejnikow stole a pocket watch from an elderly Jew during a deportation from Piaski transit camp to Trawniki, took 500 zloty from another deportee in the Lublin District, and took a wristwatch from a woman in another operation.[40] Vasili Litvinenko took valuables from Jewish prisoners at Janowska as he escorted them to be shot at a killing pit. He later spent all the money he got from the valuables on alcohol.

SS-Rottenführer Erich Lachmann, who had supervised Trawniki guards both at Trawniki itself and also at Sobibor, stated after the war that "The Ukrainians were uncouth and unreliable, especially under the influence of alcohol. While they were actually on duty, they had to stay in line, but otherwise they did pretty much whatever they wanted."[41] In September 1943, Streibel stated that he wanted to recruit more men for Trawniki service from among the western Ukrainian community, because of the 3,600 or so men that he had, many of the eastern Ukrainians among them were unreliable.[42]

There were disciplinary problems with the Trawniki guards assigned to the "Heinkel" aircraft factory in Rostock. Charges included drunkenness, assaults on superiors, fraternization with female laborers, and theft of supplies from the factory.[43]

In December 1943, the Trawniki camp staff noted sternly in a daily order that it had been repeatedly observed that members of the camp, especially over the weekends, had been found in Trawniki village in severely drunken states.[44]

In the Reinhard camps, a number of Trawniki guards were summarily shot by the SS for various reasons. In Sobibor, two were shot in front of their comrades. In Treblinka, Wirth beat and whipped the guards into submission in a way that disturbed even the SS. Wirth's treatment of the Trawniki guards was discussed by the SS, who came to the conclusion that should the guards join up with the Jews, they—the SS—would all be killed. According to historian Michael Tregenza, in 1942, in Belzec, Wirth on one occasion repeatedly whipped the face of one of Hackenholt's Trawniki guard assistants, Ivan Huzij, at the gas chamber, when he failed to get the engines started during a gassing demonstration for SS officers. Huzij was admitted to the local hospital with facial lacerations. After he recuperated he was reassigned to Treblinka. On many occasions, Wirth and Hering reacted to the excesses of the Trawniki guards by beating, whipping, and imprisoning them in a punishment bunker in Belzec, where they remained for several days without food or water. Two Trawniki guards, who violated security regulations by talking about what went on in Belzec to outsiders, were arrested. Wirth had them dressed in clothing bearing the Jewish yellow star and then had them gassed with the victims of an incoming transport. This incident broke many of the Trawniki guards who witnessed it. They cried out in despair.

SS NCO Heinrich Unverhau later stated that Commandant Hering ordered that two Trawniki guards be shot for stealing Jewish property in the camp. They were forced to put on jackets that had the Star of David on them. They were then shot at the edge of a mass grave. The other Trawniki guards were forced to observe the execution.[45]

On one occasion, two Trawniki guards were imprisoned in the punishment bunker in Belzec for theft of valuables. Hering ordered SS-Scharführer Heinrich Gley and SS-Scharführer Fritz Irrmann to shoot them. The two guards attacked Irrmann when he went into the bunker, and in a panic, Gley opened fire, accidentally killing Irrmann, and the two guards escaped:[46]

I would like to provide details on the death of SS-Oberscharführer Jirmann. As far as I remember, I came to Belzec in July or August 1942. One night, two to four weeks after I arrived at the camp, we were finishing dinner, and Jirmann got up and said to me, "Gley, come with me." It was pitch dark outside, and I was carrying a flashlight. Across from the camp headquarters, there was a small forest with a bunker that was used as a detention facility for the Trawniki guards. Jirmann and I went to the detention facility. In front of the facility, Jirmann asked for my flashlight. On the walk over to this bunker, we did not talk at all. I did not ask where we were going and what was supposed to happen. I did not even know that there were people locked up in the bunker. With flashlight in hand, Jirmann went into the bunker. He kept his gun holstered. I saw a shadow jumping him from behind and throwing him to the floor. The flashlight dropped out of his hand and went out. When I saw this attack, I pulled out my gun and released the safety catch. All this happened in only a few seconds. Then I saw a shadow jumping out of the bunker, trying to escape. Without recognizing the escapee, I shot at him. A second later, another shadow ran out of the bunker. I shot at him as well, without recognizing who he was. The man fell to the floor, groaning, hit by the bullet. Almost simultaneously, a third shadow came out of the bunker. I am not sure if I shot at him as well. Everything happened very quickly, within seconds. When the third shadow appeared, I almost simultaneously recognized that the second man, whom I had shot, was Jirmann. The shot had killed Jirmann instantly. As far as I remember, the bullet went beneath the rib cage, straight to the heart. As to why the shooting was going to be done secretly, at night, it is probably because it was supposed to be concealed from the other guards. I later learned that the two Ukrainians had supposedly broken into the storage room for valuables while they were on sentry duty. I am not sure why there had never been a formal courts-martial for this offense.

Although the Trawniki guards were threatened with death by Wirth if they dared talk about their work while outside the camp, loose talk inevitably increased when the guards were drunk in the nearby village. The undisciplined behavior of the Trawniki guards caused a lot of problems for the SS. "We were conspirators in a foreign land, surrounded by Ukrainian volunteers in whom we could not trust."[47] "Not only did they fall asleep at their assigned guard posts, but they also tended to show disrespect toward the German SS men in the camp. They spent most of their time carousing in the nearby villages, from where they would return drunk late at night, shouting, carrying on, and firing their weapons."[48]

Ivan Demjanjuk, Zaki Tuktarov, and other guards received twenty-five lashes with a whip or riding crop for having left Majdanek without authorization during a quarantine of the camp, in order to visit a local brothel (although they claimed they went out to get food). The incident was memorialized in a report:[49]

POW Camp of the Waffen-SS Lublin
January 20, 1943
Subject: Report of the Guard Dog Detachment concerning the *Wachmänner*.
1: Deminjuk, ID #1393
2: Pasenok, ID #900
3: Peretjalko, ID #1469
4: Tuktarow, ID #1730

To the
Commandant's HQ of the POW Camp of the Waffen-SS
Despite a repeatedly announced camp quarantine order, the abovenamed *Wachmänner* left their quarters and the camp grounds without permission. According to their statements, they went to the village to buy food. Please take under advisement.
25 blows with a stick.
January 20, 1943, initialed by Langleist, Trawniki Training Camp
Report administration to battalion POW Camp Detachment in Lublin
25 blows administered with a stick on January 21. Signed, Erlinger

Signed, Erlinger
SS-Oberscharführer

The following report had been filed by the SS in Majdanek regarding the camp's contingent of Trawniki guards:[50]

Waffen-SS Battalion
Lublin
January 24, 1943
Subject: Hostile Attitude of the Ukrainians
To the Commandant's HQ of the Waffen-SS
Lublin
SS-Oberscharführer Erlinger, who is assigned from Trawniki with both Ukrainian companies and is assigned responsibility for them, reported that the Ukrainians sing Communist "liberation songs about Stalin" in an intoxicated condition during evening hours. The songs would then be secretly hummed throughout the barracks. Modifications to these songs were made by Oberwachmann Timoshenko. There was talk among the Ukrainians that anyone reporting about this singing would be shot. One Ukrainian told this to Oberwachtmeister Heinsch, who is responsible for the 1st Company.

SS-Oberscharführer Erlinger does not consider the Ukrainians reliable. As soon as there is a favorable opportunity, they would mutiny without hesitation. Guard service is too boring for the Ukrainians. They say they cannot "earn" anything. The enthusiasm for serving under German command authority disappeared once the evacuation of the ghettos ended. During the work of clearing the ghettos, they were swimming in money, which they now miss. They were willing so long as there was any opportunity for robbery or murder. Erlinger stated that one cannot count on them for any other type of duty.

Stefan Bzumowski of the 1st Ukrainian Company, who made several reports to Oberwachtmeister Heinsch, stated that he was constantly threatened with being shot. He had attracted the hate of his comrades because of his exemplary service. One time, he was assigned as NCO of the day. When he was too strict with the Ukrainians, they told him, in effect, "You better stick with us, be a comrade, and be like us, or we will shoot you." Bzumowski stated that his father had fought against the Bolsheviks, he himself can hardly stand Bolsheviks, and he characterizes his comrades as such. He himself likes being in German service, although he would like some other type of duties.

Characterization of Bzumowski: Makes a good impression. According to his own statement, he attended a Polish school. He can speak and write Polish, Russian, Ukrainian, and also a little German.

Proposal: We find it appropriate to occasionally inform SSPF, SS-Gruppenführer Globocnik, or chief of staff, SS-Sturmbannführer Hofle, about the current state of morale. With Bzumowski, who can be described as an informant, it is possible that we could identify those Ukrainians, by name, who are especially radical, and perhaps transfer them back to Trawniki in exchange for replacements.

It should be noted that such behavior has not been previously observed. There has been irreproachable service, especially with regard to the Ukrainians posted as sentries in between the guard towers at night.

In the meantime, we should consider withholding special alcohol rations from the Ukrainians.

Commander of the SS-Totenkopf Battalion
Lublin POW Camp

Signed [illegible]
SS-Hauptsturmführer

On that same day in Majdanek, another report on some Trawniki guards was filed:[51]

SS-Totenkopf Battalion
POW Camp of the Waffen-SS
Lublin
January 24, 1943
Subject: Violation of Restriction to Camp–Ukrainians frequenting a Polish "cathouse"
Ref: Attached Interrogation Protocols
To the Commandant's HQ
POW Camp of the Waffen-SS
Lublin
The SS-Totenkopf battalion submits two interrogation protocols, from which it was determined that several of the Ukrainians (Vladas Amanaviczius, ID #1640, and Paul Makarenko, ID #445) regularly visit a Polish house, outside the boundaries of the camp. The purpose is unquestionably sexual intercourse, judging from the observed fact that only women reside in the house. Whether the house is to be cleared out and the residents brought to the camp needs to be resolved. Also to be decided is whether the securing of the household's effects is to be performed by the SD, the camp's own Political Section, or by the SS-Totenkopf battalion. The women are about fifty, thirty, and sixteen years old.

It is requested that a decision be made. SS-Unterscharführer Buchwald is to be used as a guide to the house in question. Also, it should be decided whether use is to be made of weapons in the future in case of insubordination by the Ukrainians.
Commander of the SS-Totenkopf Battalion
Lublin POW Camp

[signature]
SS-Hauptsturmführer

EXAMPLES OF THOSE WHO WERE INJURED OR SICK IN THE LINE OF DUTY

Viktor Bogomolow: two fingers shot off (index and middle) during a deployment against partisans or a Jewish deportation operation in Lublin, May 3, 1942; released from service at his own request, November 7, 1942[52]
Andrej Davidenko: wounded during Warsaw Ghetto uprising, April 19, 1943[53]
Petro Hawriluk: discharged from service due to hepatitis, April 5, 1944[54]
Nikolaj Huculjak: gunshot wound to the hand during the Warsaw Ghetto uprising, April 21, 1943 (after the war, he would claim that rather than having gotten the wound from Jewish insurgents, that it had been self-inflicted in order to get discharged from Trawniki service); released from service at his own request, August 30, 1943[55]

Grigor Ivanischin: wounded during Warsaw Ghetto uprising, April 23, 1943[56]

Ivan Knignitskij: wounded during Warsaw Ghetto uprising, April 21, 1943[57]

Dimitri Kobilezkyj: discharged at his own request after diagnosis of having a heart arrhythmia, November 1943[58]

Jurko Kosatschok: wounded during Warsaw Ghetto uprising, April 25, 1943[59]

Mychajlo Maximiw: discharged from service due to tuberculosis, April 23, 1943[60]

Michael Minenko: wounded during Warsaw Ghetto uprising, April 19, 1943[61]

Pavel Nestarenko: wounded during Warsaw Ghetto uprising, April 19, 1943[62]

Andrej Protschenko: wounded during Warsaw Ghetto uprising, April 19, 1943[63]

David Robertus: cut by a Jewish prisoner near the gas chambers in Treblinka II, 1942 or 1943[64]

Boris Roschdestvenskij: wounded during Warsaw Ghetto uprising, April 19, 1943[65]

Mikhail Rosqoniajew: self-inflicted gunshot wound to the head, left eye shot out; assigned to Sobibor at the time; released from service at his own request, February 2, 1944 (he originally claimed he shot himself by accident; however, after the war, he told Soviet authorities it had been a suicide attempt)[66]

Emil Schmidt: wounded during Warsaw Ghetto uprising, April 24, 1943[67]

Friedrich Schneider: wounded in Warsaw, May 19, 1943, gunshot wound to upper arm and shoulder[68]

Ivan Tellmann: discharged from service due to tuberculosis while assigned to Plaszow, February 1944[69]

Vladimir Tscherniawsky: Accidentally shot in the hand by another guard from one of the watchtowers in Treblinka II. The guard who shot him had meant to hit a Jewish prisoner who had attacked him.[70]

Vladimir Usik: wounded during Warsaw Ghetto uprising, April 27, 1943[71]

Woldemar Wutke: discharged from service while assigned to the SS "Streibel" Battalion, March 16, 1945, probably due to illness or injury[72]

Alexei Zhukov: Fell ill with syphilis and was hospitalized in Lvov until his detachment in Janowska returned to Trawniki in late September 1943[73]

In one instance, in Treblinka II, at least two Jews armed with knives stabbed two Trawniki guards at the undressing area. As a result, a Trawniki guard in one of the watchtowers opened fire with a machine gun. All the Jews at the undressing area died, but a Trawniki guard also had his hand shot off.[74] On another occasion, a Jew getting off the train at the unloading ramp threw a hand grenade, wounding Trawniki NCO Alexander Yeger and killing another Trawniki guard. On yet another occasion, a prisoner cut the throat of Trawniki NCO David Robertus, although he survived.[75]

EXAMPLES OF THOSE WHO DIED IN THE LINE OF DUTY

Olexander Babijtschuk: abducted and killed by partisans, December 1943–January 1944; at the time was assigned to an SS estate in Wisznice, Biala-Podlaska District[76]
Georg Backer: died, possibly from a gunshot wound, and possibly while assigned to Sobibor, February 2, 1943[77]
Ilya Baidin: died in an accident at a railway station while jumping onto a moving train, December 10, 1944; assigned to Flossenbürg concentration camp at the time.[78]
Nikolaj Boschko: abducted and killed by partisans while assigned to Budzyn Detachment, August 22, 1943[79]
Felix Brandezkij: killed by partisans while assigned to agricultural estate "Jablon," April 18, 1944[80]
Vasili Burljajew: committed suicide via a gunshot wound while assigned to Janowska, June 14, 1943; was intoxicated at the time and had previously made statements to fellow guards regarding thoughts of suicide[81]
Wolodymer Chytrenia: killed by partisans, November 1943[82]
Wasyl Daniljuk: shot and killed by another guard, Alexander Borodin, during service in the SS "Streibel" Battalion, November 27, 1944[83]
Myron Flunt: stabbed or throat slit by two Jewish prisoners in the forest work detail at Sobibor (after which they escaped), July 23, 1943[84]
Josef Glista: drowned while swimming in Trawniki, June 20, 1943[85]
Mikhail Gubrijenko: shot and killed by partisans in Jozefow, near Terespol, while conducting reconnaissance with German gendarmerie, May 25, 1943[86]
Andrej Hermaniuk: died of gunshot wound due to the careless handling of a rifle by another guard in the guard shack at Poniatowa, October 2, 1943; died the same day at the SS first-aid station[87]
Nikolaj Isatschenko: died while serving at Budzyn Detachment, January 12, 1943; probably shot while attempting to desert, or killed by partisans nearby[88]
Ivan Klatt: reportedly killed by Jewish prisoners during the Sobibor uprising, October 14, 1943: hit over the head with a hatchet[89]
Emiljan Kostenko: died in Trieste while serving under the HSSPF Adriatic Coast, May 15, 1944[90]
Ivan Kulak: killed by partisans in the Zamosc area, March 29, 1943[91]
Stepan Kwaschuk: died on August 20, 1943, possibly as a result of wounds sustained during the Treblinka camp uprising on August 2, 1943[92]
Josef Loch: believed to have been killed by partisans while assigned to Zamosc Detachment, February 1944[93]

Sergej Malov: committed suicide with a gunshot wound after he learned that he was about to be questioned by German police on suspicion of theft of jewelry from a house in Lvov; was assigned to Janowska at the time[94]

Ivan Mandrikow: accidentally shot and killed by another guard during a Jewish deportation operation while serving with the Radom Detachment, 1942[95]

Wasyl Martiszczuk: missing from the SS "Streibel" Battalion as of January 1945[96]

Stepan Mogilo: KIA in Warsaw, May 19, 1943[97]

Petro Nahorniak: Captured by partisans near Castelnuovo while serving under the HSSPF Adriatic Coast, May 24, 1944. However, he survived, as evidenced by his postwar trial.[98]

Boris Odartschenko: died in a military hospital in Warsaw after receiving a gunshot wound to the stomach during the Warsaw Ghetto uprising, April 22, 1943[99]

Nikolaj Olejnikow: missing from the SS "Streibel" Battalion as of January 1945; tried in Stalingrad/Volgograd, 1947[100]

Nikolaj Petriuk: died in a military hospital in Lublin due to tuberculosis, August 21, 1943; at the time, had been assigned to an estate in Tomaszow-Lubelski[101]

Jaroslau Pidlentenschuk: killed by partisans while assigned to Poniatowa, February 10, 1944[102]

Anatoli Rige: Died on December 8, 1941, while assigned to Treblinka I. Apparently he had drunk an alcoholic beverage laced with benzine.[103]

Arnold Rosenke: MIA while serving under the HSSPF Adriatic Coast, March 1945[104]

Nikolaj Rubanov: died while assigned to Budzyn Detachment, January 12, 1943; probably shot while attempting to desert, or killed by partisans nearby[105]

Rustambek Saitow: died from a self-inflicted, accidental gunshot wound to the chest while assigned to the Warsaw Detachment, June 27, 1943[106]

Ivan Saplawny: died in an accident on April 5, 1942, probably while assigned to Belzec (where he was assigned, starting one month earlier)[107]

Mychailo Sawka: killed near Trieste while serving under the HSSPF Adriatic Coast, June 2, 1944[108]

Wasyl Scheftschuk: died in a military hospital in Lublin of heart failure (age twenty-three), June 1944[109]

Christian/Heinz Schmidt: allegedly committed suicide in Trieste while serving with HSSPF Adriatic Coast, April 9, 1944[110]

Kuzma Sokur: died of appendicitis while assigned to Flossenbürg concentration camp, December 28, 1943[111]

Willi Stark: KIA during Warsaw Ghetto uprising, April 22, 1943; gunshot wound in the back, lower left arm broken by gunshot, and arterial injury to both thighs[112]

Mychajlo Tomaczuk: killed by partisans, April 15, 1944[113]

Nikolaj Uchatsch: killed by partisans at the Kazimierz railway station as he was escorting a Jewish prisoner, September 15, 1943; assigned to Poniatowa at the time[114]

Ivan Walnyskij: died of heart disease while assigned to Plaszow[115]

Eduard Wlasiuk: killed by AK partisans in the Lublin area in July 1944, or died in a car accident in or near Vienna after having been remobilized into the Red Army, May 1945[116]

CHAPTER 3

DESERTIONS

According to Dr. Peter Black, up to 30 percent of all Trawniki guards eventually deserted from German service (that would be up to about 1,500 of the known 5,082 guards).[1] As many as 1,000 Trawniki guards may have deserted by the end of the war.[2] Dr. Sergej Kudryashov gave a different figure of precisely 469 guards having deserted (about 9 percent of them), but he noted that the real figure is actually slightly higher because some of them deserted in the final weeks of the war, "too late for the desertions to be registered by the German authorities." Death, desertion, disciplinary problems, and discharges may have reduced the number of Trawniki guards by 1,000 by September 1943.[4]

Initially, Trawniki guards were punished on the spot, and in any way that the punishing German official arbitrarily saw fit. However, by mid-1943, German police disciplinary regulations were applied, and from that point on, the guards were subject to formal proceedings before SS and police courts just like any other members of the SS or police.[5] The courts with most frequent jurisdiction were the SS and Police Court in Lublin and the SS and Police Court in Krakow. Punishment for desertion was generally several weeks or several months of imprisonment, which could be served in a jail, a labor camp, such as the one in Debica, or a concentration camp, such as Majdanek (for an example of jail imprisonment, see the case of Wolodymyr Shur, below; for an example of imprisonment in the labor camp in Debica, see the case of Vladimir Bruchaki, below; for an example of imprisonment in Majdanek, see the case of Petro Hul, below). However, this was the case only if the guard deserted unarmed and had gone back to his family residence. In cases where guards escaped armed or joined the partisans, they were generally shot, since it was expected that they would resist capture. Guards would also be shot if they attempted mutiny, since this was regarded as hostile and they could not be expected to submit to arrest.

Whenever a guard deserted, a report would be filled out and filed. Since the Trawniki guards were under the jurisdiction of Trawniki camp, the Trawniki camp authorities would be responsible for filing the report. Trawniki camp, in turn, was subordinate to the SS and police commander of the Lublin District until August 1943, and from then on, to the SS Main Economic and Administrative Office (SS-WVHA). The report would generally include information on the guard in question, including his name, date of birth, place of birth, last known residence, location he had been assigned to when he deserted, and date of the desertion. The standard report also had a space where it was to be stated whether the desertion was believed to be benign (in other words, if the man had simply gone back home to his family) or whether it was believed to be hostile (to join a bandit/partisan unit). In fact, as the war was coming to an end, some former Trawniki guards even reentered the Red Army (or, for the civilian recruits, began entering the Red Army for the first time). A copy of each desertion report was generally forwarded to several offices, including the SS and police commander

(SSPF), Lublin District; SS Garrison Administration, Lublin; SS and Police Court Lublin; commander of the security police and SD Lublin; Waffen-SS Leadership Main Office (SS-FHA), Berlin-Wilmersdorf; and the Criminal Police (Kripo) Office, Berlin.

The report was also attached as an addendum to each Trawniki guard's personnel file, and a notation would be made on the top of the first page of the file indicating that he had fled. If the guard was recaptured or shot, that was noted too, in order to keep the file as current as possible. The notation was generally signed by Albert Drechsel, Helmut Leonhardt, or other Schutzpolizei NCOs assigned to the Trawniki Administrative Office who were responsible for keeping track of all the guards and maintaining their files (akin to a human resources department).

Searches for escaped Trawniki guards could generally be conducted by any available units that could spare the resources, and this generally meant the local police (Schutzpolizei, Gendarmerie, and the Polish "Blue" Police). For Polish "Blue" Police involvement in searching for escaped Trawniki guards, see the case of Kisilyev and Zischer). It is also known in a few instances that Trawniki guard units themselves could be used to search for their escaped comrades (see interrogation statements of Nikolaj Chernyshev and Andrej Vasilega), and at least in the case of deserters from Auschwitz-Birkenau, German SS camp guards (Waffen-SS/SS-Totenkopfverbande) were utilized in the search, in addition to the local police. In cases where an escaping guard was suspected of something other than just desertion (such as theft or assault, for example) the Criminal Police (Kripo) could get involved as well. Some guards, rather than actually deserting from their places of assignment, simply didn't return to duty after having been granted home leave. This was an easier way to flee Trawniki service than outright desertion.

It is difficult to estimate how many Trawniki guards deserted to the partisans versus those who simply tried to make their way home to their families. Others simply hid out and kept low profiles, sometimes with their girlfriends (for former Trawniki guards who hid out with their girlfriends, see the examples of Ivan Tkachuk and Nikolaj Skorokhod). Of those who did join partisan units, earlier Trawniki recruits (who were mostly of central and eastern Ukrainian, or Russian, origin) were generally inclined toward the Soviet partisans (for an example of this, see the desertion of the group of guards under the leadership of Ivan Woloshin, and the example of Ivan Kakarach), while later Trawniki recruits (mostly of western Ukrainian origin) might have had a preference for the UPA (which was specifically a movement geared toward western Ukrainians). It cannot be ruled out that some Trawnikis simply joined whatever unit that they happened to encounter on the run, and this would have included the AK (assuming the AK would accept them); for an example of a former Trawniki guard who allegedly joined the AK, see Eugeniusz Maytchenko, below. It is also not known how many former Trawniki guards who joined the partisans survived the war. Some are known to have survived because they were interrogated and put on trial (an example of this included the aforementioned Ivan Woloshin group) after the war:

We lose track of many of those who deserted or went missing, particularly in 1943–1944. I am guessing that the vast majority returned home, if they could, or went underground in German-occupied Poland until they got the opportunity to return home. Many who did get across Soviet lines passed themselves off as forced laborers and were recruited back into the Red Army. It is possible that some were recorded as AWOL who had actually been kidnapped or killed by the partisans. Moreover, some of the men sought contact with the partisans—although this was problematic, since the AK trusted only Poles, the NSZ was even more nationalistic, and the Trawniki guards were not always comfortable going to the GL-AL. Trawniki guards did conspire with Jewish prisoners from time to time, but it seems unlikely that they would desert to join the ZOB—for a variety of reasons. Though the UPA would seem logical on one level, I am not aware of any former Trawniki guards in its ranks. Since the Trawniki guards who deserted were motivated in part by the expectation that Germany would lose the war, the UPA would seem to be a risky choice for former collaborators who intended to return to the Soviet Union. In general, these men tended not to have been politically active before World War II, and their desertion to the partisans, when it happened, is likely to have been motivated by increasing chances of survival rather than political conviction.[6]

As for the odds of recapture by the Germans after desertion, "this depended on a variety of factors, including proximity to the front lines, whether a deserter's home area was still behind German lines, whether the Germans had sufficient manpower to search the deserter's home region, whether the deserter even went to his home region, and the timing. By early 1944, desertion was more likely to be successful and permanent than, for instance, in 1942.[7]

Regarding those who took part in mass desertions—those who were not killed in the subsequent pursuit or firefight generally tried to get back to their homes behind German lines, to join local partisan groups, or to get through the front lines and reintegrate back into life in the Soviet Union, which meant registering for the armed forces. Others had laid very careful plans to go underground, often with the help of local contacts, including girlfriends. Mass-desertion actions were not products of impulse—they were planned. Before May 1943, the Germans could simply shoot mutineers, or those who deserted with their weapons. After May 1943, captured deserters or mutineers had an SS and police disciplinary hearing.[8]

Desertion from German service was not considered a mitigating factor when Soviet and Polish authorities prosecuted former Trawniki guards after the war. They were arrested and imprisoned regardless, just for having collaborated with the enemy.

Motives: There were several possible motives for desertion. The most-common ones were the following: (1) A fear that Germany might lose the war, and the guards would then one day have to answer for their crimes to Soviet authorities. This was especially true following the German defeat at Stalingrad in early 1943, Germany's first real failure of the war (not including the earlier failure to take Moscow by early 1942). The guards were under no illusions that their own country would regard them as traitors and that they would either be executed or imprisoned once it was discovered that they had collaborated. They may have hoped that by fleeing German service, in time they could get back to their own side before it was noticed that they had worked for the enemy (for an example of this, see the case of Andrej Sergienko). (2) A fear that the Germans would one day do to the guards what they had done to the Jews. The guards may have wondered if the only reason the Germans were utilizing them was to get rid of the Jews and help police the eastern territories, and that once Germany won the war, their continued use might be superfluous and they would simply be eliminated as unwanted witnesses to German crimes (for an example of this, see the case of the Trawniki guards who deserted from Auschwitz-Birkenau). (3) Some guards were simply undisciplined in general and never really wanted to be in German service to begin with. They were opportunists who just wanted to survive and would have taken the first chance to slip away and go home. Some may have also still been loyal to the Soviet regime. (4) Those individuals who objected morally to the ill treatment and murder of civilians, or those who found it distasteful having to carry out "dirty work" (for an example of this, see the case of the group led by Mikhail Gorbatchew).

Former Trawniki guards gave statements in postwar interrogations and postwar trials regarding their motives for desertion, but the sincerity of these statements needs to be considered. In many cases, the individual in question may have said what they thought their interrogator wanted to hear in order to mitigate their level of guilt. For example, it sounds better to state that there is a moral objection to the activities being conducted as a guard than to say that one simply fled because he feared that Germany would lose the war. Starting in early 1942, Soviet partisan propaganda began promising full amnesty to Soviet POWs who had become German collaborators, so long as they switched back to the Soviet side. Those who switched back were usually enlisted into Soviet partisan units after screening by the NKVD, which arrested only those who were considered particularly suspicious or notorious, and sent them across the front lines or executed them.[9] In 1942, Panteleimon Ponomarenko, head of Soviet Partisan Central HQ, formulated a policy by which German collaborators were to be given the opportunity to switch back to the Soviet side and redeem themselves by "fighting for the liberation of the Motherland."[10] In the second half of 1943, over 10,000 German collaborators deserted back to the Soviets.[11] In October 1943, the Wehrmacht general staff became concerned at the growing unreliability and desertion of German collaborators in the East.[12]

Here will be provided numerous examples of guards who escaped or at least attempted to escape, and those who failed to return from leave. The desertions will be categorized according to the location from which they were known to have taken place. When information cannot be confirmed or corroborated, it will be stated as such.

DEATH CAMPS

BELZEC

On July 8, 1942, four guards were apparently shot in the camp. Those men were Mikhail Gorbatchew, Sergej Poprawka, Yakov Ananyev, and Timoshenko (first name not specified). During the Soviet investigations, in 1964–66, of the Trawniki guards who had served in Belzec, nearly every guard who was questioned and every guard charged with crimes mentioned the shooting of these four men. Soviet trial records that were sent to Germany in the 1960s documented that these four guards had refused to carry out an order at the camp. Some of the other former guards claimed that these four guards had been planning to escape and had convinced some Jewish prisoners at the camp to accompany them.[13] One former guard interrogated on this matter, Taras Olejnik, stated that Gorbatchew suggested to him that they should desert together. Olejnik did not attempt to desert with Gorbatchew and stated that he was shocked to learn that Gorbatchew and the other guards who were to desert with him were betrayed by a Jewish prisoner. However, questions posed by Soviet investigators suggest that Olejnik himself had been blamed for betraying Gorbatchew and the others when he learned of their planned escape.[14] Whatever the case may be, it is clear that Gorbatchew had made critical remarks about his duties at Belzec. Dr. Dieter Pohl assumes that the escape was planned together with Jewish prisoners, since some of these prisoners were apparently shot together with the deserting Trawniki guards.[15]

There were a number of desertions from Belzec in 1942 and 1943.[16] On November 18, 1942, the guard I. Maximenko was shot as he attempted to escape. Guard Grigorij Kuchichidze, a Georgian, deserted on December 12, 1942. He was immediately caught and shot.[17] On January 16, 1943, the guard N. Tsukanov was shot for apparent mutiny.

On March 3, 1943, twelve to fifteen guards fled the camp together. The names of those who were allegedly involved included Ivan Woloshin (who was apparently the ringleader of the escape), Mikhail Korshikow, Piotr Brovzev, Nikolai Leontev, Fedor Khabarov, Ivan Baskakov, Ivan Zikota, Alexander Dukhno, Alexander Melnikov, Grigorij Usenko, Dimitri Prokhin, Viktor Kirillov, and Peto Litus, a Latvian. Another guard, V. Kutikhin, was shot as he attempted to escape.[18] According to rumors that circulated in Belzec, the reason for the desertion was that Woloshin had feared punishment for an offense he had committed in the camp.[19] The guards escaped with their weapons. Before taking to the forest, they raided a nearby grocery store in order to obtain food. The group joined a Soviet partisan unit that was operating in the area. At least six local residents from the Belzec area remembered Ivan Woloshin when they were questioned over twenty years after the war ended. Five of them are cited here:

Woloshin escaped from the camp. On October 10, 1943, he came to my house as a partisan. He was with other partisans, and they had rifles. He asked me for food. I didn't let him in. I didn't see him again. I remember the date he came because fifteen days later, my granddaughter was born.[20] In 1943, some *Wachmänner* escaped to the forest with rifles. Among them, Woloshin, who became a partisan.[21] In spring 1943, some *Wachmänner* escaped from the camp. Woloshin was one of them. He hid in the Belzec area.[22] Woloshin escaped to the partisans. In summer 1943, he came to me for food. He had a rifle. I didn't let him in.[23] Twenty-nine *Wachmänner* tried to liberate the camp. The leader of this was Woloshin. There was two hours of shooting. The twenty-nine of them escaped.[24]

Misiewicz, in her testimony, apparently went on to speak of members of the Belzec Jewish *Sonderkommando* revolting and escaping along with the Trawniki guards. However, no other witnesses corroborate this, and there is no known documentation to support it.[25] In his 1947 interrogation, former guard Mikhail Korshikow recalled some of his fellow guards who escaped Belzec with him:

In March 1943, Ivan Khabarov escaped along with us and joined the partisans. In fall 1943, he died in combat against the Germans. Nikolai Leontev escaped from Belzec along with us in March 1943. He served in the partisan group of Major-General Vershigor. He [Leontev] was evacuated as wounded in 1944. I do not know where he is currently. He [Alexander Bakatanov] remained in Belzec after we escaped. He had intended to escape along with us, but he did not have an opportunity. I do not know where he is currently. He [Alexander Melnikov] escaped with us from Belzec and joined the partisans. He was killed in combat against the Germans in April 1944. I participated in his funeral.[26]

In an interrogation seventeen years later, Korshikow once again stated the names of several guards who were alleged to have been part of the desertion from Belzec with him.[27] Another former guard, Piotr Browzew, was asked about the mass desertion he took part in at an interrogation over thirty years after the war:[28]

Q: What happened on March 3, 1943?
A: I fled.
Q: Where did you go?
A: I went to the partisans and remained with them until the end of the war.
Q: You named a very exact date for your escape from Belzec. Why is this date so exact in your memory?
A: It was a big deal to get away from such a camp.
Q: Did you escape by yourself?
A: No, there were thirteen of us.
Q: Do you remember their names?
A: I remember, but half of them are no longer alive. They were killed.
Q: Were they captured?
A: No, they died as partisans.
Q: Name those you remember.
A: Woloshin, Korshikow, Leontev, and Baskakov. They are alive. I went to visit one of them on vacation. The others are dead, killed.
Q: What was going on in Belzec at the time of your escape?
A: They were beginning to burn the bodies.
Q: Were you posted as a guard at the pits or at the site of burning?
A: Yes, sometimes.
Q: Members of various nationalities carried out guard duty?
A: Yes.
Q: Were there any Latvians among them?
A: Yes. I fled with one of them.

[*Author's note*: This is probably a reference to the guard Peto Litus.]

In 1964–66, the individuals from this escape who survived the war, including Woloshin himself, were the primary witnesses in the trial against their former comrades who had served at Belzec.[29] This mass desertion resulted in the entire Trawniki guard unit in the camp being transferred out and replaced by a new seventy-five-man guard unit on March 27, 1943.[30]

From the March 27 replacement unit, on April 10, 1943, at least seven or eight guards had planned to mutiny within the camp. That same day, they were shot. They included Oberwachmann Eugen Binder (a *Volksdeutsche*), Grigorij Yezhov, Ivan Bondar, Peter Ivanov, Boris Khaylov (?), Alexei Sivochenko, Nikolai Kudryavtzev, Alexander Golubchik, Ivan Puzanov and Naum Markosenko [*Author's note*: for undetermined reasons, Markosenko wasn't shot until May 16, 1943, possibly kept alive longer than the rest of them in order to be interrogated].[31] Exact details are sketchy, but apparently these guards had planned to raid the camp armory and shoot their way out of the camp. The plan never came to fruition, because on the day it was to occur, the SS camp staff promptly arrested and executed those involved. A likely scenario is that the plan was betrayed by one of the guards involved (who may have gotten cold feet at the last minute) or another guard who knew of the plan but was not involved.[32] The guard Dmitrij Pundik, who served at Belzec, had this to say about the events in question:

On our fifteenth or sixteenth day in Belzec, our group spent the morning bathing. We then took up our guard duty in the woods in the vicinity of the camp. An hour and a half later, the other guards and I saw a group of Germans and a few guards in a chain, moving from the edge of the woods toward the camp. They came to us, relieved us of guard duty, and led us back to the camp. We all gathered in the camp dining hall. Germans and translators entered the hall after an hour or an hour and a half. They ordered us to name all the individuals who wanted to escape. They told us if we didn't name the ringleaders within ten minutes that we would all be shot. None of us revealed anything about a planned escape. The Germans came back ten to fifteen minutes later and took two guards away, one of whom was [Maxim] Komaschka and another who went by the nickname "Gypsy." A few minutes later the Germans came back in with a list and called out the names of sixteen guards. They didn't call them all at once, but one at a time. This went on until evening. None of those who were called came back. I remember some of the names called—Jeschow, Tischenko, and Golubschik. The guard standing next to me, Vasili Kotelewiz, was ordered out of the room. As he was walking out, two men grabbed him and hit him with their guns. Kotelewiz came back late that night. I saw that he had been beaten up pretty badly. The other guards and I laid him down on a table. He then told me that they had wanted to call me up and that someone had made a mistake in calling him. The next morning, a few Jews from a work detachment came to the dining hall where we were and showed us the uniforms of our comrades who had been taken away. There were blood spots on the clothing. From this, we understood that these men had been taken away and shot. One of the Jews, a girl, confirmed this and told us that our comrades had been shot. They were shot in the camp zone at night. They were bound by their hands, in pairs, with wire. As they were led from the commandant's office to the camp, in pairs, Jeschow, who was tied to Golubschik, struck a German in the side with his head. The German then shot Jeschow and Golubschik on the spot. We were ordered to line up. We returned to the barracks. In the barracks, we looked out the window. A car arrived. A German officer got out of the car and pulled the guard Ivan Bondar out of the car by his collar. He was tied up. The German then shot him. A few days earlier, Bondar had been injured while he was messing around with some explosives that he had found. He had been treated at the hospital and then returned to the camp. About forty to fifty of us guards were loaded onto two trucks and returned to Trawniki. As far as we could figure, about seventeen guards had been shot. Komaschka and "Gypsy" were among us when we returned to Trawniki. They both later got permission to marry Polish women. We considered them traitors and believed that they were guilty of betraying our seventeen comrades who had been shot.

Q: From captured documents available to us, we gather that Ivan Bondar and Grigorij Jeschow, as well as some other guards that you identified, were shot in Belzec because they took part in an insurrection on April 10, 1943. What can you say about this?

A: I believe the date of the executions is correct. It's clear that my statement that I was in Belzec for fifteen or sixteen days corresponds to reality. I was thus in Belzec from March 27 to April 10 or 11, 1943.

Due to the planned mutiny, this guard unit was replaced, just as the one before it had been, only two weeks earlier. A new sixty-man Trawniki guard unit arrived on April 12, 1943, to complete cremations and the dismantling of the camp.[33]

SOBIBOR

An escape of five Jewish prisoners, two of them women, together with two Trawniki guards, took place on Christmas night, December 25, 1942. The escape took place in Camp III, the extermination area. It was said to be a well-planned and well-organized escape, but the details are unknown. The escapees' choice of Christmas was no accident—that night the German staff and Trawniki guards would be celebrating and drunk. After the escape the group separated into at least two groups. The two Trawniki guards, Viktor Kisilyev and Wasyl Zischer (possibly a *Volksdeutsche*), together with one of the young woman, Pesia Lieberman, found refuge in the home of a Polish farmer near the village of Olchowiec in Kozia Gorka, 20–30 miles southwest of Sobibor, on the night of December 31, 1942. The farmer informed the nearby police station of Wierzbicy about the escapees, and three Polish policemen, Meisnerowicz, Piescikowski, and Kwiatkowski, surrounded the farm and killed the three as they tried to flee.[34]

Another, slightly different version states that Meisnerowicz, rather than dealing with the matter himself, informed the gendarmerie in Chelm. Three gendarmes arrived at the farmer's house at 4:00 a.m. As they approached, the three escapees fled outside, and one of the former Trawniki guards fired a shot. The policemen returned fire, killing all three of the fugitives. The Jewish woman, Pesia, who was with the two Trawnikis, was twenty-six years old and was from Chelm. The former Trawniki guard who was armed reportedly had nearly 100 rounds of ammunition with him for his rifle. The weapon and ammo were confiscated by the police and returned to the commandant of Sobibor.[35] The names and fates of the other four Jewish escapees remain unknown, but they did not survive the war. In reprisal for this escape, a few dozen prisoners in Camp III were murdered.[36]

On March 15, 1943, guard Anton Solonina fled the camp.[37] He was tried after the war.

On June 30–July 1, 1943, two guards, Konstantin Demida[38] and Ivan Kakarasch (or Karakach), flee.

On July 19, 1943, Karakach joined the "Zhukov" Soviet partisan unit (there is no mention of what happened to Demida). A report of the desertion was filed:[39]

SS-Sonderkommando, Sobibor
July 1, 1943
To the SS and Police Commander, Lublin District
Operation Reinhard
Inspector of the *SS-Sonderkommandos*
Lublin
The SS *Wachmann* (guard) Ivan Kakarasch, ID #1790, born in Krasnodarsk, a Russian, and the SS *Wachmann* (guard) Konstantin Dimida, ID #443, born in Baranovichi, a Belorussian, ran away from the Sobibor camp on the night of June 30–July 1, 1943. Patrols conducted so far have not been able to identify their route of escape. Both of them took along a Russian rifle with ammunition. The gendarmerie in Chelm and Wlodawa, the security police in Chelm, and the Customs and Border Patrol in Zbereze were notified in writing immediately and requested to assist in the search.
Signed,
Niemann
SS-Untersturmführer and deputy camp commandant

In a memo of October 7, 1943, Zachar Poplawski, a Soviet partisan, informed a Communist Party official in the Brest region that certain crimes committed by the Germans had been brought to his attention while he was serving in the "Voroshilov" and "Zhukov" partisan units. Reports from partisans reached the political officer of the Voroshilov unit. Captain Abdulaliyev and a partisan named Zukowski or Bukowski reported about the Sobibor death camp, situated along the Brest-Chelm railway line. They reported that it had gas chambers. In summer 1943, Poplawski was also informed about the camp by individuals who had crossed the Bug River to join the Zhukov partisan unit. Captain Abdulaliyev informed Poplawski that there was an eyewitness from Sobibor camp among his partisan unit, a former guard there who had deserted and had written a detailed report about the camp for his partisan superiors. It was Ivan Karakach. He identified himself as Ukrainian, a Komsomol member, and a former Red Army sergeant. He would eventually become a platoon commander in the partisan unit. In addition to writing a report about Sobibor, he also drew a map of it. He reported that all the Trawniki guards at Sobibor were armed with Russian rifles and that the camp armory contained two Russian machine guns, including a Degtyarev machine gun, a Polish heavy machine gun, about thirty German grenades, and 5,000 rounds of ammunition. He also reported that the camp had gas chambers, cremation pits, and a watchtower equipped with a heavy machine gun.[40]

Also sometime in July 1943, guard Ivan Ivschenko escaped from the camp.[41] He was tried in Kharkov (his birthplace) after the war.

Maria Pazyna, who lived in the village of Osowa, near Sobibor, provided the local Soviet partisans with food on a regular basis. She met Anatoly Pankov, who told her that he had recently served as a guard at Sobibor but had managed to run away and join a Soviet partisan unit (date unknown). After the liberation of the area, Pankov visited Pazyna several times, wearing his Red Army uniform. Pankov told her that in the fall of 1943, a transport of Soviet POWs had arrived in Sobibor. He stated that they had organized an uprising, that it had been successful, and that all the prisoners in the camp had escaped. The camp soon thereafter ceased to exist, he told her. He also stressed to her that the POWs had been in constant contact with partisans.[42]

The camp kitchen in Sobibor was run by a Jewish prisoner named Hersz Cukierman. The kitchen was frequented by a Trawniki guard named Kaszewadzki (first name possibly Volodia), who was allegedly from Kiev. Cukierman and Kaszewadzki talked often, and Cukierman tried to feel him out to see if he was trustworthy. Gradually, Cukierman came to trust him, especially when he was told by other prisoners that Kaszewadzki had contact with a nearby partisan group. Allegedly, Kaszewadzki even assured some of the prisoners that one day he would help them escape from the camp. Kaszewadzki told Cukierman that from time to time he would sneak out of the camp to meet with a partisan group. He wanted Cukierman to arrange to hand over enough money to buy some weapons. Later, Cukierman learned from Kaszewadzki that the nearby partisan unit had had a plan to liberate Sobibor but had given up on the idea because it would have been too risky—the camp was under heavy German surveillance, and if the attempt failed, all the prisoners would be killed in retaliation.[43]

Romuald Kompf, who became commander of the 3rd Battalion of the AK's 7th Infantry Regiment, described in his memoirs that it was very difficult to conduct any systematic observation of the Sobibor camp. Sometimes, however, the partisans managed to get some valuable information from drunk Trawniki guards. AK intelligence passed this information on to its Lublin and Warsaw branches, which in turn passed information on to the Polish government in exile in London.[44]

In summer 1943, some Jewish prisoners in the camp apparently made a deal with some Trawniki guards that, one night while on duty, the guards would provide a few trucks, which would be parked not far from the camp. Cukierman, who was in on the plan, recounted later that the number of trucks was supposed to be adequate to allow all prisoners in the camp to escape. The prisoners were to be driven to the other side of the Bug River, where they would form a partisan group. The Trawniki guards were offered a huge amount of money for this undertaking. However, some of the prisoners doubted if they could really trust the guards. Therefore, they decided to pay only half the money up front and withhold the other half until the escape had succeeded. The deposit was 700 dollars. In a meeting with one of the guards, the guard stated that he would be able to help a maximum of only fifteen prisoners escape. Cukierman then told him the deal is off. He realized then that the Trawniki guards were going to cheat the prisoners by probably driving them away from the camp, robbing them, and then killing them. The next day, however, several prisoners had changed their minds and agreed to the plan. That night, they were driven away hidden in a truck and were taken to the Bug River. However, when they got there, the truck simply turned around and drove back to Sobibor after unloading some boxes at the river. Soon, the Trawniki guards who had been in on the plan disappeared. It was later discovered that a large number of items were missing from the camp storage barracks. The guards must have stolen them, and that is what they had offloaded from the truck at the Bug River. The whole plan had been for the group of Trawniki guards to escape and use the prisoners just to get their hands on some money.[45]

Cukierman soon resumed talks with Kaszewadzki, who continued promising to help him work out an escape plan. Then, it was decided to withdraw thirty Trawniki guards from Sobibor, and Kaszewadzki was one of them. Before he left, he warned Cukierman to be very careful and not to have contact with any other guards. On the day that the Trawniki platoon was to transfer out of the camp, Kaszewadzki and eleven other armed guards (including one who used to stand guard by the gas chambers) deserted. This was later confirmed by Irena Sujko in her testimony in 1968. From 1934 to December 1943, she had lived next to the Sobibor railway station. At the station, she sold food items, and Trawniki guards from the camp frequented her food stand. They would tell her about the camp. She had made friends with Kaszewadzki. She described him as about forty-five years old, medium height, and sturdy build. Despite allegedly being from Kiev, he told her that he was actually Russian and that he had been a major in the Red Army.

Sujko knew that he had run away from the camp. She provided him with some civilian clothing and also gave him some money that she had been holding for him that he had taken from the camp.[46]

At least three guards are known to have deserted in the days leading up to the camp uprising: Friedrich Neumann (a *Volksdeutsche*) and Vasili Puschkarew, both on October 4, 1943, and Alexander Semenow on October 12, 1943.[47]

According to an earlier plan for a camp uprising (around August 1943), after killing the German SS staff, the Trawniki guards were supposed to join the prisoners and escape with them to the forest and join the partisans.[48] To carry out a successful escape from Sobibor, a way had to be found to eliminate the SS. The camp underground hoped that if the Germans were liquidated, the Trawniki guards, or at least some of them, would not act against the prisoner uprising and that some of them would even join in the escape.[49] However, bearing in mind previous cases in which Trawniki guards had shown themselves to be untrustworthy, the uprising conspirators gave up on the idea of bringing them into the plans.[50]

Alexander Pechersky learned a very important fact when he studied the layout and routine in Sobibor in preparation for the uprising—only the Ukrainians who were on guard duty received ammunition for their weapons, and only a small amount: in some cases, no more than five bullets. All the others who were off-duty carried no ammunition in their rifles. This was the result of the Germans reducing their firepower as a result of guards who had deserted to the partisans with their weapons.[51]

After the Sobibor uprising, SS-Oberscharführer Karl Frenzel realized it was important to take security measures in case partisans, taking advantage of the situation, overran the camp. Therefore, in the evening of October 14, 1943, he informed Hans Wagner, commander of the German army's Security Battalion 689, stationed in Chelm, about the uprising. Frenzel contacted Wagner's aide, Wiertz, and asked him to send reinforcements. He told Wiertz that prisoners had raided the camp armory, and that some of the camp's Trawniki guards had been in collusion with the prisoners during the uprising.[52] (Frenzel apparently did not elaborate on what he meant by "collusion," or how many guards were supposed to have been involved, and what was done about it.) Similar information stated, "The last remaining Jews [in Sobibor] had beaten to death all the German camp staff and had then made off together with their Russian guards."[53] After the Sobibor uprising, in an "after-action" report, it was claimed that twenty-eight of the camp's Ukrainian guards were unaccounted for and had "fled for fear of German reprisals."[54]

As Sobibor was just on the verge of closing down, once dismantling was complete, three guards deserted together on November 17, 1943. They were Wolodymyr Shur, Wolodymyr Scharan, and Peter Glusch. All three were from the Hrubieszow region, and all three had previously been assigned to the Lublin Detachment. Both Shur and Scharan were captured and imprisoned in Lublin on December 17, 1943. Scharan returned to Trawniki service as of April 19, 1944. Shur probably also returned to Trawniki service and is known to have deserted once again as of June 16, 1944.[55]

TREBLINKA II

According to Soviet documents, there was a GL partisan unit in the Wyszkow Forest consisting of Ukrainian camp guards who had fled from their posts in Treblinka. Supposedly, this group was so corrupt that it had to be destroyed by Soviet partisans. Another report indicated that units in the Wyszkow Forest avoided all real military action and relegated themselves only to the securing of provisions.[56]

On October 21, 1943, a thirty-man Trawniki guard detachment accompanied about 200 Jewish prisoners on a train from Treblinka II to Sobibor. The prisoners were executed in Sobibor.[57] On October 22, 1943, that same thirty-man Trawniki detachment left Sobibor for Trawniki. The detachment was accompanied by four Trawniki *Volksdeutsche*, including Josef Loch and David Robertus, and a German, SS-Oberscharführer Herbert Floss. Floss was killed on the train as it traveled between Chelm and Zawadowka, about 2 miles southwest of Chelm. It was determined that Floss had been shot by the guard Wasyl Hetmaniec. Hetmaniec then fled from the train at Zawadowka station, along with four other guards. They took with them Floss's submachine gun with two or three full magazine clips, and their own rifles. The following day, two of the guards showed up back at Trawniki and turned themselves in. The fate of the remaining three is uncertain.[58] Josef Loch gave a more detailed account of this incident when he was questioned about it in Trawniki on October 23, 1943. Some of the points he made are summarized or paraphrased here:

I was assigned to Treblinka II, June 1942–November 1943. I was promoted to *SS-Zugwachmann* on October 1, 1943. On October 22, 1943, on the train from Sobibor back to Trawniki, the guards were drinking vodka and schnapps. As the train passed through Chelm and Zawadowka, I heard two or three gunshots coming from another train car. Someone on the train pulled the emergency brake, and the train came to a halt. We all got off the train, and SS-Unterscharführer Schumpf, a staff member from Trawniki who happened to be on the train by chance, took command of the situation. The three other platoon commanders and I were ordered to assemble the guards in formation and conduct a roll call / head count. Once this was done, it was determined that five guards were missing. They must have jumped off the train following the shooting I had heard. An inspection of the train cars found that SS-Oberscharführer Herbert Floss, who had been on the train as an escort to the guard platoon, had been shot and killed. He was slumped over, and his sidearm, a submachine gun, was missing.

Someone else who was questioned from the actual train car in which the shots took place identified Floss's killer as the guard Wasyl Hetmaniec. As a security measure, all of the twenty-five guards still present were disarmed for the continuing journey back to Trawniki. One of them was apparently shot as he resisted being disarmed.[59] It is not clear from the available evidence whether the guard who had shot Floss did so deliberately as part of a preplanned desertion, or whether, intoxicated, he accidentally discharged his weapon and he and the other guards then fled spontaneously in a panic.[60] SS-Unterscharführer Otto Horn alluded to this incident in a postwar statement:

I questioned their [the guards'] political reliability: during 1943, a number of them deserted to the Russian partisans. When Treblinka was closed down in 1943, the Ukrainian guards there were transferred to Sobibor, escorted by a German. They murdered their escort and joined the partisans.

On November 7, 1943, as the camp was about to close down, guard Ivan Tkachuk deserted. He later stated that he had fled "because it was very difficult to endure the horrors that were being carried out there." He had a Polish girlfriend he hid with, whom he later married. Soviet authorities tracked him down and arrested him on a ship that was leaving Danzig for Stockholm in 1950.[61] He stated: "I served at Treblinka until 1943, and then with the help of a Polish female acquaintance I escaped from the camp, having obtained false papers. Along with this woman, I went to the city of Lublin. Later, we went to the city of Gdynia, where the woman had a house. We lived there until 1950, and then I was exposed as a former SS man by the Polish government and handed over to Soviet authorities."[62]

SS-Oberwachmann Nikolaj Demediuk, who was assigned to a manor estate that had been established on the former site of Treblinka II, had his living quarters searched. Discovered was cash in an amount equivalent to nearly $5,000 in US money (about $50,000 today), thirty gold coins, and a treasure trove of jewelry. Demediuk's superior, Oswald Strebel, a *Volksdeutsche*, had the search conducted because he suspected that Demediuk was planning on deserting.[63]

AUSCHWITZ-BIRKENAU

On the night of July 3, 1943, fifteen to seventeen Trawniki guards deserted. They were part of a 150-man Trawniki company that had formed the SS-Totenkopf guard battalion's 8th Company in Birkenau (a.k.a. Auschwitz II) on March 31, 1943.[64] The names of those involved were Oberwachmann Taras Lukjanenko, Terentij Gordienko, Alexander Chrushchev, Nikolaj Batdanenko, Ivan Pavlov, Stanislav Komar, Wasyl Beschewitz, Maxim Shopelnik, Wasyl Chomko, Ivan Romanenko, Jefim Kiritschok, Sergei Sergienko, Paul Petkowsky, Peter Rebane, Philip Wergun, and Chernobayev (first name not specified).[65] "After a massive search involving 500 SS men from the camp and police and gendarmerie from three neighboring districts, eight of the escapees were killed following a shoot-out, and one was captured."[66] "Fifteen men deserted with their rifles and sixty rounds of ammunition each. They left the camp in civilian clothing a few at a time and headed east across the Vistula River, guided by a local civilian camp employee."[67] One of the escapees, Sergei Sergienko, was soon captured and brought back to the camp. A German gendarmerie patrol challenged the rest of the escapees and opened fire on them. A pursuit force of four SS-Totenkopfverbande companies joined in the search. It included 455 SS men, including the camp's canine unit, and thirty SS men of the camp's internal staff. Over the following day, a massive dragnet was conducted in the district. The deserters killed two of their pursuers and wounded another, who died a few days later. The search units killed eight of the escapees and captured one more, Maxim Shopelnik.[68] According to what one of two captured men said under interrogation, the motive for the desertion was that duty in the camp was too hard and that it would be better to join the bandits (i.e., the partisans). According to SS-Rottenführer Pery Broad, a member of the Auschwitz Political Section (i.e., the camp Gestapo), the desertion was the result of the conviction among the guards that one day the Germans would get rid of them when they were no longer of any use.

An additional account of the incident stated the following:

During the pursuit and skirmish that ensued in the area of Chelm-Wielki, near Bierun, eight of the guards were killed and one captured. Of the pursuers, three were killed, including SS-Scharführer Karl Reinicke and SS man Stephan Rachberger. On the basis of this event, the remaining members of the unit are transferred for guard service in Buchenwald. The SS-WVHA, Office D-1, ordered that in the future, *Volksdeutsche* and foreign members of the SS should not be formed into a company of their own but should be integrated into already-existing German units.

The bodies of the eight guards killed in the pursuit were brought to the main camp and burned in Crematorium I. They were among the last bodies to be burned in this crematorium, which ceased being used later that month.[69]

Another reported stated (and is here paraphrased):

> On the night of July 3, 1943, sixteen foreign guards, who had been under the command of SS-Untersturmführer Theodore Lange, escaped Auschwitz with firearms and plenty of ammunition. They took off in the direction of Gross-Chelm and were attempting to cross the Przemsza River to hide in the forests in the Jaworzno region. The *feldgendarmerie* from neighboring localities pursued, and a skirmish ensued. Additional troops had to be summoned from Katowice and Myslowice, including SS men manning armored vehicles. Two SS men were killed and twelve were wounded.[70]

The two captured guards, Sergienko and Shopelnik, were sent to Munich (probably Dachau concentration camp or the SS–Penal Camp Dachau). They were tried and convicted by an SS and police court and were shot in late summer 1943.[71] Of the five escapees who the Germans never caught, only one is known to have been tried after the war by Soviet authorities—Terentij Gordienko. He was sentenced to twenty-five years of hard labor (ITL), a common sentence for former Trawniki guards, and died while serving that sentence.[72] Two other guards were mistakenly arrested by the Germans after Sergienko wrongly denounced them: Ivan Kozlovskij and Petr Alexeyev.[73] The remainder of the Trawniki guard unit in Auschwitz-Birkenau was transferred to Buchenwald, because after this incident, the Auschwitz commandant, Rudolf Hoss, no longer wanted the unit in his camp.

CONCENTRATION CAMPS

MAJDANEK
On November 23, 1942, the guard Kundischew (first name not specified) deserted with his rifle.[74]

Guard Fedor Tartynskij had this to say in a postwar interrogation: "On December 31, 1942, our company was sent back to Trawniki. There were rumors at the time that Russian POWs were to be exterminated at Majdanek, and that the Germans sent us away out of fear that we would mutiny. Only German SS remained in the camp."[75]

On January 23–24, 1943, the guard Boris Platonow deserted. The report of his escape read as follows:[76]

Subject: Flight of Ukrainian guard Boris Platonow, ID #2383, allegedly a Russian from Moscow. To the Commandant's HQ, POW Camp of the Waffen-SS, Lublin:
While conducting a check of the guards on January 23, 1943, at about 7:30 p.m., I observed at a distance the Ukrainian guards Besmerki, #2428, and Platonow, #2383, who were stationed between watchtowers #2 and #3, approaching each other. Besmerki gave Platonow a light and Platonow smoked. When I confronted them right after that, guard Platonow threw his cigarette away. Because of the language difference, my volume was no doubt the only reason he understood the nature of my admonition. On January 24, 1943, at about 7:30 a.m., the duty officer reported that guard Platonow had left the guard quarters without permission during the time he was not on guard duty. The search already conducted has been fruitless. SS-Oberscharführer Ehrlinger was again ordered to conduct a thorough search of all the guard quarters. Platonow's whereabouts have still not been determined, so it can be concluded without doubt that he has fled. He took his rifle with him.

Commander of SS-Totenkopf Battalion,
SS-Hauptsturmführer Langleist

On the same day, January 24, 1943, another report was filed by SS-Hauptsturmführer Langleist, titled: "Hostile Attitude of the Ukrainians." The report stated [paraphrased here]: SS-Oberscharführer Ehrlinger, who came from Trawniki with both Ukrainian companies and is assigned responsibility for them, reported that he does not consider the Ukrainians to be reliable. *As soon as there is a favorable opportunity, they would mutiny without hesitation.* [author's emphasis][77]

On March 27, 1943, the guard Grigorij Koslow, who had deserted, was recaptured and shot. Although it is not definitive that he had specifically escaped from Majdanek, it had been his last known place of assignment as of November 10, 1942. (Two other guards, Nikolaj Timin and Grigorij Stoilow, were also shot for desertion that same day after having been recaptured. It is not certain where they deserted from, but this author believes that they knew each other, had deserted together, were captured together, and were shot together. They were both from the same region—Turijsk, Ukraine; they both had the same occupations prior to Trawniki service—agricultural laborer; and they were both recruited for Trawniki service on the same day—July 12, 1942. Furthermore, the Trawniki personnel file of one of them indicates that he was shot in front of his own guard unit—probably the unit assigned to wherever he had deserted from, and he was shot in front of them probably in order to serve as an example of what happens to deserters.)[78]

SSPF WARSAW / WARSAW CONCENTRATION CAMP

Sometime between January and March 1944, guard Ivan Gubenko deserted.[79]

FLOSSENBÜRG

On September 30, 1943, eight guards who were to deploy from Trawniki to Flossenbürg on October 1 deserted. This was determined during a routine roll call in Trawniki. A report of the incident was made to the SS and Police Court Krakow. Their names were not identified in the available report. They might have previously served at Sobibor.[80] In an interrogation after the war, guard Ignat Danilchenko told his Soviet interrogators that he had fled from guard service:

> In October or November 1944, Demjanjuk and I transferred to Regensburg with other guards. We escorted 200 political prisoners. We guarded prisoners doing construction work until April 1945. We evacuated toward Nuremburg. I escaped along the way, but Demjanjuk continued escorting prisoners. He refused to escape with me. I never saw him again.[81]

SACHSENHAUSEN

On November 20, 1943, three guards deserted from a train transport deploying to Sachsenhausen for guard duty.

Those men were Evgen Tymchuk, Michael Wowk (or Wolk), and Petro Tschaplinski. Tymchuk was arrested by the police and put in Lublin prison on December 17, 1943.[82] A report highlights the incident:

> Commander of the Security Police and the SD,
> Lublin District
> January 4, 1944
>
> Protocol of Interrogation—
> Eugen Tymtschuk made the following statement: "I was an SS guard in the Jewish camp in Sobibor. On November 20, 1943, we were transported away from Sobibor. We were told that we would be en route for three days but were not told where we would be going. In Deblin, while my comrade Wolk and I were fetching water, the transport train left without us. We then went on foot to Jaszczow. My comrade traded his overcoat for two work shirts, which we were wearing when we were captured. We did not report in because we were afraid due to our having remained in Deblin, and in addition, my comrade wanted to go home. I do not know where his parents live since they were resettled, as were my parents. My parents currently

live in Siedliszcze, Hrubieszow District. In Jaszczow, in the area of the railway station, we were taken prisoner along with some other people. My comrade, however, managed to run away again. I do not know where he will stay. He probably went to his relatives. I had nothing to do with the tobacco smugglers who were arrested with me."

Signed,
Secretary of the Criminal Police

Additionally, the following report was filed:

Waffen-SS
SS and Police Court VI
Lublin
To SS guard Eugen Tymchuk,
Trawniki Training Camp

Order for Punishment: You are accused of the following: In Deblin, on November 20, 1943, you were on a transport from Trawniki to Oranienburg, together with your unit. During a fifteen-minute stop of the train in Deblin, you went to drink water with your comrade Wowk. Due to negligence you missed the departure and did not come back. Rather than continuing the trip with the next train to Oranienburg, you resolved to go back home first and only then to continue to your garrison. However, you were discovered during an inspection in Szaczczbuw and arrested. Your comrade Wowk successfully escaped. Misdemeanor: Crime punishable under Section 54 of the Military Criminal Code.

Signed,
Schonfeldt,
Oberwachtmeister of the Schutzpolizei Reserve

The evidence was: your confession
You are sentenced to six weeks of confinement
This order for punishment shall be executed if you do not appeal it within three days after you were notified of it. You may appeal in writing or orally with the court, the next level in your chain of command for disciplinary purposes, or the person who informed you of the Order for Punishment. You may waive the appeal within the three-day period.

Convening Authority:
Signed, Sporrenberg
SS-Gruppenführer and Major-General of the Police
Investigating Officer:
Signed, Woellmer
SS-Untersturmführer and SS Judge of the Reserves

Tymchuk served his imprisonment from December 17, 1943 to February 10, 1944. After that, he was turned back over to the Trawniki camp by SS-Unterscharführer Zellner. Sometime in February 1944, Tymshuk deserted once again, this time from Trawniki itself. From available documentary evidence, it is not possible to determine where along the train route Petro Tschaplinski fled,[83] but his escape seems to have been separate from the other two men because his desertion was not mentioned in the same report as theirs.

DACHAU-LANDSBERG
In September 1944, guard Peter Klemeschow deserts. This was his last known posting as of April 1944. Prior to that, he had been assigned to Plaszow.[84]

BUCHENWALD
Guard Andrej Kuchma, who had previously served at Belzec and Auschwitz-Birkenau, says that he escaped from a transport going to Germany (probably in July 1943), and he then resided in the city of Kassel until 1945 when the area was occupied by American forces.[85]

At least four guards are known to have deserted shortly before the war ended. Those men were Ivan Kurynyj, Nikolaj Malagon, Evdokim Parfinyuk, and Ivan Sisoj. They all fled in early 1945, probably around the time that the camp was evacuating, and they took advantage of the chaotic situation to disappear among the flood of prisoners, forced laborers, refugees, and other displaced persons roaming through Germany as the war came to its conclusion. All four of them had previously served at Auschwitz-Birkenau, three of them had served at Treblinka II, two had served at Belzec, and two had served at Sobibor.[86]

MAUTHAUSEN-GUSEN
This camp was located in Austria near Linz, and a group of guards here planned a desertion in April 1945. An informant among them reported the plot to the camp authorities, and the entire guard detachment was placed under arrest and the ringleaders of the plan were executed (the whole incident sounds like a mirror image of the attempted mutiny by the guards at Belzec on April 10, 1943; see above). The arrested guards were taken to a nearby camp in Steyr, and the SS abandoned them there. Those guards fled just before the arrival of American forces and returned to Soviet lines.[87]

Labor Camps

TRAWNIKI

"We knew that guards had contact with partisans. There was an instance when the weapons storeroom was opened with a duplicate key and weapons were stolen. They went out the back window. Men and weapons ended up with the partisans."[88]

SS-Rottenwachmann Nikolaj Chernyshev stated in a postwar interrogation: "In fall 1942, about seven *Wachmänner* escaped from the camp. My company was deployed to search for them, but we did not find them."[89]

In a postwar interrogation, SS-Gruppenwachmann Andrej Vasilega stated the following:

In spring 1943, I participated in a roundup. It was organized because ten *Wachmänner* had fled from Trawniki camp. The escapees were not located. In August 1943, I took part in another roundup in which we searched for other *Wachmänner* who had escaped. Five of them were caught. I brought them back to Trawniki and imprisoned them. In summer 1944, I took part in a search for partisans after two *Wachmänner* went missing. The *Wachmänner* were later found to have been killed by Poles.[90]

In March 1943, guard Wasyl Bojchuk attempted to desert, resulting in his either being assigned to, or imprisoned in, Majdanek for two months. In September 1943, he overstayed his home leave by ten days before returning to his post at Budzyn labor camp.[91]

Petro Hul, a young farmhand from the Chelm area, was conscripted for Trawniki service. Shortly after arriving at Trawniki for training, he apparently decided that he wanted nothing to do with the place and refused to undergo conscription procedures. He was then physically pressured to cooperate, to the point that he submitted. However, in July 1943 he attempted to flee. He was then imprisoned in Majdanek, where he died of alleged "heart failure" on November 9, 1943. When his father complained, in writing, to the governor in Krakow, about the brutal treatment of his son in Trawniki, Streibel requested that the father be punished for making such allegations against the Trawniki authorities.[92]

On September 2, 1943, the guard Wasyl Djomin, a Russian, failed to return from leave from Zhytomyr, Ukraine.[93] Exactly one month later, on October 2, 1943, nineteen-year-old guard Stepan Schpak deserted.[94]

On September 25,1943, guard Marian Bachulski, a Polish Goralian, deserted from the camp.[95]

On February 7, 1944, guard Ivan Tolotschko failed to return from leave.[96] A month later, on March 30, 1944, guard Nikolaj Zezulka failed to return from leave. He was from Stulno, a town near Sobibor, in the Chelm region.[97]

A few weeks before the liberation of the Lublin area by the Red Army, guard Ivan Knysch deserted on June 11, 1944.

After the war, he stated that he had fled due to the declining morale at Trawniki and the fear that the Soviet advance was soon to overrun the camp: "I conspired with Wachmann Solovskij, and we escaped from the camp and joined the partisans. We remained with the partisans until 1945."[98] On June 15, 1944, the guard Ivan Saniuk, a late Trawniki recruit (ID# 4819) from Chelm, fled the camp.[99]

The guard Eugeniusz Maytchenko, at his postwar trial, claimed that he had deserted from Trawniki in July 1944 and joined the AK. He was arrested by the Polish Communist Secret Police (UB), released after several weeks, and enlisted in the Polish army. He was promoted to sergeant and served at the front, being decorated for bravery. After the war, he served as a political officer.[100]

Guard Ivan Grigorchuk, who had served in the unit that helped suppress the Warsaw Ghetto uprising, was asked the following in a postwar interrogation:

Q: Under what circumstances did you return to the Motherland?
A: In mid-1944, during the German retreat, I escaped and crossed the front lines near Lvov with my girlfriend (now my wife). I arrived back home in Kolomiya District. I began working on a state farm and then as a stable boy.
Q: Why did you not serve in the Red Army?
A: I was registered with the Kolomiya District Military Commissariat in 1945, but I was not called up for service.[101]

The guard Mikhail Moskalik spoke of his desertion from Trawniki service in a postwar interrogation:

I served at Trawniki for ten months. I was then sent with forty others to the Rava-Russkaya station. We were tasked with guarding the railroad line, checking trains, and catching deserters. I remained there until July 1944. I was then sent to Mogilev, where we dug trenches and ditches for the German army. The same month, we were sent to the area near Ternopol. There I served as a messenger for a German unit. I then retreated with the Germans into Poland. I hid with a local resident named Olga Marusyak. She lived near Kovel. When the Red Army arrived in the area, I went to the Kovel District Military Commissariat and stated that I had worked in a German labor battalion. I was drafted into the Red Army and sent to a reserve regiment in Yanov. I then transferred to the 186th Mortar Regiment and served as a loader until I was wounded on January 31, 1945. I was sent to an army hospital in Prussia and then another hospital in Gleiwitz. I remained in hospital until March 1946. I was then discharged and went home.[102]

On many occasions I saw that Streibel had Ukrainians shot without having any proceedings carried out against them. They were known to be somewhat unrestrained and wild, particularly when drinking. Occasionally, some ran away. When they were caught, Streibel would put them in confinement for three days, and he would then have them shot in the camp by other Ukrainians. They would then be dumped in a dirt hole. I saw this with my own eyes several times.[103]

Kollaritsch, a member of the Trawniki staff, was killed by his own Ukrainians toward the end of the war. He had a guard detachment assigned to guard bridges. The Ukrainians organized a mutiny. They obviously deserted. Kollaritsch was hated by the men for his severity.[104]

According to guard Mikhail Laptev:

The commander of our squad was Oberwachmann Mikhail Yankovskij. From what he told me in 1957, after helping suppress the Warsaw Ghetto uprising, he escaped to the partisans, where he was decorated with the Red Star Medal.[105]

PONIATOWA
Guard Ivan Lukanyuk stated the following in a postwar interrogation:

In fall 1942, I was drafted by the German military. But I had no desire to serve, so I escaped from the assembly point in Kolomiya and hid at home. In spring 1943, the Ukrainian-German police arrested me, and I was sent to the Kolomiya prison. In the prison, a Gestapo officer offered to release me if I would join the guard service. I agreed and was sent to Trawniki.

After serving in Poniatowa, he was transferred to guard service in Germany:[106]

When Germany surrendered, we discarded our uniforms and weapons and scattered in various directions. I was captured in civilian clothing by American forces. I was put in a civilian camp for about two weeks, then I was handed over to Soviet authorities.
Q: Have any of your relatives also betrayed the Motherland?
A: My brother Mikhail was a member of the OUN, and he engaged in armed battle against Soviet authorities. In 1945, he was killed during an armed encounter with Red Army troops.

My other brother Dimitri was drafted into the Red Army in 1944, but he did not appear to serve. He deserted and joined the UPA. He also engaged in battle against the Soviet authorities, and I know nothing about his fate.

Q: Did you yourself participate in the OUN movement?

A: In 1945, when I returned home, my brother Mikhail asked me to join. I told him I needed to recover from my stay in the internment camp and would think about it later. Soon after this, my brother was killed, and no one else ever brought up the subject with me.

On February 23, 1943, eighteen guards deserted, taking weapons and ammunition with them. The escapees consisted of nine Russians, six Ukrainians, one Belorussian, one Tatar, and one "apparent" Greek.[107]

On July 24, 1943, guard Juri Dutko fled the camp. Less than a month later, guard Petro Kuschnir deserted on August 10, 1943. He was asked about this in a postwar interrogation:[108]

Q: How long were you in Trawniki service?

A: Three weeks. I escaped and hid at home in Stanislavov region.

Q: Describe under what circumstances you escaped from Trawniki service.

A: One evening, before lights-out, I went out into the yard of the barracks, crawled over the wire fence, and escaped.

Q: What did you do after you escaped?

A: I hid in my hometown in the Stanislavov region until 1944. That is, until the district was liberated by the Red Army. I then went to work building barracks in the eastern regions of the Soviet Union.

Q: How long did you do this work?

A: Three months, in summer 1944, and then I was returned by train to the western Ukraine. At one of the train stations in the Tarnopol region, I got off the train to go to the market, and the train ended up leaving without me. I set off on foot with a few others who had also been left behind by the train. We spent the night in the forest, and we then ran into about twenty armed men who asked us where we were going. We told them, and one of them said that they would take us to the NKVD. They led us to two peasant houses in the forest. Here they questioned us and then told us that they were bandits and invited us to stay with them. We agreed to stay. Two days later, I ran away from them and made my way home to the Stanislavov region. After my mother died, my brother and I gave ourselves up to the MVD.

Q: While you were in hiding, did you have any connection with the OUN or the UPA?

A: No.

Q: You are giving a false statement. We know that you had a connection with the bandits.

A: I had no connection with the bandits.

Q: What happened after you gave yourself up to Soviet authorities?

A: From February to August 1946, I lived and worked as a farmer in my home village in the Stanislavov region. In August 1946, I was sent by the MVD to the eastern regions of the Soviet Union because of my collaboration with the Germans [Trawniki service].

Q: Where were you sent, and what did you do there?

A: I was sent to the Marevo settlement in the Gorki (Nizhni-Novgorod) region. I worked in forestry there.

Q: How did you end up back in the Stanislavov region again?

A: In November 1946, I was released from work. I returned home to the Stanislavov region.

Q: We have information that after you returned to your home village, you committed robberies in the area. Do you corroborate this information?

A: No, I do not. I committed no such robberies.

Q: Do you remember the names of any of the men who served with you at Trawniki?

A: Yes. One in particular I remember is Ivan Kushnerik. He was from the same village as me in the Stanislavov region. He is now in the UPA.

At least fourteen guards deserted the camp or failed to return from leave in the weeks shortly before and shortly after the "Erntefest" massacre, which took place on November 4, 1943: the guard Grigorij Yevseyev was declared a fugitive after he was supposed to have been transferred back to Trawniki on September 27, 1943. On October 9, 1943, guard Nikolaj Tkachuk failed to return from leave. On October 19, 1943, guard Vladimir Terletskij failed to return from leave. He had previously been assigned to the unit that helped in suppression of the Warsaw Ghetto uprising. In his postwar interrogation by Soviet authorities, Terletskij was questioned regarding his desertion from Trawniki service:[109]

Q: Why did the Germans grant you leave?

A: I requested it because my mother was ill.

Q: Why did you not return from leave?

A: While on leave, in my hometown, I met with the head of the local unit of the OUN. He persuaded me to join the OUN. So I did. I remained in an OUN underground unit until 1945. I worked for the military intelligence arm of the OUN, and I collected weapons for the movement.

Q: Do you know of any other men in Trawniki service who defected to the Ukrainian Nationalists?

A: Yes. Mikhail Svistun. Like me, he was from the Stanislavov region and served as a Trawniki guard from February to September 1943, and like me, he had deployed to the Warsaw and Bialystok Ghettos. He went on leave with me in fall 1943 and, like me, did not return to Trawniki service. The last time I saw him was in early 1944 in a UPA unit.

These details were repeated at Terletskij's trial:[110]

In 1943, I was granted leave and went home. After going home, I did not return again [to Trawniki service], and in response to an offer by a regional leader of the OUN, Mikhail Luchkiv, I joined the OUN-UPA in October 1943 and served as a scout. I was armed with a pistol and grenades. Upon the arrival of Soviet units in our village, I was already a member of the OUN-UPA and continued to reside illegally. In summer 1944, I turned myself in out of guilt to the regional office of the MVD.

On October 27, 1943, three guards deserted: Jaroslaw Lohyn, Ivan Luzek, and Wolodymyr Torba.

On October 30, 1943, guard Mychajlo Pankiw deserted the camp. On November 11, 1943, guard Stanislau Swidrak fled in Lvov before he was supposed to escort a train back to the camp. On November 15, 1943, four guards deserted: Stanislaw Kosak, Stefan Hawryluk, Jaroslau Hura, and Jaroslau Demtschuk. On November 21, 1943, Eugen Maliart left the camp with eight other guards (although it is not clear if they deserted as well, or if he was the only one among them who left without permission); however, he returned to Trawniki service on March 18, 1944. On November 26, 1943, guard Dymtro Korzynski failed to return from leave. In December 1943, guard Wasyl Shyndykevskj had overstayed his leave. As a result, he was put in confinement for two weeks.

Shortly after his release, he deserted, on January 7, 1944. In a postwar interrogation, he was asked about this:[111]

Q: When did your Trawniki service cease?
A: In January 1944, when I fled back to the Motherland [the Soviet Union].
Q: Under what circumstances did you flee?
A: While in Trawniki I was notified in November 1943 that my father had died. For this reason I received leave for eleven days and went home. I overstayed my leave by nine days and then returned to Trawniki. Not only did I return late, along the way back I also caused an incident with a policeman. The Trawniki command gave me twelve days' confinement as punishment. After completing the punishment, I escaped from the camp and went home. I escaped because I was now convinced of Germany's defeat. In May 1944, I was mobilized into the Red Army. I served as a private in the 247th Rifle Regiment. In the area of Danzig, I received a shrapnel wound in April 1945. After treatment ended in August 1945, I went home. When I recovered, I was deemed fit for duty in the construction service.

On February 23, 1944, guard Olexa Tarasiuk failed to return from leave. The following month, two more guards deserted: Wolodymyr Kazaj on March 2 or 4, 1944, and Wolodymyr Stryhun on March 27, 1944.

PLASZOW

On May 2, 1943, three guards deserted: Ivan Kostinow, Yevgenij Prigoditsch, and Andrej Keliwnik. They were all captured, and on June 24, 1943, they were shot in Majdanek.[112] Upon arrest, the three guards gave a statement to the police. One of those statements is given below:

Kazimierz, May 1943
After the end of my shift on May 2nd, I went to a woman in the Plaszow suburb of Krakow with my comrades Andrej Keliwnik and Yevgenij Prigoditsch. There we drank homemade schnapps that the woman had procured from elsewhere. We took our weapons with us. My two comrades persuaded me to go on a trip to the village of Ludwinow, in the city of Chodel, Pulawy District, where Prigoditsch had a lover. We went that day to Lublin by rail. From Lublin, we went on foot to Chodel and then on to Ludwinow. We spent the night in Chodel in the mayor's house. At our request, the mayor gave us the use of a horse and carriage for the trip to Ludwinow. We didn't locate Prigoditsch's lover in Ludwinow. I tried to persuade my comrades that we should return to Krakow, but to no avail. We then went to the village of Ratoszyn, where Prigoditsch met with another woman to obtain some more schnapps. The woman ran away. Prigoditsch shot his rifle twice in anger. I accidentally broke a window with my own rifle, since I had been drunk ever since we left Ludwinow. My comrades reportedly stole 180 zloty from a local resident. A little later, Keliwnik and I ran into five Polish policemen in the village, who ordered us to hand over our weapons. We complied without putting up any resistance, and we stressed that we were not bandits, just drunken idiots. Two of the policemen went off to find Prigoditsch and arrested him too, about ten minutes later. I did not steal anything. Food and drink were always provided for by Prigoditsch, procured by acquaintances of his, and never taken under armed threat. I committed no acts of violence or theft. I stress that my actions are to be attributed to the influence of Prigoditsch and of alcohol. I deeply regret my behavior and request leniency in being judged.

Signed,
Ivan Kostinow
Geisler
Kriminal Oberassistant, Criminal Police
Taranda
Polizei-Angestellter

Kazimierz, May 8, 1943
Andrej Keliwnik Statement
I categorically deny having broken open the gate of a farmstead with my comrades during our stay in Ratoszyn. When I stated in my interrogation of May 7th that Kostinow had given a woman in Ludwinow ninety zloty to buy schnapps, this was an error. Before our trip we had 150 zloty at our disposal, which we used to buy the train tickets. We drank away the rest in Krakow before we set off. So our journey was conducted without using any cash. We obtained food from acquaintances, and the money for the return journey to Krakow.

Signed,
Andrej Keliwnik
Geisler
Kriminal-Oberassistant, Criminal Police

Kazimierz-Dolny, May 10, 1943
Report: On May 4, 1943, a Polish police patrol from Opole, Pulawy District, arrested the following foreign guards from the Jewish camp in Krakow [Plaszow]: Ivan Kostinow, Yevgenij Prigoditsch, and Andrej Keliwnik.
Cause of the arrest: On the basis of witness statements, they were strongly suspected of looting and robbing individual farmsteads in the village of Ratoszyn, Chodel, Pulawy District.
    The accused were handed over to the Gendarmerie station in Opole, along with the preliminary findings of the investigation, and were brought from there to the office here in Kazimierz for further consideration.
    The accused are members of the Trawniki Training Camp in Lublin District and were on assignment as guards at the Krakow camp for Jews. On May 2, 1943, they took Jews to a worksite and then deserted.
    On May 4, Sergeant-Major Waclaw Zakrzewski from the Polish police station in Chodel, Pulawy District, conducted an investigation into the matter of the robbery of three farmsteads in the village of Radoszyn, Chodel, Pulawy District. He determined that three bandits armed with rifles and wearing Ukrainian coats and caps arrived from the village of Ludwinow on a borrowed horse and cart. They went into a woman's house and stole 180 zloty, smashed four windows, and fired two shots in the house. One of these bandits attempted to rape another local woman but did not succeed. They entered another house and stole twenty-five zloty, and the resident of the house fled. In another house they demanded schnapps but came up empty handed. They also stole some clothing—a shirt, a jacket, and a pair of pants.

The bandits were arrested by Polish police officers based in Chodel. One of the bandits was in possession of the stolen pants. His name is Ivan Kostinow. The second bandit, Yevgenij Prigoditsch, had possession of the stolen jacket and shirt and the twenty-five zloty. All of the stolen items were returned to their owners in exchange for a receipt. The bandits reported that they had been guards at a Jewish camp in Krakow and that they had run away. The men are currently imprisoned by the Gendarmerie in Opole, and their three rifles along with thirty-three rounds of ammo were confiscated and turned over to the police in Opole.

Signed,
Zakrzewski
Sergeant-Major

May 31, 1943, Commander of the Security Police and SD Lublin District IV E 1 b–Gestapo to the SS and Police Commander, Lublin District
I enclose a file on the foreign guards named below, regarding their unauthorized absence from their unit and acts of robbery: Ivan Kostinow, Yevgenij Prigoditsch, Andrej Keliwnik.
These men are members of the Trawniki training camp. On May 2nd they left their post at Plaszow camp, without authorization, and took with them their rifles and ammunition. On May 5th they were arrested in Ratoszyn, Chodel, Pulawy District, and are currently being held at the Lublin prison. With regard to their offences, I refer to the enclosed investigation file. The items taken from these men include three Russian rifles, thirty-three shells of ammunition, one bayonet, and one belt. I have notified the commander of the security police and SD in Krakow of the arrest of these three men.

June 9, 1943
SS and Police Commander
Lublin District
Trawniki Training Camp
Re: The guards Kostinow, Prigoditsch, and Keliwnik, who deserted from their camp
Ref: Report–IV E 1 b [Gestapo] of May 31, 1943
To the Commander of the Security Police and SD
Lublin District
With regard to the above report, it is requested that the guards Ivan Kostinow, Yevgenij Prigoditsch, and Andrej Keliwnik, who are currently being held in the Lublin prison, be immediately taken for special treatment [i.e., execution]. It is also requested that their uniforms be turned over to our depot on Warsaw Street in Lublin, along with notification of the completion of this task.

Commander of Trawniki Training Camp
SS-Hauptsturmführer

July 10, 1943
Commander of the Security Police and SD
Lublin District
IV E 1 b–Gestapo
To the SS and Police Commander
Lublin District
Trawniki Training Camp
Re: The guards Kostinow, Prigoditsch, and Keliwnik, who deserted from their camp.
Ref: Letter of June 9, 1943
On June 24th the abovenamed guards were taken to the Lublin concentration camp [i.e., Majdanek] for special treatment [i.e., execution]. The special treatment took place there on the same day. Their uniforms were immediately turned over to SS-Unterscharführer Scheithauer, a driver with the Lublin Detachment.

On August 18, 1943, sixteen guards[113] and over 300 Jewish prisoners allegedly escaped in two trucks belonging to the camp command. According to the police, the fugitives took enough arms and ammunition with them for 100 people. An investigation was conducted and the camp was put on lockdown. In retaliation for the escape, German and Ukrainian police reportedly shot 200 Jews. On August 31, 1943, three trucks loaded with bodies of the dead left the camp, according to the Department of Internal Affairs of the Polish government delegation. The number of prisoners who escaped and, even more so, the quantity of arms taken appears to be exaggerated. Yet, there is no doubt that an armed resistance movement organized by Jewish prisoners in collaboration with the Trawniki guards did exist. The fate of its members is not known, as is the fate of those who escaped from the camp. A search in the archives for testimony of members of the camp underground regarding this escape has been fruitless. Therefore, it is possible to conclude that none of these people survived.[114]

Guard Mikhail Laptev took part in suppressing the Warsaw Ghetto uprising and also served at Plaszow, stating the following in a postwar investigation:

I remember Petr Krasnobaj as having served with me in Plaszow camp. In 1943, he escaped along with a group of sixteen others. During the night of the escape, he offered me an opportunity to run with them. He and I, however, did not come to a firm agreement, and during the night of the escape, he did not wake me up. Thus, I remained in the camp. The escape included Lukyanchuk, Lysak, Ivan Gubenko, and a certain *Gruppenwachmann* who, from what I heard, was from Kiev. I do not remember the names of the others.[115]

On August 29, 1943, guard Vasili Slowjagin deserted. On September 1, 1943, he was shot.[116] In August 1944, guard Boris Babin deserted. It is not certain that he fled specifically from Plaszow; however, that was his last known place of assignment as of August 1943. He was captured and imprisoned by the Soviets in September 1944. He reentered the Red Army and served from January 1945 to July 1946.[117] In September 1943, guard Vladimir Emelyanov, from the Moscow region, who had previously served at Belzec, escaped from the camp.[118]

JANOWSKA

On July 27, 1943, the guards Nikolaj Grishchenko and Nikolaj Zhivotov, the latter a Russian from Orlov region, fled.[119] They were allegedly last seen in the company of two Ukrainian women in Lvov.[120] At least eleven guards deserted in September–November 1943.[121] On September 29, 1943, guard Alexander Sajdakow deserted[122] (available documentation does not make it definitively clear whether he deserted from here or Sobibor; however, the author has opted to believe that he had been transferred here from Sobibor on September 25, 1943, since other guards who had been assigned to Sobibor on August 2, 1943, as he had, had also been transferred to Janowska on this date.) At least three guards were known to have deserted in October 1943. That month, a mass execution of Jewish prisoners took place in the camp. Those known deserters are Nikolaj Butenko,[123] Nikolaj Gordejew (on October 25, 1943),[124] and Nikolaj Skorokhod. Gordejew, who was apparently recaptured and imprisoned sometime in 1944. Skorokhod stole from the camp storage depot and passed on the stolen items to a Polish friend in order to pay for false papers and finance his own desertion in late October, after the mass shootings in the camp. After escaping, Skorokhod hid out with his Polish girlfriend in Lvov until Red Army troops liberated the city in 1944.[125]

In November 1943, guard Jakob Zechmeister[126] (possibly a *Volksdeutsche*) fled. (See the explanation for Sajdakow above. Zechmeister had also served at Sobibor as of August 2, 1943, but this author believes he was transferred to Janowska on September 25, 1943). Also in November 1943, guard Wasyl Kartashew deserted. He had previously served at Sobibor.[127] On November 23, 1943, Nikolaj Bukowjan deserted. He had recently been promoted to *SS-Gruppenwachmann* and had served at Janowska for nearly two years.[128] The guard Andrej Sergienko deserted from the camp on an unknown date. At least one of his motives for fleeing from Trawniki service was fear of Soviet authorities returning to the area, following German defeats.[129]

DOROHUCZA

On March 25 or May 25, 1944 (available documentary evidence is contradictory), the guard Vasili Rjaboschapka, deserted. He took with him a firearm and hand grenades and is believed to have joined the partisans. He had previously served at Sobibor.[130]

TREBLINKA I

On March 17, 1943, there was a report of escaped guards (the author did not have access to the report, and so it has not been determined if the desertions were from Treblinka I or Treblinka II). On April 11, 1944, at least three guards fled the camp: Ivan Chapayev, Ivan Filipow, and Boris Safronow. They took weapons with them and are believed to have joined the partisans.[131]

Gruppenwachmann Anatol Munder (a *Volksdeutsche*) is said to have fled to the partisans.[132] Another guard elaborated on Munder in a postwar interrogation:

As I remember, Munder left the camp. I knew about his departure even before he actually left. He told me himself that he was preparing a group and was going to leave the camp. This conversation occurred between us face to face in a café. Having drunk a bit, he told me about this. And it came to pass just as he stated. About ten *Wachmänner* went with him. I cannot remember their names. On the eve of Munder's escape, I was placed in the punishment cell. I do not know what I was placed there for. Another *Wachmann* besides me was also in the punishment cell. I don't remember his name. When Munder and his group escaped, they broke the locks to the punishment cells, but the other *Wachmann* being held in the cell was closer to the entrance than I was, so they managed to break his lock and did not manage to reach mine. Someone from among the German officers heard noise coming from the punishment cells. He was the duty officer, and he fired in our direction. The *Wachmänner* who were preparing to escape jumped from the punishment cell and took cover. During this night, Munder left the camp with a group of *Wachmänner*.

Q: How long before the camp was liquidated did Munder conduct his escape?
A: Not long before the camp was liquidated, but I cannot exactly say how long this period was. After his escape, I spent about a month in the punishment cell.[133]

The remaining political prisoners in the camp (estimates vary between 300 and 700) were taken out to the nearby forest, where they were shot and buried in groups. On July 23, 1944, as the German SS staff and Trawniki guards fled the camp upon imminent approach of the advancing Red Army, at least five guards took advantage of the chaos to break away from the rest of the unit. They were Nikita Rekalo, Valentin Roshanski, Mikhail Poleschzuk, Grigorij Sirota, and Pavel Kozlov. There may have been others in this desertion group, because they soon stumbled into Soviet troops, who opened fire on them and may have killed some of their number. These five men, and Ivan Shevchenko, who had deserted in October 1943, were among the first Trawniki guards to be captured, interrogated, and tried by Soviet authorities. Proceedings against them took place before the war ended.[134]

AGRICULTURAL ESTATES

A Wehrmacht monthly report of May 4, 1943, stated: "The success of the bandits is frequently due to the unreliability of the guards assigned to lumber mills and agricultural estates, many of whom desert to the partisans, as have a number of the *Volksdeutsche Sonderdienst*."

TARNAWATKA

Located not far from Belzec, this is where the guard Grigorij Nesmejan was assigned after he transferred out of Belzec on March 27, 1943. He deserted from there at some point in April 1943 or later.[135]

OLBIESZCZYN

Located in Krasnik District, five guards who had transferred out of Belzec on April 12, 1943, were sent here, and they all deserted on May 2, 1943. They were Alexej Schamordin, Stepan Sierakow, Daniil Tadyschewkow, Ivan Tschistaljow, and Nurgali Nurmuchametow.[136]
A report was filed for Trawniki training camp:[137]

At the state farm in Olbiencien, Krasnik District, the five *Wachmänner* escaped, and Oberwachmann Wekschins shot himself and left a note that he could not live any longer. The *Wachmänner* took weapons and ammunition with them.

Signed by [illegible signature],
SS-Unterscharführer

Schamordin and Sierakow were Russian; Tschistaljow was Komi (an ethnic group from northern Russia with origins in Finland); Tadyschewkow was Oirot (an ethnic group from the central Asian region of the Soviet Union, near such places as Kazakhstan and Mongolia); and Nurmuchametow was a Tatar (an ethnic group from the Crimean and Caucasian regions of southern Russia).[138]

BYGODA

Located 7 miles northwest of Lublin. On July 2, 1944, guards reportedly fled (the number is not specified) after an attack and robbery by partisans.

KLUCZKOWICE

On July 14, 1944, six guards fled to the partisans with their weapons after killing their *Volksdeutsche* NCO.

POLICE/DEPLOYMENT UNITS

LUBLIN DETACHMENT

Eight Trawniki guards deserted from here, a few days after having transferred back from Janowska. They were Gruppenwachmann Waldemar Lesik, ID #165; Oberwachmann Andrej Babitsch, ID #776 (possibly a former NKVD officer, and the Germans knew this); Wilhelm Paruschewskij, ID #310; Semen Nasarenko, ID #341; Vladimir Priwarskij, ID #634 (?); Paul Paschuk, ID #794; Konstantin Nasarenko, ID #863; and Dimitrij Hoschko, ID #1404. They had taken with them eight rifles and 455 rounds of ammo, suggesting their intent to go over to the partisans.[139]

In August 1943, the guard Jan Pilipiuk, from the Chelm region, apparently went missing for a time after being deployed from the Lublin Detachment to the Bialystok Detachment. Trawniki authorities wrote to the Gendarmerie office in his home region of Chelm, asking them to search for him and arrest him as a deserter if he were found. Based on a letter he wrote to his sister in September, it was suspected that he had gone home due to possible homesickness. However, as of late September 1943, the search was called off when it was determined that he was still in Trawniki service and had been deployed to Sobibor on September 16, 1943.[140]

On September 19,1943, guard Pawlo Jurtschenko killed a policeman and was shot as he attempted to flee. He had previously been assigned to the unit that helped suppress the Warsaw Ghetto uprising.[141] A report of the incident was filed:

Lublin, September 26, 1943
To the Trawniki Training Camp
Re: Execution of the SS-Wachmann Pawlo Jurtschenko (ID #1843) following a traffic stop carried out by the Lublin Mounted Police Squadron
On September 19, the SS-Wachmann Pawlo Jurtschenko, who had been assigned to an escort detachment of the German Equipment Works in Lublin, abandoned his post without permission. Police Officer Wilms, a member of the Lublin Mounted Squadron, told me that an *SS-Wachmann* had shot Zugwachtmeister Akamwischer, another member of the Lublin Mounted Squadron, as he was conducting a traffic stop. Other members of the police conducting the traffic stop

subsequently shot and killed the *SS-Wachmann*. Upon examining the body, it was determined that the *SS-Wachmann* in question was Pawlo Jurtschenko, ID #1843, from Trawniki Training Camp. He was a Belorussian national, born on September 10, 1920, in Mogilov.

Signed,
Wachtmeister, Schupo

On December 1, 1943, Vladimir Bruchaki fled. He had previously been assigned to Sobibor. He was captured on December 17, 1943, and tried by the SS and Police Court in Lublin. He was sentenced to five months' imprisonment, which he served at a prison labor camp attached to the SS training camp (Heidelager) in Debica, Poland, March–August 1944. As foreigners (excluding *Volksdeutsche*), the Trawniki guards were presumed "not to possess the military bearing and loyalty to duty that is characteristic of Germans."[142]

According to a report submitted by the Lublin Detachment to Trawniki training camp, from March 6 to April 2, 1944, a total of nineteen guards either deserted or failed to return from leave. These men were as follows: Osyp Kuc, Vitaly Woytschuk, and Wolodymyr Wosnjak on March 6, 1944; Sergej Soptschuk, who failed to return from leave on March 10, 1944; Josef Demchuk and Kasimir Antonjuk on March 20, 1944; SS-Zugwachmann Eugen Ponkratow and SS-Gruppenwachmann Paul Malinowski on March 21, 944; Stefan Martynjuk and Nikolaus Dejnek on March 25, 1944; Alex Kotczora and Stefan Olschewski on March 27, 1944; Michael Dzysa, Alex Luchtaj, and Roman Jusypchuk, who failed to return from leave on March 28, 1944; Josef Borolejko and Georg Antonjuk, detailed to the Pulawy sawmill, on March 28, 1944; and Osyp Popko and Ivan Trotz, on April 2, 1944. All of these guards were later recruits (with ID numbers in the 4,000 range) except for Zugwachmann Ponkratow (#142) and Gruppenwachmann Malinowski (#2469). The report ended with the following observations:

Through the repositioning of the front to the rear, the political situation in the home territory of the *SS-Wachmänner* has also changed. Some of the home territories have been occupied by the Russians or infested by bandits. The two events have not been without influence on the SS guards. In addition, the guards' relatives are encouraging them to desert. Thus the large desertion figures in the reporting period. In addition, a certain unreliability in the *SS-Wachmänner* has become noticeable through this situation.[143]

Signed,
Majowski,
SS-Oberscharführer

Signed,
Basener,
Oberwachtmeister, Schupo
Commander of Lublin Detachment

On January 6, 1943, guard Vladimir Pronin, who had been deployed to guard Soviet POWs employed at construction work in Rostov, Mariupol, Stavropol, and Armavir, took advantage of the distraction caused by the Soviet offensive at Stalingrad to desert and seek refuge with his family (paraphrased here):

In September 1942, I was sent in a group of seven *Wachmänner* from Trawniki to Lvov as a member of an SS vehicle convoy. I was then sent with the SS vehicle convoy to the German-Soviet front, where I served in Mariupol, Rostov-on-the-Don, Stavropol, and Armavir. In Rostov-on-the Don, we were quartered in a building that was a former artillery academy. Available laborers were hired to restore the building. I served as a guard over the vehicles and performed other administrative tasks. In Stavropol, we were also quartered in a building in which restoration was carried out by Soviet POWs who had been brought from a camp that was located in a former jail building on the outskirts of Stavropol. Five other *Wachmänner* and I escorted the POWs to and from work and guarded them while they restored the building. I was then in Armavir for one day, after which I headed west because, in the area, units of the Red Army had struck a blow against German forces, and some German units began to withdraw westward. Along the way in Zaporozhe, I left the train and returned to my family.[144]

Guard Ivan Tscherkasow, a Ukrainian who lived in the Semipalatinsk region in Kazakhstan prior to the war, had several disciplinary problems while in Trawniki service. This culminated in his desertion from his assignment at the Waffen-SS Troop Supply Depot in Lublin on November 17, 1943. He was captured, but deserted again, and was shot on March 17, 1944.[145] A report was filed on the November 1943 desertion:

Waffen-SS Supply Depot
Lublin, November 17, 1943
Re: Desertion of SS-Wachmann Ivan Tscherkassow, #774
To the SS Garrison Headquarters,
SS Legal Officer
Lublin

The Waffen-SS Supply Depot reports the desertion of SS-Wachmann Ivan Tscherkassow. Tscherkassow was sentenced to three days of detention on November 16th for being absent without leave and was admitted to the detention center. On November 17th around 1 p.m., it was discovered that Tscherkassow had broken out of the detention center. He had deserted from the grounds of the Waffen-SS Troop Supply Depot Lublin.

Tscherkassow was born in the Kirovograd region and lived in Semipalatinsk. He had entered Trawniki service on October 10, 1941. His girlfriend is Stanislawa Marjefska, who lives in Lublin. She has a child of about six months old and is currently expecting another. Tscherkassow was unarmed at the time of his desertion and was wearing a fatigue uniform, a black forage cap, and long boots. He had left all personal effects behind.

Signed,
Commander of the Waffen-SS Supply Depot Lublin
SS-Hauptsturmführer

On November 24, 1943, guard Stefan Ciucki deserted from the Gendarmerie post Bilgoraj. He was captured and imprisoned in the Lublin jail.[146] On December 10, 1943, guard Johann Jankowsky deserted from the Gendarmerie post Krasnystaw.[147] On February 12, 1944, guard Stefan Choruk deserted from the Wizniza Detachment.[148]

On March 6, 1944, at the Stary-Dwor outpost in Wysokie District, which had been established to watch over a grain warehouse, an attack was conducted by a group of 150 men led by a former Trawniki *Wachmann*, Fedor Cernicki. During the attack, the outpost was set on fire. In the process, the following five Trawniki guards assigned to the outpost fled: Ivan Szczerbacz, #4170; Wasyl Petrusiak, #4175; Nikolaus Lewkowitsch, #4187; Alex Martschuk, #4240; and Vladimir Jartisch, #4243. They took their weapons with them. The German Gendarmerie lieutenant in charge of the outpost believed they had joined the group that had conducted the attack, and he filed a report to Trawniki to that effect.[149]

On March 28, 1944, guard Sergej Schewtschuk deserted from the Rejowiec Detachment.[150]

On March 30, 1944, guard Jan Tschup deserted from the Skierbjeschow Detachment. He took a rifle and ammunition with him.[151]

SS-STREIBEL BATTALION

Guard Fedor Vyshavanyuk stated the following in a postwar interrogation:

In fall 1943, I was sent as a member of a five-man detachment to the village of Yastkov, about 8 miles from Lublin. There we guarded a German estate where wounded German soldiers were being taught how to farm. I remained there until summer 1944. I remained there until the advance by units of the Red Army on Lublin. Then, a member from our five-man detachment deserted. The remaining four of us were arrested and taken to the SD in Krakow. There they conducted an investigation for two weeks. We were then sent 15–20 miles from Krakow to dig trenches. About a month later, we were sent back to the SD in Krakow and interrogated. We were then sent to join our unit in the city of Gorlitz. Our company withdrew in the direction of Dresden. We stopped about 12 miles from Dresden. The company spent the spring of 1945 digging defensive positions. After Dresden was bombed by American aircraft, we went to Dresden to clear rubble from the streets. After that, we were to deploy somewhere else, but we all scattered along the way because units of the Red Army and American forces were approaching from all sides. Having escaped from my company, I was captured by the German police and was placed in a column of Soviet POWs who was being sent somewhere. I escaped to Czechoslovakia along with other Russian POWs and joined the Czech partisans. I remained with them until the end of the war.[152]

In a postwar interrogation, guard Petr Koval stated the following:

I was sent in September 1942 to guard Lublin concentration camp [Majdanek]. I was there until the end of January 1943. In March 1943, as a member of a group of about fifty *Wachmänner* from Trawniki, I was sent to guard Treblinka labor camp until August 1944, when the Red Army advanced on Poland. After fleeing to the rear of the retreating German forces, we were used by the German command to mobilize the Polish population to carry out defensive labor for the Germany army. After we halted west of Poznan, we deployed to nearby villages and mobilized Poles and Czechs to worksites and then guarded them. In November 1944, all *Wachmänner*, including me, were sent to Germany.

In January 1945, we arrived in Dresden and halted there. We cleared roads and cleared the bodies of those killed during bombings, and buried them. In March 1945, our unit was transferred to Czechoslovakia, to a village. I escaped from this village during early April 1945, along with Reznichenko, Galyaskarov, Kondratenko, and Wagner, and we then joined up with partisans. Before our departure, we took weapons and changed into civilian clothing, and then we walked through the woods for six days until we found the partisans. After we joined a group of partisans that numbered about thirty people in the woods, commanded by Major Subbotin, a Czech officer, we remained with this group until the end of April 1945, until the occupation of Czechoslovakia by Soviet forces. The partisan group we belonged to included Ukrainians, Russians, and Czechs who had been POWs. While serving in this group, I frequently lay in ambush by the main road along which German vehicles passed, and I fired upon them with a rifle. On one occasion I remember that at night, we went to a village, where we blew up an ammunition supply point.

We did not have any direct engagements with regular German units, but on one occasion when a company of German soldiers entered the woods, planning to clear the area, we engaged them with weapons and the Germans retreated, leaving several killed. We did not have any other actions against the Germans, because soon after, Soviet forces took Prague and we entered the city. We were then sent by the Soviet command to Osventsim [Auschwitz], where there was an inspection and screening point. There we were subjected to examination by counterintelligence [SMERSH]. I concealed information about my criminal activities [Trawniki service] and about the fact that I was a traitor to the Motherland [the Soviet Union] because I feared being punished. In September 1945, I was mobilized into the Red Army, and I was sent to a vehicle recovery unit, where I served as a rifleman until August 1946, after which I was transferred to a labor battalion. In May 1947, I was demobilized on the basis of a decree from the Presidium of the Supreme Soviet and was returned home to my village in the Zaporozhe region.[153]

OTHER ASSIGNMENTS

BIALYSTOK DETACHMENT

On August 10, 1942, guard Paul Garin (a *Volksdeutsche*), assigned as a driver/mechanic to the motor pool, fled. A report that was filed provides details[154] (paraphrased here):

Chief of the Order Police
Police Vehicle Maintenance Workshop
Subject: Desertion of a *Wachmann*
To: Commander, Trawniki Training Camp
According to my detachment in Bialystok, Wachmann Paul Garin left the post on August 10, 1942, and has not returned since. The Search Department of the Criminal Police has been informed.

Signed,
Kaiser,
Major of the Schutzpolizei

Three days later, a follow-up report was filed (paraphrased here):

Bialystok,
August 13, 1942
To: Vehicle Maintenance Workshop, Lublin
Wachmann Garin was arrested and detained by us on August 12, 1942. On August 9, 1942, Wachmänner Garin and Malyschev went to the city. A few hours later, they returned drunk. Malyschev had started an argument with some Poles for no reason, resulting in a fight. The following day, Wachmann Garin disappeared. A sweep of the city was unsuccessful. On August 12, Garin was sighted near the barracks. He was chased and captured. He was drunk and was confined to the barracks. When he sobered up, he was interrogated. He admitted having fled and had also tried to persuade Wachmann Malyschev to do so. Malyschev, however, did not get involved. Garin had stolen another *Wachmanner's* overcoat and had sold it along with his own uniform boots and shirt. He used the money to buy alcohol. After being administered a beating, Garin admitted having sold the uniform items to a farmer about 5 miles outside Bialystok. He had also stolen a hammer and a pair of pliers from the toolbox in the carpentry shop and sold these items as well.

Garin had already been punished with three days' confinement on July 28, 1942, for being drunk on duty. Since he is useless for any duty and it is feared that he will flee again and commit theft again, he should be returned to Lublin. Garin is to be considered a destructive element and, because of his Bolshevik ideas, could easily act as an influence on the rest of the guard force and poison their morale. In consideration of these tendencies, the strictest sentence on Garin is called for.

Signed,
Horndasch,
Wachtmeister, Schupo

On September 8, 1942, Garin was discharged from Trawniki service and returned to Stalag 319 POW camp in Chelm.

HSSPF ADRIATIC COAST
In 1945, guard Ivan Marchenko apparently deserted to the Yugoslav partisans in or near the city of Fiume (modern-day Rijeka), in modern-day Croatia. He had previously served as one of the gas chamber operators at Treblinka II.[155] Similarly, the following statement was made: "In spring 1945, Marchenko and a man named Grigorij, who had been a mechanic of the

gas chambers at Sobibor, seized an armored personnel carrier in Fiume [today, Rijeka] and fled to the partisans over the border in Yugoslavia."[156]

Regarding another guard who may have deserted in this area, a statement by former *SS-Oberscharführer* Kurt Bolender is relevant: "The gassing engine [in Sobibor] was worked by a Ukrainian named Emil and a German named Bauer. I know that the Ukrainian, later in Italy, joined the partisans. I don't know what happened to him."[157]

(*Author's note*: It is unclear whether Emil and Grigorij might have been one and the same person, or whether these were two different guards in charge of the Sobibor gassing engine.)

In April 1945, SS-Zugwachmann Emanuel Schultz (a.k.a. Emanuel Vertogradov) fled as the SS and police unit he had been attached to withdrew from the Adriatic region into Austria. He had previously been one of the highest-ranking Trawniki NCOs serving at Treblinka II.[158] At his trial in Kiev in 1961, he claimed that he had joined the Yugoslav partisans.

"Information on desertions is extremely scarce." The Trawniki company reportedly had four deserters; however, this was not counting the last days of the war before the German retreat from Trieste, when several men left the unit and went into hiding.[159]

EBENSEE CAMP

Guard Vasili Bronov, from Gomel region in Belorussia, who had previously served at Belzec and Plaszow, stated the following in a postwar interrogation:

Ivan Shurayev and I served at Plaszow together until April 1944. Then we were sent to the Gusen camp [Austria]. From the camp in Gusen, we were sent in October or November 1944, to the concentration camp in Ebensee [Austria]. At the end of March 1945, Shurayev, Ivan Krestov, and I escaped in the area of the Ens River near the city of Steiermark [Styria/Austria]. For the next month, we made our way through the mountains and valleys of Austria in the direction of Red Army forces. In early May 1945, we crossed over to the side of Soviet forces. We were then sent to an assembly point near the city of Amstetten [Austria]. In June 1945, we were assigned to the 210th Reserve Rifle Regiment. I did not meet Shurayev again until September 1946. I visited him at his residence in Kuznetsk, Penza region, so he could help me find a job.[160]

REGENSBURG

Guard Nikolaj Akhtimijchuk, who had served in the unit that helped suppress the Warsaw Ghetto uprising, stated the following in a postwar interrogation:

From May through August 1944, I served as a guard at a cement factory. My responsibilities included protecting the factory from attacks by partisans, who fired upon the factory almost every night. In August 1944, I retreated along with the Germans to the city of Regensburg. There, I was left to serve as a guard at a rubber factory. I served there until the arrival of American forces in December 1944. I then removed my uniform and went to the outskirts of the city. There, I began working for a German landowner for two months. In February 1945, the Americans announced that all foreigners who wanted to return to their homelands were to gather at the Red Cross. So I went to the Red Cross. I was registered and put on a train to Czechoslovakia with about 400 other people. I was then put on another train and sent to the city of Przemysl. There, I underwent screening. I stated that I had been a forced laborer in Germany. I was issued a certificate, and I returned to the Soviet Union in late May 1945.[161]

VLASOV ARMY

In a postwar interrogation, guard Vasili Litvinenko, who had served at Janowska, stated the following:

In fall 1944, I was sent as a member of a detachment of *Wachmänner* numbering about twenty-five men, to the city of Chomutov, near Prague. There we guarded a castle in which imprisoned members of the Romanian government were held. There were about thirty people held there. They were not required to work, and we were only required to guard them. In late January 1945, we were again sent to Flossenbürg. I spent about two months guarding the camp there. Then the Germans began to send us to serve in the so-called Russian Liberation Army (ROA) commanded by Vlasov. Wachmann Beseda and I arrived in the city of Goldberg, where the Vlasov units were located. We did not want to join these units, so we escaped and ran to Austria. I found work with a farmer in the city of Grieskirchen. On May 7, 1945, American forces entered the area. Officials of the Red Army command arrived in the city in the same month. I concealed my service with the Germans from the Soviet authorities, and I was called up to serve in the Red Army. In December 1945, I was demobilized and arrived home to my family in the Kiev region."[162]

CHAPTER 4

UNIFORMS

A combination of internal Trawniki memos, eyewitness accounts, and photographic evidence indicate that there were at least five uniforms worn by the Trawniki guards. These included black, black with gray collar and cuffs, earth brown, earth gray, and the combination uniform (earth-brown or earth-gray tunic with black pants).

One thing that all the uniforms had in common was that they were always worn with a black side-cap, or black forage cap, that had on it a plastic or aluminum button with the *Totenkopf* (skull and crossbones) insignia. This black cap was worn regardless of what color the rest of the uniform was. All the uniforms were also all worn with black boots, and all uniforms would also eventually come to have black shoulder boards.

When Red Army POWs recruited for Trawniki service were first brought to Trawniki, they apparently initially kept their Red Army uniforms prior to being issued their Trawniki uniforms.[1] In addition to the color of uniforms noted above, different eyewitnesses have variously described uniforms in a variety of colors. This could be due to the actual existence of additional uniforms in additional colors, faulty memory of witnesses recalling details over time, the subjective nature of each witness's recollection of a particular color, and the difficulty of ascertaining color in cases where black-and-white photographs from the war period are being scrutinized. Other colors that the Trawniki guards' uniforms have been described as khaki,[2] dark khaki,[3] dark brown,[4] green,[5] forest green,[6] yellow green,[7] gray,[8] and gray green.[9]

A wartime memo stated the following:[10]

SS and Police Commander, Lublin District
Trawniki Training Camp
October 19, 1942
Trawniki rank and rank insignia are the following:
Wachmann: private, plain shoulder boards
Oberwachmann: private 1st class, shoulder boards with 1 stripe
Gruppenwachmann: sergeant, shoulder boards with 2 stripes
Zugwachmann: sergeant major, shoulder boards with 3 stripes
Gruppenwachmänner and *Zugwachmänner* are also to have collar patches with piping.

Signed,
Streibel,
SS-Hauptsturmführer
Commandant, Trawniki Training Camp

In addition, photographic evidence demonstrates that NCOs had not only stripes on their shoulder boards and collar piping on their tunic lapels, but also the SS sleeve eagle patch on their left shoulders (Something that the rank-and-file *Wachmänner* were not entitled to on their uniforms).

Another wartime memo stated the following:[11]

Lublin
May 10, 1943
Order: For now, guard units will receive black or earth-gray uniforms. Eventually, field-gray uniforms are planned.

Signed,
Streibel,
SS-Sturmbannführer

Signed,
Globocnik,
SS-Gruppenführer and Major-General of the Police

In a postwar interrogation, former *SS-Sturmbannführer* Karl Streibel had this to say about the uniforms:

First, black uniforms were worn; later, captured uniforms were worn, probably Belgian, with black tabs and field caps. The Belgian uniform was brownish, earth colored, similar to the uniform of the labor service (RAD: Reich Arbeits Dienst). Initially, the personnel had various uniforms even within the same units. In mid-1942, the black uniform was entirely eliminated.[12]

(*Author's note*: Streibel is incorrect, since the black uniform continued to see service after 1942, as demonstrated in photographs of black-uniformed Trawniki guards at the scene of the Warsaw Ghetto uprising in 1943.)

Former *SS-Zugwachmann* Heinrich Schaefer, a *Volksdeutsche* who served as a clerk and paymaster in the Trawniki Administrative Office, stated this: "We had black uniforms, then we had gray-brown uniforms. They tended to be more brownish, I guess one could call them beige. I also had silver-gray stripes on my shoulder boards."[13]

THE BLACK UNIFORM

According to Dr. Peter Black, this uniform probably originated from Polish army uniforms that were dyed black. This uniform (and its variation with the gray collar and cuffs) is frequently cited in eyewitness testimony of what Trawniki guards wore, and apparently made enough of an impression that because of it, the guards were often referred to as " the Blacks."[14] Another possible origin of these uniforms is that they formerly belonged to the Allgemeine-SS, since this same uniform was distributed to the *Schutzmannschaften*—local auxiliary police units recruited by the German police on Soviet territory to assist the Germans in enforcing their occupation laws (as well as hunt for Jews and partisans).[15]

THE EARTH-BROWN UNIFORM

This uniform was apparently confiscated from captured stocks of Belgian army uniforms. It may also be the one that some eyewitnesses refer to as "khaki." A uniform of the same color had also been worn by early recruits of the Waffen-SS in training, and at least one member of the Waffen-SS assigned to Trawniki believed that this uniform worn by the guards was in fact the same Waffen-SS uniform.[16]

THE EARTH-GRAY UNIFORM

The existence of this uniform is confirmed by official wartime documentation from the Trawniki authorities, just as it is with the black and earth-brown uniforms. However, its origin is not known, and whether or not it has ever been shown in a wartime photograph is difficult to tell, considering that photos from that era are in black and white. Suffice it to say that although the color has the word "gray" in it, it is the author's opinion, on the basis of descriptions and known examples of this color seen in a color photo book, that the color tends to look more brown than gray.[17] Several instances exist in which Trawniki guards were issued the black uniform but also had an overcoat in earth gray.[18]

THE COMBINATION UNIFORM

This uniform consisted of black pants with some other color of tunic, probably the earth-brown or earth-gray one. Why some guards wore a combination of the uniforms is not known. Perhaps it had to do with whatever uniform parts happened to be available, and some guards simply were unable to get themselves issued a matching-color uniform.[19] The distribution of the uniforms to the guard recruits in Trawniki was the responsibility of SS-Oberscharführer Ernst Teufel (who first started out in Trawniki as an *SS-Rottenführer*). He was in charge of the camp's clothing storehouse. The clothing storehouse in turn came under the jurisdiction of the SS Garrison Administration Lublin, to which the Trawniki training camp was a branch office.[20] As far as it is known, recruits at the Trawniki training camp wore tunics described as black or gray green.[21] According to one source, "the Trawniki men were initially issued gray-green uniforms, and after the end of the training period they received black uniforms."[22] The gray-green uniform referred to here was probably the earth-gray or field-gray one.[23] On the basis of photo evidence, a pretty heterogeneous mix of uniform elements were in use for the Trawniki guards:

The Model 1932 black *SS-Dienstrock* made for the Allgemeine-SS, SS-Verfugungstruppe, and SS-Totenkopfverbande, standard SS Model 1937 tunics, tunics cut in the style of the Army model 1940 or 1941 tunic, and the earth-gray model 1934 tunic originally used by the SS-Verfugungstruppe.

According to some trial depositions, at least the Trawniki guards serving at Belzec were issued uniforms described as earth brown or *lehmbraun* (clay brown).[24] These may have been the obsolete earth-brown model 1934 tunics used by personnel of the SS-Totenkopf regiments that guarded concentration camps.[25] In most cases, no collar tabs were worn on their tunics. NCOs wore a peculiar short, lower-collar *Tresse* that was silver colored, and rank stripes, also made of *Tresse*, on black shoulder boards.[26] Photos show up to a maximum of three *Tresse* stripes worn by Trawniki personnel on their shoulder boards to indicate rank. These were probably of the same type used by the Waffen-SS and were used to indicate ranks by several foreign units in the service of the Germans such as the Osttruppen, the Sonderdienst in occupied Poland, and the Trawniki guards (*SS-Wachmannschaften*), sometimes together with collar piping or collar *Tresse*. The collar *Tresse* seemed to be the standard one used by NCOs in the German army. A peculiarity of the collar *Tresse* on Trawniki uniforms is that it did not go all the way around the collar but instead stopped at shoulder level.[27]

In some cases, the SS eagle was worn on the upper left sleeve of the tunic, as it was with German SS personnel. Photo evidence also indicates that some Trawnikis wore the yellow-blue national shield of the Ukraine on the left sleeve of the black tunic. Also confirmed by photos was the use of the bicolor combination uniform generally worn by the Schuma. These black uniforms, often obsolete *SS-Dienstrock* model 1932 uniforms originally produced for the SS, were modified for use by the Schuma and Trawnikis by adding collar, sleeve cuffs, and lower tunic pocket flaps in light blue, blue gray, or green.[28] The Schuma uniforms worn by the Trawniki guards can be seen in the photos taken during the suppression of the Warsaw Ghetto uprising.[29]

The Trawniki guards generally wore black side caps with a simple metallic tunic button sewn on to the front of it. In some rare cases, this plain button was replaced by a button with the *Totenkopf* insignia on it. These side caps were probably obsolete ones used by the Allgemeine-SS, SS-Verfugungstruppe, and the SS-Totenkopfverbande in the 1930s. In rare cases it appears that the black side cap in use was the one issued to Waffen-SS Panzer troops starting in 1940, with standard SS eagle and *Totenkopf* embroidered patches attached. It also seems that *Volksdeutsche* Trawnikis, in some cases, used the field-gray side cap with embroidered SS eagle and *Totenkopf* patch attached.[30]

Photos taken during a parade for Hitler's birthday on April 20, 1944, and during Christian Wirth's funeral in May 1944, both held in the Adriatic coast region, seem to indicate that the Trawniki personnel assigned there were issued SS-style collar tabs for their uniforms. The collar tabs were rhomboidal, black, and outlined, but without the sig runes insignia, like those used by the Sipo/SD. It also appeared that at that point, the NCO collar *Tresse* now went completely around the collar.[31] This uniform was "very likely produced with Italian gray-green wool cloth." The tunic, produced in slightly different variants, was cut in the style of the German army's model 1940/41 tunic but also "had a distinctive and unusual collar made of black cloth."[32]

Aside from the Trawniki guards, the Italian, Slovenian, and Croatian members of the *SS-Wachmannschaft* battalion in the Adriatic coast region also wore, mainly during training, Italian fatigue model 1940 uniforms, dyed khaki or sand color, without insignia.[33] These uniforms were made of gray cotton fabric. They were widely used in the summertime by the Italian army in order to preserve the dwindling stock of gray-green uniforms. These tunics were also used in the Adriatic coast region by the SS Training and Replacement Battalion stationed in Valcanale, Udine Province, the Landschutz in Udine Province, the SNVZ (Slovenian Landschutz), Police Battalion "Fiume," and the Civic Guard in Trieste.[34]

APPENDIX

ASSIGNMENT LOCATIONS

AKTION REINHARD DEATH CAMPS
SSPF Lublin District
Sobibor
Belzec
Treblinka II

CONCENTRATION CAMPS
SS-WVHA
Auschwitz-Birkenau
Majdanek
Warsaw concentration camp
Stutthof
Sachsenhausen
Buchenwald
Flossenbürg
Neuengamme
Mauthausen subcamp Gusen

LABOR CAMPS
Janowska: under the jurisdiction of SSPF Lvov District
Plaszow: under the jurisdiction of the SSPF Krakow District
Treblinka I: under the jurisdiction of the SSPF Warsaw District
Lipowa Street labor camp: under the jurisdiction of the SSPF Lublin District
Trawniki: under the jurisdiction of the SSPF Lublin District
Budzyn: under the jurisdiction of the SSPF Lublin District

Krasnik: under the jurisdiction of the SSPF Lublin District
Poniatowa: under the jurisdiction of the SSPF Lublin District
Dorohucza: under the jurisdiction of the SSPF Lublin District

CITY AND DISTRICT OFFICES
Lublin Detachment: under the jurisdiction of Orpo Lublin to facilitate deportations from the Lublin Ghetto; SS Garrison Administration HQ Lublin; Waffen-SS Troop Supply Depot Lublin; Rejowiec Detachment; Gendarmerie Biala-Podlaska; Security Police, Branch Office Radzyn; Security Police Warsaw; Warsaw Detachment: to facilitate deportations to Treblinka II and to help suppress the Warsaw Ghetto uprising; SS Training Camp Trawniki / SS Garrison Administration HQ Lublin–Branch Office Trawniki: initially under the jurisdiction of the SSPF Lublin District, and later under the SS-WVHA; Radom Detachment: to facilitate deportations to Treblinka II; Zamosc Detachment; Bialystok Detachment; SS Garrison Administration HQ Lublin: Branch Office Zamosc; HSSPF Adriatic Coast (Yugoslav/Italian border region), Trieste: San Sabba concentration camp and antipartisan duties. Withdrawal into Carinthia region, Austria, April 1945.

SS AGRICULTURAL ESTATES
Trawniki guards were also assigned to several SS estates that Globocnik, working with the SS-WVHA, had hoped to turn into SS and police bases. On some of these estates, Jewish

or Polish laborers did agricultural work or mining. By the summer of 1942, the Lublin District had two agricultural training schools, one in Jastkow, and one at Okszow in the Chelm region, and fourteen SS and police bases:[1]

1) Kosice-Dolne, Lublin
2) Rachow, Janow-Lubelski
3) Wytyczno, Chelm region
4) Horodyszcze, Chelm region
5) Serebryszcze, Chelm region
6) Okszow, Chelm region
7) Panska-Dolina, Zamosc
8) Wola-Zolkiewka, Krasnystaw
9) Turow, Radzyn
10) Simion, Radzyn
11) Suchawola, Radzyn
12) Jablon, Radzyn
13) Sarny, Pulawy
14) Sobieszyn, Pulawy

PARAMILITARY UNITS

SS "Streibel" Battalion—under the jurisdiction of SS Special Staff "Sporrenberg"—fighting withdrawal from the Lublin District in the wake of the Red Army advance through Poland beginning in July–August 1944, and culminating in the Vistula-Oder Offensive in January 1945. Participated in cleanup duties in Dresden following a severe bombing of that city in February 1945. Disbanded near the German-Czech border region, April 1945.

OTHER

Heinkel Aircraft Factory, Rostock, Germany

EXAMPLES OF DEPLOYMENT ROSTERS

GERMAN STAFF IN TRAWNIKI CAMP, 1942–1944[1]

SS-Sturmbannführer Karl Streibel
SS-Sturmbanführer Hans Mickeleit
SS-Obersturmführer Willi Franz
SS-Untersturmführer Johann Schwarzenbacher
SS-Oberscharführer Hermann Erlinger
SS-Oberscharführer Josef Mayevskij
SS-Oberscharführer Josef Napieralla
SS-Oberscharführer Rolixmann
SS-Oberscharführer Johann Struck
SS-Scharführer Ernst Teufel
Stefan Baltzer
SS-Unterscharführer Burkhardt
SS-Unterscharführer Robert Kollaritsch
SS-Unterscharführer Lehnert
Herman Reese
SS-Unterscharführer Rudolf Reiss
SS-Unterscharführer Fritz Rings
SS-Unterscharführer Willi Sautter
Kurt Reinberger
Police Oberwachtmeister Albert Drechsel
Police Oberwachtmeister Konrad Heinsch
Police Oberwachtmeister Koziol
Police Oberwachtmeister Helmut Leonhardt
Police Oberwachtmeister Theodor Pentziok
Police Oberwachtmeister Roman Pitrow
Police Oberwachtmeister Herbert Schafer
Police Wachtmeister Bieniek
Police Wachtmeister Michael Janczak
Police Wachtmiester Erich Lachmann
Police Wachtmeister Ernst Mohr

SECURITY POLICE WARSAW, APRIL 8, 1942[2]

Reference: Order from SS-Hauptsturmführer Hermann Hofle

Karl Schaubert, #40
Konrad Maier, #62, Armavir
Gregorij Mironjuk, #267
Kuzma Bojko, #280, Vinnitsa
Leontij Bokovenko, #285, Zhytomir
Michael Kobolenko, #298
Paul Jarmak, #349, Sumsk
Fedor Chilko, #351
Alexei Korovjanko, #395, Vinnitsa
Vasili Mirnenko, #412, Chernigov
Andrej Sles, #414, Zaporozhe
? Lavrenenko, #420, Chernigov
Jakob Iskaradov, #458, Kharkov
Pawlo Kudrin, #511, Zaporozhe
Nikita Tjutjunik, #520
Vasili Andrijenko, #527, Zhitomir
Alexander Valizin, #633, Ivanovsk
Michael Kurilo, #637, Dnepropetrovsk
Petro Gretscheniuk, #638, Zhitomir
Ivan Kosatschenko, #642, Zhitomir
Peter Slovenko, #675
Dimitri Besotosnyj, #688, Poltava
Alexei Golenko, #733, Stalino/Donetsk
Jakob Saitschuk, #808, Kiev
Alexander Prozenko, #815, Chernigov
Dimitri Belov, #826, Sumsk
Ivan Kamenov, #834, Stalino/Donetsk
Gavrilo Meljuschke, #970, Dnepropetrovsk
Alexei Grigoryev, #1103, Odessa
Stepan Prilipka, Kiev

Signed, *Oberwachtmeister*, Schupo

TREBLINKA II, 1942–1943[3]

Franz Bienemann
Dimitri Borodin
Albert Braun
Fedor Duschenko
Ivan Gapotij
Ignacy Gardzinski
Pavel Golovashin
Petro Goncharov
Mikhail Gorbachev
Ivan Gorpinchenko
Alexei Govorov
Franciszek Hajczuk
Wasyl Hetmaniec?
Leonid Ilnitskij
Alexander Jager/Yeger
Wasyl Jelentschuk
Dimitri Korotkikh
Ivan Kurrinij
Anani Kuzminski
Stepan Kwaschuk
Nikolaj Lebedenko
Pavel Leleko
Filip Levchishin
Josef Loch
Nikolaj Malagon
Nikolaj Malischeff
Ivan Marchenko
Moisej Martoschenko
Nikolaj Nedozrelov
Alexander Paraschenko
Evdokim Parfinyuk
Nikolaj Payushchik
Leonid Pevtsov
Andrei Pokotilo
Alexander or Vasili Popov
Samuel Pritsch
Emil Pusch

Danil Onoprijenko
Alexander Rittich
David Robertus
Boris Rogosa
Fedor Ryabeka
Prokofij Rjabzew
Grigorij Rubez
Vasili Rudenko
Nikolaj Scherbak
Wasyl Schischajew
Emmanuel Schultz/Vinogradov
Ivan Schwidkij
Nikolaj Senik
Nikolai Shalayev
Vasili Shilov
Nikolaj Skakodub
Georgi Skydan
Oswald Strebel
Ivan Terekhov
Ivan Tkachuk
Vladimir Tscherniawsky
Jakob Unrau
Sergei Vasilenko
Wasyl Woronkow
Trofim Zavidenko

BELZEC, 1942–1943[4]
Andrei Akkermann
Peter Alexeyev
Yakov Ananjew
Philip Babenko
Luka Bardachenko
Ivan Baskakov
Wasyl Belyakov
Genrikh Benzel
Ivan Bessmertnj
Piotr Browzew
[?] Budziak
Grigorij Bulat

Prokofij Busennij
Alexander Bychkow
Alexander Chruschev
Alexander Dukhno
Karl Diener
Vladimir Emelyanov
Mikhail Gorbachow
Fedor Gorun
[?] Gruzin
Vasili Gulij
Timofej Gura
Michael Huber
Stefan Jadziol
Yakov Keresor
Fedor Khabarov
Vasili Kipka
Andrej Kirillov [?]
Mitrofan Klotz
Grigorij Kniga
Mikhail Korzhikow
Ivan Kotscherga
Ivan Kozlowskij
Grigorij Kuchichidze
Andrei Kuchma
Ivan Kulak
Mikhail Kuschniruk (November 1941)
Boris Kutykhin
Samuel Kunz
Alexei Lazorenko
Nikolai Leontev
Grigorij Linkin
Peto Litus
Grigor Lowinow
Vladimir Lomow
Peter Lukyanchuk
Nikolaj Malagon
Nikita Mamchur
Nikolaj Matwijenko
Anastasi Mawrodij

I. Maximenko
Alexander Melnikov
Stepan Mogilo
Vladimir Morozov
Sadygula Motygulan
Grigorij Nesmejan
Pavel Nestarenko
[?] Netschaj/Nechayev?
Ivan Nikiforow
Taras Olejnik
Vasili Orlovskij
Franz Pamin
Nikolaj Pavli
Grigorij Petschonij
Alexei Pietka
Yurij Plechow
Wasyl Podenok
Franz Podessa
Andrei Pokotilo
Wasyl Popov
Sergei Poprawka
Ivan Poprushnij
Dimitri Prochin?
Kiril Prochorenko
Alexander Pruss/Zakharov
Emil Pusch
Pavel Redens (November 25–December 26, 1941)
Boris Rogosa
[?] Rosenholz
Arnold Rosenko
Viktor Sabat
Ivan Saplawny
Alexander Schaeffer
Heinz/Heinrich Schmidt
Freidrich Schneider
Vasili Schuller
Reinhard Seibert/Seivert
Alexander Semenow

Alexander Semigodow
Ivan Sisoj
Profirij Szpak
Ivan Tellmann
Fedor Tichonowskj
[?] Timoshenko
Dimitri Timoshkin
Luka Tobolski
Karl Trautwein
N. Tsukanov
Alexander Twardochleb
Grigorij Usenko
Jakob Wesota
Edward Wlasiuk
Ivan Woloshin
Viktor Wowk
Ivan Zagrebajew
Ivan Zaitsev
Grigorij Zakharov
[?] Zhuravlev
Ivan Zikota
Akim Zuev

SOBIBOR, 1942–1943[5]

Boris Babitsch
George Backer
Franz Bienemann
Ivan Bilik
Dimitri Borodin
Prokofij Busennij
Alexander Chruschev
Karl Dzirkal
Jakob Engelhardt
Fedor Gorun
Alexei Govorov
Alexander Kaiser
Friedrich Kaiser
Volodia Kaszewadzki
Viktor Kisiliev

Ivan Klatt
Ivan Kozlovskij
[?] Krupka
Ivan Kurrinij
Stepan Kwaschuk
Vladimir Morozov
Vasili Pankov
Evdokim Parfinyuk
Franz Podessa
Emil Pusch (Sobibor, October 4, 1942;
  Treblinka, November 1, 1942; Belzec,
  March 1, 1943; Lublin Detachment, May
  7, 1943)
Mikhail Rosgonjajew
Fedor Ryabeka
Nikolaj Skakodub
Anton Solonina
Ivan Tellmann
Ivan Werdenik
Philip Wergun
Wasyl Zischer

JANOWSKA, 1942–1943[6]

[?] Aleksejew
Boris Babitsch
Nikolaj Bubyr
Nikolaj Bukowjan
Vasili Burljajew
Nikolaj Butenko
Wasyl Djomin
Vyacheslav Dmitriev
Mikhail Ermilov
Alexander Fedchenko
Nikolaj Gordejew
Ivan Juchnowskj
Vasili Karptsov
Wasyl Kartaschew
Alexander Kirelacha
Stefan Kopytyuk

Peter Kovalyuk
Stepan Kwaschuk
Vasili Litvinenko
Yegor Lobyntsev/Lobanzow
Sergei Malov
[?] Matwijenko
Alexander Minochkin
[?] Naryzhnyj
[?] Nechayev
Friedrich Neumann
Andrei Ostapenko
Georgi Pankratov
Vasili Pochwala
Vladimir Pronin
Peter Rasstrigin
Dimitri Rjasanow
Yakov Sagach
Chassion Salachetdinow
Petro Sbeshnikow
Peter Sergeyev
Andrej Sergienko
S. Shirgaliev
Pawlo Sidortschuk
Nikolaj Skorokhod
[?] Solomka
Nikolaj Swjatelnik
Ivan Tarasov
Mikhail Titow
Ivan Volkov
Waldemar Wutke
Jakob Zechmeister
Nikolaj Zhivotov

MAJDANEK, FEBRUARY 15, 1943[7]

Oberwachmann Nikolaj Leitsch, #1672
Peter Pichodko, #595
Ivan Isaak, #665
Nikolaj Pavlenko, #741

Ivan Tscherkasow, #774
Karl Weiper, #833
Nikolaj Goroschko, #1250
Alexei Kanayev, #1254
Mikhail Malyshev, #1372
Georgi Semikolenow, #1597
Demian Januk, #1766
Vladimir Senzow, #1812
Dimitri Podbira, #1878
Anatoli Rumjanzew, #1996
Vasili Slowjagin, #1999
Grigorij Nediljko, #2074
Nikolaj Martinenko, #2079
Boris Babin, #2158
Ivan Ovtschinnikov, #2271
Nazar Zakotnij, #2318
Afanasij Ponomarenko, #2323
Ivan Ostapenko, #2336
Ivan Tschapljak, #2337
Wasyl Olyunin, #2428
Myron Flunt, #2804
Ivan Panasiuk, #3040

Signed, Philip Grimm
Oberwachtmeister, Schupo Reserve

Heinsch
Oberwachtmeister, Schupo

PLASZOW, MARCH 18, 1943[8]

Oberwachmann Johann Telmann, #96
Oberwachmann Emil Adam, #379
Oberwachmann Anifat Demedenko, #878, Kiev
Dimitri Pastevenski, #430, Zhitomir
Pader Stepanenko, #512, Dnepropetrovsk
Andrej Wdawitschenko, #528, Vinnitsa
Grigorij Krasilnik, #684, Kiev
Mikhail Ignatowsky, #701, Orel

Ivan Koljaka, #736, Sumsk
Ivan Labunskij, #762
Semyon Jakovizki, #876, Kirovograd
Nymofej Skidan, #972
Fedor Babatenko, #1091, Zhitomir
Ivan Stezenko, #1128, Krasnograd
Mikhail Sklyar, #1172, Poltava
Stepan Podolskij, #1416
Fedor Nykytyn, #1418, Orlovka
Wasyl Petschenskyj, #1425, Kharkov
Wasyl Piatkovskyj, #1586, Balta
Georgi Semikolenow, #1597
Mikhail Grekov, #1607, Odessa
Bronislaw Karpovitschus, #1646, Vilkaviskis
Feysi Valiyev, #1683, Kazan
Hanwar Jakubow, #1696
Grigorij Kiriyuschkin, #1701
Achad Mursagalanov, #17??, Tatar Republic
Konstantin Wykonynowski, #1743
Dimitri Podbira, #1878
Peter Sirschenko, #1910
Viktor Tscherbatiuk, #1928, Zhitomir
Wasyl Kolomyjec, #1932
Nikolaj Krut, #1950, Silo Ruska
Nikolaj Matschuskij, #1982, Dnepropetrovsk
Junus Chansevirov, #2032, Yalta
Ilja Gajfulin, #2056
Sergej Krasnoschok, #2064, Nikolayev
Grigorij Beskrownij, #2071, Dnepropetrovsk
Augustynas Vilbekas, #2142
Filimon Sokolov, #2185
Wasyl Schyrnov, #2238, Kazan
Wasyl Toporkin, #2257
Nikolaj Kolesnik, #2310, Kharkov
Stepan Jutschenko, #2321
Afanasij Ponomarenko, #2323
Alexander Baran, #2327, Dnepropetrovsk
Ivan Ostapenko, #2336, Kharkov
Grigorij Kravschenko, #2346

Trofim Wlasiuk, #2358, Kamenets-Podolsk
Kuzma Krykun, #2359
Michael Ovornyk, #2362
Mikhail Kolombar, #2366
Yakov Djatschok, #2368
Ivan Taz, #2374
Ivan Bessmertnyj, #2421, Voroshilovgrad/
    Lugansk
Ivan Nahornyj, #2423
Ivan Shevschenko, #2400, Novo-Arkhangelsk
Alexei Ivanenko, #2439

Signed, *Oberwachtmeister*, Schupo Reserve

SOBIBOR, MARCH 26, 1943[9]

Gruppenwachmann Jakob Wasem, #799:
    ended up remaining behind
Oberwachmann Friedrich Lorenz, #87,
    Donbas: ended up remaining behind
Oberwachmann Karl Dzirkal, #1629, Moscow:
    ended up remaining behind
Oberwachmann Tadas Rimkus, #1641: ended
    up remaining behind
Vladimir Sirotenko, #1?, Odessa
Jefim Gonscharow, #300
Alexander Karpenko, #386
Alexei Isajenko, #408, Kharkov
Konstantin Demida, #443, Baranovichi
Pawlo Makarenko, #445
Anatoli Gontscharenko, #56?, Odessa
Peter Rudenko
Kuzma Sokur, Kiev
Ivan Fedorenko
Ivan Bilik, #61?, Kiev
Efim Wolinez, #744
Ivan Ivschenko, #780, Kharkov
Josef Netschaj, #814
Anatoli Olexenko, #843
Gregor Lyachov, #987

Ignat Danilchenko, #1016, Dnepropetrovsk
Ivan Vakutenko, #1154, Kharkov
Nikolai Judin, #1158, Voronezh
Ivan Zhukov, #1281
Ivan Tischenko, #1332
Nurgali Kabirov, #1337, Tatar Republic
Semyon Sokorev, #1343, Kursk
Petro Sbesnikov, #1370, Avdeyevka, Stalino/
    Donetsk region?
Ivan Demjanjuk, #1393, Vinnitsa
Fiodor Vedenko, #1413
Chariton Chromenko, #1420
Andrei Nagorny, #1428
Ginnadi Frolov, #143?
Mikhail Reschetnikov, #1488, Kalinovka,
    Kursk, Vinnitsa, or Kiev region?
Jakob Domeratzki, #1531
Wasyl Antonov, #1678, Kazan
Nikolaj Gordienko
Aglam Batartinov, #1684, Tatar
Achmed Chabibulin, #1688, Tatar
Wasyl Yepifanov, #1698
Fetich Karimov, #1699
Bari Nabijew, #1712, Tatar
Dimitri Pischerov, #1717
Kamil Schigapev, #1719, Tatar
Chares Sabirov, #1726
Igor Besverche, #1786
Ivan Kakorasch, #1790
Nikolaj Gontscharenko, #1832
Pawlo Karas, #1837
Alexander Jasko, #1842
Nikolaj Medvedev, #185?
Kuzma Vaskin, #2161
Nikolaj Martinov, #2166
Ilya Baidin, #2345
Konstantin Savertnev, #2348
Dimitri Schevschenko, #2353
Peter Ivaschenko, #2354

Maxim Sirenko, #236?
Wasyl Ryschkov, #236?
Semen Mykolajenko, #2387
Ivan Indyukov, #240?
Mikhail Kusevanov, #2414
Ivan Yermolayev, #2415
Nikolai Seleznev, #2416
Mikhail Belyj, #2418
Nikolai Krupinevich
Yakov Koschemajkin, Lubyanka
Dimitri Bogunov
Grigorij Serik
Leonid Kurakov, #2431
Wasyl Deptyarev, #24??
Fedor Gorlov, #2434
Ivan Ustinnikov, #24??, Kiev
Grigorij Sergienko, #2440
Ivan Ljachow, #2441
Pavel Schichavin, #2442, Rjabski Zavod
Pavel Kudin, #2448, Kiev
Philip Kravschenko, #246?
Pavel Mordvinichev, #2463, Uralsk
Andrej Maschenko, #2466
Terentij Martynov, #2467
Sabit Bagandtimov, #2496, Tatar
Myron Flunt, #2804, Drogobych
Ivan Panasiuk, #3040

Signed, *SS-Untersturmführer*

BELZEC, MARCH 27, 1943[10]
Gruppenwachmann Vladimir Usik, #91
Oberwachmann Eugen Binder, #81
Oberwachmann Nikolai Malischeff, #82
Oberwachmann Fritz Stolz, #106, Saratov
Oberwachmann Artur Baumgart, #182
Dimitri Pundik, #264
Wasyl Kotoleviz, #268
Wasyl Mirgorodskij, #497

Sergei Schafolov, #544
Ivan Listopad, #553
Ivan Wownjanko, #568
Alexander Golubchik, #676
Ivan Bondar, #751
Ivan Polochov, #810
Nikolaj Scharandin, #918
Ivan Lisenko, #985
Nikolai Pavlov, #1030, Nizhny-Gorki
Fedor Monin, #1041, Zaporozhe
Todos Zikun, #1132, Siomaki, Vinnitsa region
Peter Berezowskij, #1165
Ivan Boblo, #1301
Dimitri Jasenko, #1313
Grigorij Yezhov, #1351
Jurko Danilov, #1408
Wasyl Komarnitzky, #1411
Kiril Tischenko, #1417
Fjodor Kuschik, #1421
Ivan Tschistalyov, #1435
Wasyl Krupnow, #1496
Grigorij Wowk, #1505
Ivan Stepanov, #1537
Ivan Savlutschenko, #1580
Nurgali Nurmuchemetov, #1714
Zibogad Orlov, #1715
Danil Tadyschekov, #1731
Nazibuk Schaichulin, #1732
Mikhail Babitsch, #1740
Ivan Zajcenko, #1750, Voronezh
Vladimir Makarcik, #1751
Ivan Gorpinchenko, #1784
Wasyl Oschepkov, #1867, Perm region?
Grigorij Welikodnyj, #1890
Peter Rybalka, #1908
Wasyl Porchomenko, #1925
Fedor Horbuk, #1938
Ivan Dudjenko, #1944
Sergej Titarenko, #1948

Alexander Liplenkov, #1955
Alexei Schamordin, #1961
Stepan Sierakov, #1962
Nikolaj Kurinnij, #1976
Grigorij Popov, #2004
Viktor Severentschuk, #2005
Alexei Jolkin, #2008
Wasyl Schlapakov, #2010
Boris Khaylov, #2011, Akulino,Vitebsk?
Maxim Komaschka, #2012
Stepan Shevschenko, #2014
Ivan Chatko, #2016
Fedor Tkatschenko, #2017
Filip Kornijenko, #2019
Alexander Popov, #2026
Savat Mochonjko, #2033
Naum Markusenko, #2037
Peter Smorudov, #2039
Peter Ivanov, #2044
Alexei Sivotschenko, #2047
Ivan Filindasch, #2053
Ivan Puzanov, #2054
Konstantin Agayev, #2063
Nikolai Kudryavzev, #2065, Novosibirsk
Fedor Schugin, #2081
Boris Babin, #2158, Petropavlovsk
Peter Iljin, #2178
Wasyl Mironov, #2181

Signed, SS-Untersturmführer Schwarzenbacher

AUSCHWITZ-BIRKENAU, MARCH 29, 1943[11]

Gruppenwachmann Viktor Sabat, #192
Gruppenwachmann Vasili Schuller, #223
Gruppenwachmann Peter Alexeyev, #1294, Berdyansk, Zaporozhe region
Oberwachmann Reinhold Brendel, #232
Oberwachmann Feodor Oblja, #337

Oberwachmann Vladimir Lomow, #437
Oberwachmann Grigor Lohwinow, #620
Oberwachmann Ivan Kozlowsky, #653, Odessa
Oberwachmann Ivan Sisoj, #761
Oberwachmann Vasili Popov, #812
Oberwachmann Gregorij Tschegrinetz, #1094, Kharkov
Oberwachmann Taras Lukjanenko, #1318
Oberwachmann Ivan Orlovskij, #1544, Berdichev, Zhitomir
Oberwachmann Wilhelm Mednis, #1604, Baltic region
Peter Noschka, #196
Peter Rabano, #201
Woldemar Rodjen, #216
Grigorij Polowienka, #242
Ivan Dazenko, #248, Nikolayev
Nikita Kanjuka, #251
Nikolaj Malagon, #263
Wasyl Beschewez, #27?
Ivan Kotscherga, #279
Michael Andrejenko, #288
Andrej Zjuma, #299
Paul Kiritschenko, #302
Andrei Kuchma, #306
Roman Sautschuk, #311
Vladimir Tschereslenko, #317
Ivan Dmitrienko, #328
Peter Stepanov, #336
Semyon Dovgoljuk, #352
Daniel Kosub, #353
Wasyl Kwaschnij, #362
Terentij Gordienko, #389
Alexander Chrushchev, #413, Kursk
Alexei Netschaj, #417
Gerasim Scheremeta, #423
Lavrentij Plechow, #460
Leonid Kaplan, #463

Andrei Pokotilo, #491
Fedor Ryabeka, #498
Naum Romaschenko, #506
Tanas Varetsch, #521
Polikar Oseschnyuk, #538
Afanasi Bujval, #575
Alex Schwab, #592
Nikita Mamchur, #618
Maxim Shopelnik, #626
Evdokim Parfinyuk, #632
Alexander Semeneschin, #645
Akim Zuev, #667
Fedor Korotnichenko: replaced by Dubenskij,
    #690
Wasyl Guntschenko, #695
Ignat Shuk, #707
Eugen Duritzky, #710
Jakob Glischinski, #715
Gerasim Pavlenko, #717
Kiril Saretschnyj, #718
Andrej Janischelski, #720
Wasyl Shegelitj, #722
Nikolaj Martynyuk, #750
Philip Wergun, #796
Jefim Bolakar, #824
Wasyl Chomko, #827, Kamenets-Podolsk
Ivan Zaitsev, #830
Ivan Romanenko, #842
Viktor Wowk, #845
Jefim Kiritschok, #861
Charlampi Naumenko, #873
Taras Olejnik, #874
Ivan Zacharow, #882
Gregor Zakharov, #883
Mitrofan Klotz, #887
Grigorij Bulat, #888
Timofej Gura, #903
Daniel Slusar, #935
Denis Tschumak, #936

Michael Starodub, #949
Jakob Ptucha, #951
Timofej Sidortschuk, #955
Trochim Stepko, #957
Sergei Sergienko, #994
Ivan Besguba, #995
Ivan Djatschenko, #1002
Vasili Kipka, #1018
Jakiew Straschko, #1020
Luka Bardachenko, #1025
Nikolaj Tatarenko, #1027
Anton Stezkow, #1031
Mikhail Madwien, #1042
Vasili Geidak/Gajdich, #1049
Vasili Titschenko, #1057
Paul Detkowsky, #1063
Philip Michailenko, #1090
Pawlo Bakalo, #1098
Mykola Bogdanenko, #1100
Grigorij Lynkin, #1105
Vasili Fomenko, #1106
Ivan Pavlov, #1107, Kharkov
Fedor Tikhonovsky, #1110
Grigorij Kniga, #1114
Andrej Chimintschuk, #1121
Ivan Wdowenko, #1134
Grigorij Gapienko, #1138
Nikolaj Skakodub, #1142
Yegor Chorin, #1156
Alexei Govorov, #1202
Georg Tschansow, #1206
Wasyl Abramov, #1230
Dimitri Borodin, #1236
Nikolaj Dolja, #1244
Sylvester Muschta, #1268
Wasyl Trubenko, #1285
Michel Bacholenko, #1295
Vladimir Belinski, #1297
Prokofij Busennij, #1303

Stefan Dabischko, #1305
Stanislaw Komar, #1312
Georg Malinowsky, #1320, Kiev
Vsevolod Radschenko, #1324, Zarskoja-
    Sloboda
Andrei Schugal, #1327
Jakob Wasota, #1335
Ivan Safonow, #1348, Krasnodar
Wasyl Podenok, #1359
Alex Petuchow, #1360
Konstantin Dubrow, #1376, Kiev
Grigorij Petschonij, #1389
Fedor Gorun, #1441
Semyon Busiwskou, #1443
Luka Tobolski, #1444
Roman Boschenko, #1454
Ivan Bolschakow, #1457, Kiev
Anastasi Mavrodij, #1466
Wasyl Pankov, #1468, Kramatorsk, Stalino/
    Donetsk region
Semyon Subschenko, #1484
Ivan Zagrebayev, #1518
Grigorij Buchajenko, #1551, Melitopol
Alexander Reschetnik, #1563
Wasyl Luzenko, #1576
Anton Kawalewski, #1737, Baranovichi
Grigorij Tschernikow, #1745, Kursk
Mikhail Gorbachev, #1772
Ivan Kurynnyj, #1802
Timofej Kovalenko, #1902
Viktor Chamulin, #1903
Yakov Keresor, #1929
Alexander Retnino
Michel Erdmann, Karlstadt
Alexander Sellmann, Odessa

Turned Over by: *Oberwachtmeister*, Schupo
Reserve
Received by: *SS-Unterscharführer*

BELZEC, APRIL 12, 1943[12]

Zugwachmann Jakob Bretthauer, #50
Gruppenwachmann Albert Braun, #20
Gruppenwachmann Johann Dorschinski,
    #121
Oberwachmann Gustav Klug, #84
Oberwachmann Friedrich Lorenz, #87,
    Donbas
Oberwachmann Jakob Dachno, #809
Oberwachmann Vasili Bronov, #2127
Petro Gorezkij, #3403
Ivan Piguljak, #3404
Mykola Kryschavskij, #3406
Yakov Melnitschuk, #3408
Mykola Slowak, #3409
Wasyl Daniljuk, #3410
Sawko Ivanischyn, #3411
Mychajlo Wytwickij, #3415
Hryzko Prymak, #3418
Wasyl Schlapak, #3420
Mychailo Sydoruk, #3421
Gregor Pintorak, #3422
Wolodymyr Mosyak, #3425
Ivan Salinski, #3426
Petro Popeliuk, #3427
Pawlo Hrenkiv, #3428
Wasyl Tarnovezkij, #3430
Yakov Boitschuk, #3432
Dmytro Sawchuk, #3435
Mychajlo Sapototschnij, #3438
Wasyl Lytvyniuk, #3444
Petro Diduch, #3445
Mykola Klemjuk, #3447
Nikolaj Terentiak, #3449
Wasyl Schkatulyak, #3450
Ivan Huminiuk, #3451
Mikhail Boitschuk, #3453
Mikhail Grenyak, #3454
Wolodymyr Bolechiwskij, #3456

Mychailo Onufrijtschuk, #3458
Wolodymyr Kozlowskij, #3459
Dmytro Hajdeschuk, #3460
Wolodymyr Turjanskij, #3462
Stefan Zaruk, #3463
Dmytro Mokan, #3465
Dmytro Makarschuk, #3467
Mykola Hutyn, #3468
Ivan Tkatschuk, #3472
Wasyl Piguljuk, #3476
Mychailo Bodnariuk, #3478
Ivan Oleksiuk, #3479
Mikhail Grygoruk, #3480
Wasyl Popiliuk, #3481
Mychajlo Boryschkevich, #3482
Mykola Babiuk, #3484
Wasyl Myksymschuk, #3485
Mykola Hojdesch, #3490
Petro Niniovskij, #3491
Dmytro Ost[??]tscuk, #3493
Stefan Wyciden, #3496
Mychajlo Bronevich, #3498
Michas Demydiuk, #3499
Josef Babij, #3502
Petro Huzuliak, #3508

WARSAW DETACHMENT, APRIL 17, 1943[13]

Zugwachmann Friedrich Kaiser, #6
Zugwachmann Abraham Thiessen, #15
Zugwachmann Johann Klassen, #16
Zugwachmann Otto Keil, #21
Zugwachmann Mikhail Wagner, #47
Zugwachmann Jakob Brettkauer, #50
Zugwachmann Josef Khusselman, #56
Zugwachmann Mikhail Murashko, #239
Zugwachmann Genrikh Ulrich, #243
Gruppenwachmann Johann Varkentin, #28: quartermaster's assistant

Gruppenwachmann Vladimir Usik, #91
Gruppenwachmann Vladas Zajankauskas, #122 [?]
Gruppenwachmann Jakob Englehardt, #228
Gruppenwachmann Jakob Vazem, #799
Gruppenwachmann Peter Madamov, #1440
Oberwachmann Jakob Varkentin, #25
Oberwachmann Gerhard Blendowskij, #69
Oberwachmann Nikolaj Malyshev, #82
Oberwachmann Fritz Stolz, #106
Oberwachmann Franz Karvot, #109
Oberwachmann Artur Baumgart, #182
Oberwachmann Wilhelm Dederer, #220
Oberwachmann Anatolij Elman, #236
Oberwachmann Anton Vygovskij, #241
Oberwachmann Ivan Tretyak, #380
Oberwachmann Arkadij Sirenko, #529
Oberwachmann Evgenij Shevchenko, #822
Oberwachmann Stepan Borovik, #1238
Oberwachmann Ivan Michajlov, #1482
Oberwachmann Emil Shweichelt, #1614
Oberwachmann Vasili Grigorev, #1660
Oberwachmann Moisej Mikalajchuk, #2123
Oberwachmann Oleg Stolovnik, #2125
Oberwachmann Janis Graube, #2140
Oberwachmann Marian Lukasevich, #2549
Oberwachmann Evgenij Mochus, #2550
Edward Chrupowitsch, #145: clerk
Robert Shimurra, #70
Eugen Kauzer, #83
Otto Olenburg, #88
Alexander Fuchs, #92
Anatolij Getzman, #158
Pavel Romanchuk, #170
Viktor Pichler, #198
Grigorij Ovchinnikov, #210
Edward Wlasiuk, #218
Friedrich Schneider, #231
Anatolij Elman, #236

Dimitri Pundik, #264
Vasili Kotelevitz, #268
Konstantin Gunya, #273
Yuri Pazenkovskij, #289
Maxim Klyakhin, #295
Anton Goncharuk, #303
Grigorij Evseyev, #304
Mikhail Tkachuk, #325
Arkadij Sirenko, #329
Nikifor Marchenko, #354
Nikolaj Bojko, #372
Nikolaj Bondarenko, #416
Ivan Reznikov, #418
Petr Krasnobaj, #447
Fedor Zaulak, #456
Vasili Mirgorodskij, #469
Isaak Demchuk, #474: medic
Alexei Gorbuza, #496
Fedor Dmitrenko, #502
Afanasij Mojsejenko, #518
Ivan Listopad, #553
Trofim Sucharyba, #557
Ivan Wownjanko, #568
Andrej Tkachenko, #577
Andrej Ischenko, #593
Vasili Gulij, #596
Dimitri Rybak, #603
Pavel Nestarenko, #672
Nikolaj Gribinjuk, #681
Wasyl Moroz, #683
Vasili Shevchuk, #698
Jakob Vazem, #799
Ivan Naboka, #804
Nikolaj Suslov, #805
Ivan Polokhov, #810
Josef Koleda, #829
Vladimir Malyshev, #836
Ivan Romanenko, #852
Filip Babenko, #869

Yakov Butenko, #877
Peter Lukyanchuk, #885
Alexander Semenov, #915
Vasili Evtushenko, #916
Nikolaj Sharandin, #918
Peter Kiriljuk, #934
Nikolaj Boschko, #952
Timofej Korin, #1032
Alexander Volobuev/Kuris, #1037
Fedor Monin, #1041
Fedor Efremenko, #1083
Todos Zikun, #1132
Mikhail Lapot/Laptev, #1161
Theodor Berezovskij, #1165
Mikhail Markovets, #1199
Stepan Borovik, #1238
Nikolaj Kvach, #1261
Petr Kosjanov, #1258
Nikolaj Kvach, #1261
Mikhail Lysak, #1263
Ivan Majstrenko, #1265
Boris Rozhdestvenskij, #1273
Andrej Taran, #1283
Friedrich Vetregan, #1288
Alexander Bychkov, #1300
Dimitri Yatsenko, #1313
Maxim Tkachuk, #1333
Fedor Banin, #1345
Emil Schmidt, #1367
Mikhail Dukhnich, #1384
Stepan Mogilov, #1402
Jurko Danilov, #1408
Vasili Komarnitzky, #1411
Fedor Kushik, #1421
Pavel Grichanik, #1432
Josef Kshos, #1453
Semen Chubar, #1459
Grigorij Vedmedev, #1473
Ivan Mikhajlov, #1482

Vasili Krupnov, #1496
Grigorij Wowk, #1505
Nikolaj Rydko, #1511
Nikolaj Dobrodeyev, #1519
Ivan Gubenko, #1520
Ivan Maryakovskij, #1526
Ivan Stepanov, #1537
Josef Furmanchuk, #1538
Vasili Khomenko, #1543
Andrej Evenko, #1547
Vladimir Makarchuk, #1551
Peter Onishchenko, #1552
Vasili Plikha, #1556
Vladimir Kovalets, #1558
Viktor Rjabchinskij, #1559
Boris Odartschenko, #1573
Ivan Zavluchenko, #1580
Roman Kolamets, #1587
Alexander Syrokvasha, #1590
Evgenij Kozintsov, #1592
Andrej Makarenko, #1596
Grigorij Doshenko, #1599
Zibogat Orlov, #1715
Nazibuk Shaichulin, #1732
Ivan Zaitsenko, #1750
Ilya Matwijenko, #1754
Anatoli Oskolkov, #1770
Ivan Gorpinchenko, #1784
Ivan Khorev, #1809
Ivan Salchenko, #1816
Mitrofan Tsitrov, #1818
Andrej Protchenko, #1824
Ivan Zhukov, #1826
Andrej Davidenko, #1828
Mikhail Minenko, #1829
Pavel Yurchenko, #1843
Ivan Yastrebov, #1845
Vasili Kovalchuk, #1846
Viktor Dobrowolskij, #1847

Vasili Oschepkov, #1867
Grigorij Welikodnyj, #1890
Peter Rybalka, #1908
Dimitri Kharchenko, #1916
Ivan Dudenko, #1944
Sergej Titarenko, #1948
Nikolaj Kurinnyj, #1976
Sergei Kulachko, #1979
Grigorij Merva, #1980
Grigorij Popov, #2004
Viktor Severentchuk, #2005
Alexei Elkin, #2008
Vasili Shlapakov, #2010
Stefan Shevchenko, #2014
Ivan Khatko, #2016
Alexei Grabok, #2025: arrested
Savat Mykhonko, #2033
Ivan Filindash, #2053
Konstantin Agayev, #2063
Fedor Shugin, #2081
Grigorij Schubin, #2082
Vladas Karpovichus, #2119
Alexander Pesnosyuk, #2153
Boris Babin, #2158
Peter Iljin, #2178
Vasili Mironov, #2181
Nazar Zakotnyj, #2318: released April 20
  1943
Mikhail Pichkurenko, #2334
Grigorij Shishmanets, #2342
Afanasij Khomenko, #2352
Alexei Lesha, #2408
Nikolaj Zaitsev, #2451
Roman Petrov, #2791
Stepan Bzumovskij, #2805
Vladimir Luzak, #2909
Willi Stark, #2910
Vladimir Dashkevich, #2952
Stepan Kravchuk, #2969

Nikolaj Novosad, #2970
Bogdan Ukrainets, #2974
Evgenij Bednarskij, #2981
Peter Muzykiwskij, #2987
Bogdan Kogut, #2990
Demyan Stakhurskij, #3004
Vasili Zamojskij, #3008
Nikolaj Sokolskij, #3016
Ivan Sheremenda, #3017
Roman Brunets, #3030
Christoph Shinalik, #3062
Eugen Rippel, #3087
Marian Pajerskij, #3092
Josef Glista, #3094
Aloizij Jankovskij, #3096
Vasili Nikipanchuk, #3181
Vasili Semak, #3182
Josef Masjuk, #3183
Peter Semovonjuk, #3184
Nikolaj Tkachuk, #3186
Dimitri Grigorchuk, #3187
Nikolaj Kostjuk, #3188
Mikhail Matljuk, #3189
Peter Demjanchuk, #3190
Mikhail Fostun, #3191
Nikolaj Gutsulyak, #3192
Josef Tomenchuk, #3195
Stefan Simak, #3196
Myron Belbas, #3197
Myron Zamyljuk, #3198
Peter Zamyljuk, #3200
Ivan Ostafijchuk, #3201
Vasili Gudyma, #3202
Vasili Lytwyn, #3204
Stepan Bakaj, #3205
Peter Gritsenko, #3206
Roman Kobezka, #3208
Vasili Prodanjuk, #3209
Gavrilo Berbenchuk, #3210

Mikhail Turjanskij, #3211
Dimitri Petrushak, #3212
Andrej Germanjuk, #3214
Alexei Tikhonjuk, #3215
Dimitri Korzhinskij, #3216
Vasili Korenjuk, #3217
Nikolaj Domashevskij, #3218
Vladimir Terletskij, #3219
Vasili Magis, #3220
Fedor Kmposhchuk, #3221
Fedor Klochak, #3222
Mikhail Bosovich, #3224
Nikolaj Bojchuk, #3226
Ivan Merenda, #3227
Yuri Demedjuk, #3229
Peter Tuchapskij, #3230
Vasili Romanjuk, #3231
Dimitri Veledzjuk, #3232
Nikolaj Jasmichuk, #3234
Ivan Knignitskij, #3235
Stefan Melnichuk, #3236
Mikhail Makarchuk, #3239
Artimon Yatskiv, #3241
Nikolaj Semenjuk, #3242
Fedor Vyshivanyuk, #3243
Dimitri Makovijchuk, #3244
Vladimir Revjuk, #3246
Peter Nepijvoda, #3247
Mikhail Chovgan, #3248
Peter Semenjak, #3249
Mikhail Guminjuk, #3250
Nikolaj Potyatynyk, #3251
Vasili Mitsak, #3252
Nikolaj Slobodjan, #3253
Mikhail Batjuk, #3254
Mikhail Babjak, #3255
Vasili Motruk, #3257
Nikolaj Nepejvoda, #3259
Yaroslav Salinskij, #3260

Vasili Futulujchuk, #3261
Grigorij Chelonjuk, #3262
Jurko Budnitskij, #3263
Peter Martynyuk, #3265
Vasili Alexandruk, #3266
Marian Gudima, #3267
Ivan Orobets, #3269
Alexei Dolishnyj, #3270
Ivan Prodanjuk, #3271
Jurko Vorotnjak, #3272
Peter Luchka, #3273
Jurko Gumychuk, #3274
Mikhail Gavretskij, #3275
Stepan Korbutyak, #3276
Dimitri Kharuk, #3277
Ivan Grigorchuk, #3278
Peter Gritsenko, #3280
Nikolaj Kishkan, #3283
Ilko Tsotsman, #3285
Mikhail Moskaljuk, #3286
Ivan Kiselitsa, #3289
Vladimir Vindjk, #3291
Nikolaj Kubaj, #3294
Mikhail Zademlenjuk, #3295
Gritsko Bojchuk, #3297
Nikolaj Shekerek, #3298
Andrej Ivanchuk, #3300
Vasili Ursul, #3405
Vasili Lazarenko, #3437
Stefan Lukhnich, #3495
Grigorij Ivanishin, #3516
Wladislaw Petrovskij, #3536
Eugen Fedjuk, #3602
Roman Ryshka, #3603
Roman Bilan, #3604
Vasili Krojter, #3605
Vasili Povch, #3607
Ivan Moskaljuk, #3608
Yakov Dosin, #3609

Stepan Andrusenko, #3610
Dimitri Vovchuk, #3611
Mikhail Sinyatovich, #3612
Vladimir Ziomjak, #3613
Ivan Sova, #3614
Vasili Melnichuk, #3615
Theodor Kasjan, #3616
Vasili Smetanjuk, #3617
Vsevolod Kokhan, #3618
Peter Prokop, #3619
Eugen Duchuk, #3620
Mikhail Kostiv, #3623
Danilo Rubich, #3624
Jurko Kozachuk, #3627
Leo Pilavskij, #3628
Yaroslav Kropelnitskij, #3630
Emelyan Slipko, #3631
Mikhail Maslij, #3632
Myron Ptashnik, #3633
Nikolaj Gonderuk, #3634
Ivan Protsjuk, #3635
Nikolaj Gipich, #3636
Roman Burachiskij, #3637
Nikolaj Kostjuk, #3638
Stanislav Kordyk, #3639
Erich Kuhn, #3644

Signed, *Oberwachtmeister*, Schupo Reserve

Translated by: Lt. Bazilevskaja, MGB, 4th Department
True Copy: Investigator, Investigations Department, KGB, Dnepropetrovsk Region Captain Shkonda, September 21, 1965

SOBIBOR, AUGUST 2, 1943
Oberwachmann Georg Schneider, #115: Basch
Nikolaus Pavlij, #727: Stalino/Donetsk

Jakob Zechmeister, #838: Kharkov
Wasyl Grebelny, #846: Sumsk
Anton Simka, #849: Kiev
Wasyl Kartaschew, #1185: Lewenka
Peter Butkow, #1239: Stalinsk
Ivan Tschurin, #1287: Penza
Alex Sajdakow, #1423: Leningrad
Chassion Salachadinow, #1724: Gorki
Grigorij Knjasew, #1736: Pensenskaja
Oleksa Oleksejiw, #1742: Leningrad
Hryharyj Tanko, #1757: Kiev
Peter Karobka, #1912: Kharkov
Valentyn Bohdan, #1915: Zaporozhe
Wasyl Meschtscherow, #2183: Smolensk
Nikolaj Bereschnoj, #2232: Dnepropetrovsk

SOBIBOR, SEPTEMBER 16, 1943[14]

Gruppenwachmann Nikolaj Savschenko, #1192
*Franz Podessa (holdover from a previous deployment)
Oberwachmann Friedrich Neumann, #173
Oberwachmann Peter Muzykivskij, #2987
Oberwachmann Theodor Schinalik, #3062
*Alexander Kaiser (holdover from a previous deployment)
*Ivan Klatt (holdover from a previous deployment)
Yuri Duchov, #117
Nikolaj Svjatelik, #150
Ivan Mistjuk, #265
Boris Babitsch, #391
Ivan Wownjanko, #568
Georg Pavlenko, #605
Alexander Ross, #713
Ivan Jaremenko, #807
Peter Lukjanchuk, #885
Alexander Semenov, #915
Wasyl Polyakov, #1000

Kiril Lenjuk, #1082
Alexander Kosatschenko, #1155
Ivan Wolembachow, #1211
Vasili Puschkarev, #1272
Wasyl Komarnitzky, #1411
Peter Supronenko, #1489
Ivan Gladkij, #1492
Vasili Krupnow, #1496
Michel Kornyakov, #1700
Ivan Dibriwnij, #1782
Ilja Artemenko, #1958
Viktor Severentschuk, #2005
Grigorij Schubin, #2082
Peter Jazenko, #2098
Arsen Rasdoroshnyj, #2217
Ivan Gudema, #2243
Alexander Boldin, #2328
Michel Patschkowski, #3867
Wolodymyr Levschuk, #3874
Vladimir Tschernezki, #3905
Anton Sawula, #3994
Paul Maximjuk, #3997
Vladimir Mucha, #4000
Vladimir Sholnatsch, #4010
Stepan Senio, #4011
Vladimir M[?]tschjuk, #4019
Alexander Dantschuk, #4023
Wolodymyr Onyschuk, #4024
Vasili Martschuk, #4029
Stefan Petrikowski, #4038
Anton Dudko, #4051
Stefan Koschulat, #4054
Josef Semenjuk, #4058
Jan Pilipiuk, #4065
Nikolaj Telenko, #4071
Wasyl Filipschuk, #4075
Josef Kaminski, #4076?
Vladimir Antonjuk, #4076?
Stefan Maximjuk, #4079

Sergej Martynjuk, #4081
Wolodymyr [?]ilipschuk, #4086
Peter Klemjuk, #4129
Nikolaj Djatschuk, #4142
Eugen Sherebez, #4180
Tadeusch Filipschuk, #4205
Ostap Kucharuk, #4225
Stepan Gluj, #455?
Josef Demjan, #4511
Josef Sholnatsch, #4516
Michel Bajkevich, #4532
Wolodymyr Shur, #4542
Vladimir Bruchaki, #4545
Nikolaj Musytschuk, #4546
Eugen Kondratjuk, #4555
Michel Paluch, #4564
Michel Tschaban, #4568
Michel Kapysj, #4569
Michel Stavrosski, #4572
Ivan Chilinski, #4573
Eugen Harasjuk, #4576
Leon Demtschuk, #4578
Woldymyr Scharan, #4585
Anton Michaltschuk, #4589
Sergei Tschubscheruk, #4594
Peter Teschkevich, #4595
Konstantin Michaltschuk, #4598
Stepan Savschuk, #4601
Daniel Misjuk, #4603
Josef Teschkevich, #4605
Wolodymyr Woroshbit, #4609
Michael Wowk, #4610
Eugen Kutscha, #4613
Alexei Wojtys, #4619
Nikolaj Bekalo, #4624
Stepan S[?]dlyj, #4627
Nikolaj Tschop, #4628
Miroslav Kljusjak, #4632
Anatoli Duma, #4633

Eugen Silinski, #4634
Wasyl Prystupa, #4644
Eugen Daniljuk, #4655
Eugen Glowazki, #4658
Eugen Tymchuk, #4659
Michael Lichotop, #4732
Alex Chwitsch, #4738

The SS guards have the following clothing and equipment with them: military tunic, one each; military pants, two pairs; black tunic, one each; belt, one each; forage cap; boots, one pair each; blankets, two each; rifle, one each

Signed, Karl Basener, *Oberwachtmeister*, Schupo Commander of the Lublin Detachment

TREBLINKA I. APRIL 6. 1944[15]

Zugwachmann Alexander Yeger, #14
Zugwachmann Heinrich Stieben, #143
Zugwachmann Karl Mattus, #863
Zugwachmann Oswald Strebel, #1612
Gruppenwachmann Franz Swiderski, #26
Gruppenwachmann Alfred Poppe, #120
Gruppenwachmann Anatol Munder, #132
Gruppenwachmann Emil Gutarz, #364
Oberwachmann Nikolaj Bessubzew, #222
Oberwachmann Vasili Olschanikow, #266
Oberwachmann Nikita Rekalo, #979
Oberwachmann Vladimir Janowitsch, #1005
Oberwachmann Yegor Pisarenko, #1502
Oberwachmann Fedor Gordienko, #1570
Oberwachmann Ivan Petrischenko, #1582
Oberwachmann Dimitro Kostin, #1584
Oberwachmann Liudas Kairys, #1628
Oberwachmann Nikolaj Leitsch, #1672
Oberwachmann Grigorij Maiboroda, #1836

Oberwachmann Wilhelm Baltschys, #2113
Oberwachmann Stanislaw Ciba, #2694
Nikolaj Belous, #332
Mikhail Artemenko, #524
Grigorij Sirota, #612
Gregorij Krasilnik, #684
Gregor Garus, #755
Ivan Poprushnij, #756
Andrej Kabilka, #1022
Timofei Korin, #1052
Janik Burjak, #1127
Gregor Besklubij, #1141
Ivan Surinow, #1215
Wasyl Savitzky, #1225
Ivan Guber, #1308
Fedor Nykytyn, #1418
Dimitri Moskun, #1474
Alexei Kulinitsch, #1497
Grigorij Kartaschow, #1499
Mikhail Polischuk, #1536
Vladas Amanaviczius, #1640
Arwo Orumaa, #1662
Ivan Chapajew, #1687
Kasim Gisatulin, #1694
Anwar Galaskarow, #1702
Abdrachman Saitow, #1722
Zaki Zadikow, #1723
Alexander Moskalenko, #1753
Peter Koval, #1760
Dimitri Spak, #1767
Yakov Alexejenko, #1769
Grigorij Risnytschenko, #1794
Pavel Kozlov, #1799
Vladimir Senzow, #1812
Konstantin Stepanienko, #1838
Alexei Kolgushkin, #1860
Fedor Litvinov, #1868
Valentyn Roshanskij, #1870
Alexander Sirotenko, #1907

Ivan Kondratenko, #1909
Nikolaj Bondarenko, #1926
Andrej Demitrenko, #1945
Ivan Schapar, #1956
Anatoli Rumjanzew, #1996
Boris Safronow, #1998
Pavel Polischuk, #2031
Junus Chansewirow, #2032
Alexander Sologub, #2034
Sergej Krasnoschok, #2064
Kornej Krawtschenko, #2075
Roman Djatschuk, #2091
Ivan Filipow, #2281
Kuzma Krykun, #2359
Mikhail Manguschew, #2365
Jakob Djatschok, #2368
Egor Popow, #2372
Semen Kharkovskij, #2376
Alexander Jewtuschenko, #2377
Jakob Husnonogow, #2385
Mikhail Schewzow, #2410
Peter Bucharinow, #2446
Josef Marko, #2782
Bronislaw Hajda, #3069
Franz Hajtschuk, #3078
Chychol Novoszadenko, #4818

Signed,
SS-Oberscharführer

HSSPF ADRIATIC COAST, 1943-1945[16]

SS-Oberzugwachmann Alexander Kaiser
SS-Oberzugwachmann Friedrich Schneider
SS-Zugwachmann Franz Bienemann
SS-Zugwachmann Heinrich/Helmut Dahlke
SS-Zugwachmann Emil Kostenko
SS-[????????] Maurer
SS-Zugwachmann Arnold Rosenke

SS-Zugwachmann Christian/Heinz Schmidt
SS-Zugwachmann Emanuel Schultz
SS-Zugwachmann Reinhard Siebert
SS-[???] Heinrich Szpliny
Wasyl Antonov
Andrej Davidenko
Dimitri Libodenko
Nikolaj Makoda
Ivan Marchenko
Alexej Mihalic
Petro Nahorniak
Kiril Prochorenko [?]
Nikolai Shalayev
Vasilij Smetanyuk
Edward Wlasiuk [?]

SS "STREIBEL" BATTALION: THOSE MISSING AS OF JANUARY 12, 1945[17]

SS-Rottenführer Albert Glugert, Staff Platoon: Mauthausen concentration camp

Oberzugwachmann Xaver Rucinski, #119, Staff Platoon: did not reach his unit from leave

Zugwachmann Willi Reinhardt, #32, Staff Platoon: did not reach his unit from leave

Zugwachmann Karl Mattus, #863, Michalow Detachment (von Eupen): location unknown, missing

Zugwachmann Nikolaj Olejnikov, #2263: wounded at Czestochowa, January 1945, missing

Gruppenwachmann August Kruger, #155: SSPF Detachment Lublin/Jedrzejow, missing

Gruppenwachmann Robert Rechling, #550: missing near Dmenin Radomsko, January 1945

Gruppenwachmann Ivan Gontscharow, #2041: SSPF Detachment Lublin: location unknown, missing

Gruppenwachmann Wasyl Reschetko, #2115: SSPF Detachment Lublin/Jedrzejow, missing

Wachmann Nikolaj Nepjvoda, #3259, missing near Dmenin Radomsko, January 1945

Wachmann Michael Rostopira, #3534: missing during retreat at the Kattowitz-Beuten railroad station

Oberwachmann Wasyl Petlocha, #3686, SSPF Detachment Lublin/Jedrzejow: missing

Wachmann Wasyl Smaha, #4277: captured by bandits/partisans in Stradow, January 11, 1945

Wachmann Nikolaus Rubacha, #4352: captured by bandits/partisans in Stradow, January 11, 1945

Oberwachmann Stepan Ohon, #4379, SSPF Detachment Lublin/Jedrzejow: location unknown

Wachmann Dimitri Korolczuk, #4547: in military hospital since October 20, 1944, dysentery, missing

Wachmann Nikolaj Tschop, #4628, captured by bandits/partisans in Stradow, January 11, 1945

Wachmann Fedor Davidov, #4766, SSPF Detachment Lublin: last seen in Jedrzejow

Oberwachmann Michel Matjenko, #4828, Lublin/Jedrzejow

Wachmann Alexander Artjomenko, #4852: missing near Michalow Detachment

Wachmann Ivan Astaschevski, #4853: captured by partisans near Stradow, January 11, 1945

Wachmann Boleslaw Wachowski, #4878 separated from the unit, January 1945

Wachmann Waclaw Reymann, #4889

Wachmann Sygmund Skruba, #5057, SSPF
  Detachment Lublin/Jedrzejow
Wachmann Sergej Osinov, #5065
Wachmann Eduard Grynizki, #5070, Staff
  Platoon: location unknown since retreat,
  January 12, 1945

Photo Section

Wasyl Shyndykevskij

Alexander Yeger

Paul Garin

Eduard Chrupowitsh

Heinrich Schaefer

Willi Stark

Franz Swidersky

Woldemar Wutke

Dymytro Kobylezskij

Vladas Amanaviczius   Wasyl Sajnakow   Wasyl Scheftschuk

Wolodymyr Shur   Vladimir Bruchaki   Samuel Pritsch

Ivan Ivschenko   Petro Kuschnir   Valerian Danko

Nikolaj Boschko   Dimitro Jarosch   Vasili Pudenoks

Ivan Demjanjuk   Ivan Wolembachow   Ivan Juchnowskij

Alexander Lazarenko   Ivan Marchenko   Anton Gontscharuk

Anton Solonina   Grigorij Kuchichidze   Viktor Bogomolow

Nikolaj Chernyshev   Michael Wasilenko   Philip Wergun

Pawlo Sidortschuk   Grigorij Jeschow   Alexander Kirelacha

Pawel Gamaschow   Ignat Danilchenko   Dmitrij Rjasanow

Myron Flunt   Nikolaj Isatschenko   Vasili Pochwala

Ivan Filipow   Sydor Bandarenko   Vladimir Pronin

Jurko Danilov

Stepan Mogilo

Ilmar Haage

Rustambek Saitow

Nikolaj Gordejew

Nikolaj Rubanov

Wasyl Stoljarow

Nikolaj Timin

Grigorij Stoilow

Valentin Roshanskij

Alexei Kulinitsch

Mikhail Titow

Ivan Tschornobaj

Konstantin Balabayev

Vasili Burljajew

Liudas Kairys

Nurgali Kabirow

Mikhail Korzhikow

Ivan Chapajew

Ivan Kostinow

Yevgenij Prigoditsch

Ivan Scherbinin

Alexander Solonchukow

Alexander Wisgunow

Nikolaj Butenko

Nikolaj Soljanin

Boris Odartschenko

Wolodymyr Powch

Wiaczeslaw Malesza

Wasyl Popiliuk

Wasyl Oleksiuk

Petro Niniowskij

Bronislaw Szymanskij

Petro Popeliuk

Eugen Binder

Mykola Potyatynyk

Wasyl Bojczuk

Jan Pilipiuk

Boleslaw Maj

Ivan Marchenko, a Ukrainian guard and gas chamber operator at Treblinka II

Liudas Kairys, a Lithuanian guard at Treblinka I

Alexei Kulinitsch, a Russian guard at Treblinka I

Franz Swidersky, a *Volksdeutsche* guard at Treblinka I, complete with eye patch

159

Ivan Marchenko, gas chamber operator at Treblinka II, is the taller man. The other is Ivan Tkachuk, also a guard at Treblinka II.

The grounds of the former Trawniki camp, taken by the author in 2012

The grounds of the former Trawniki camp, taken by the author in 2012

Grafitti found on a dumpster just down the street from the former site of the Trawniki camp. Taken by author in 2012. The two lightning bolts represent the letters (sig runes) "SS," and the number "88" is a reference to the eighth letter in the alphabet, "H," written twice. "HH" = Heil Hitler.

ENDNOTES

Introduction

1. Frank Golczewski, "A Very Ordinary Henchman: Demjanjuk Trial to Break Legal Ground in Germany," *Spiegel* Online, July 10, 2009.

Chapter 1

1. Peter Black, "Foot Soldiers of the Final Solution: The Trawniki Training Camp and Operation Reinhard," *Holocaust and Genocide Studies* 25, no. 1 (Spring 2011): 4.

2. Ibid., 63, n. 94.

3. Ibid., 5.

4. Ibid., 19, and 71, n. 149. File note for Brigadeführer Globocnik re: staff discussion on August 6, 1941, signed by SS-Hauptsturmführer Gustav Hanelt, August 9, 1941, IPN Archive, RG SSPF Lublin, Central Archive File 891/6, p. 11, copy in USHMM RG 15.027. For the ongoing relationship between the SS and police bases, the tasks of SS-Hauptsturmführer Hermann Hofle, and coordination of the first major deportations of Jews, see Globocnik memo, February 12, 1942, IPN Archive, RG SSPF Lublin, p. 46; and memo of SS-Hauptsturmführer Hanelt, "SS-Mannschaftshaus Lublin," no date (although probably March 18, 1942), IPN Archive, RG SSPF Lublin, pp. 18–23. Although fragmentary documentary evidence suggests that measures were taken to initiate Operation Reinhard through planning at Globocnik's think tank in Lublin, the SS-Mannschaftshaus, in August 1941, currently available evidence is not conclusive that this included the mass murder policy at this early stage.

5. Black, "Foot Soldiers of the Final Solution," p. 5, n. 35; and Report on the Construction of SS and Police Bases, no date (possibly spring 1941), NARA, RG 242/BDC, A-3343/SSO, reel 016A, Odilo Globocnik SS Officer File, frames 89–96.

6. Black, "Foot Soldiers of the Final Solution," 5.

7. Ibid., 5.

8. Ibid., 63–64, n. 97, and 52, n. 36. The author, Schulte, has demonstrated the links between Globocnik's apparatus and the expanding role of Pohl's SS-WVHA in planning and developing the SS and police bases. See *Zwangsarbeit*, pp. 239–308, especially pp. 276–78.

9. Black, "Foot Soldiers of the Final Solution," 6.

10. Ibid., 7.

11. Ibid., 8.

12. Ibid., 9.

13. Ibid., 11.

14. Ibid., 13, and 64, n. 98. For the disciplinary jurisdiction that the Trawniki guards became subordinate to starting in early 1943, see Circular of the *Reichsführer-SS* and Chief of the German Police in the Reich Ministry of Interior, "Preliminary Service Disciplinary Regulations for Police Troops," April 19, 1940, RGVA, 1323/2/219, pp. 1–14 (copy in USHMM, RG 11.001M, reel 80).

15. Black, "Foot Soldiers of the Final Solution," 13.

16. Ibid., 15.

17. Ibid., 17.

18. Peter Black, "Police Auxiliaries for Operation Reinhard: Shedding Light on the Trawniki Training Camp through Documents from behind the Iron Curtain," in *Secret Intelligence and the Holocaust*, ed. David Bankier (New York: Enigma Books, 2006), 360.

19. Black, "Foot Soldiers of the Final Solution," 19.

20. Ibid., 19, and 71, n. 151. On the management of Trawniki personnel records, see Protocol of Interrogation of Helmut Leonhardt, July 4, 1943, Streibel Proceedings, vol. 97, p. 18,536. After Drechsel left Trawniki in 1943, Schwarzenbacher became Streibel's deputy until he was reassigned to the Adriatic coast in late 1943. SS-Obersturmführer Willi Franz then served as Streibel's deputy until the arrival of SS-Hauptsturmführer Hans Mickeleit in January 1944. Mickeleit was on probation for fraud after previously serving as a Waffen-SS welfare officer in western Poland.

21. Black, "Foot Soldiers of the Final Solution," 63, n. 94.

22. Ibid., 12.

23. Ibid., 20, and 72, n. 153. For the responsibility of looted valuables taken from Jews during Operation Reinhard, see Protocol of Interrogation of Georg Wippern, April 17, 1962, proceedings against Lothar Hoffmann et al., Hessian State Archive, Wiesbaden, Abt. 468, no. 362, File 8 Ks 1/70, vol. 36, pp. 3,425–26.

24. Black, "Police Auxiliaries for Operation Reinhard," 328, n. 2; see Bogdan Musial, "The Origins of 'Operation Reinhard': The Decision-Making Process for the Mass Murder of the Jews in the Generalgouvernement," *Yad Vashem Studies* 28 (2000): 113–53; and Dieter Pohl, "The Murder of the Jews in the General Government," in *National*

Socialist Extermination Policies: Contemporary German Perspectives and Controversies, ed. Ulrich Herbert (New York: Berghahn Books, 2000), 83–103. Musial, in "Origins," pp. 129–130, suggests that Operation Reinhard was implemented on Globocnik's initiative. Another author, Christopher Browning, suggests that Reinhard was a joint initiative between Globocnik and the senior SS authorities in Berlin. See Christopher Browning, Nazi Policy, Jewish Workers, German Killers (Cambridge, UK: Cambridge University Press, 2000), 4.

25. Black, "Foot Soldiers of the Final Solution," 1.

26. Ibid., 3.

27. Ibid., 4.

28. Ibid., 21, and 75, n. 172. For Trawniki guard participation in the fall 1942 killing operation in Majdanek, see Protocols of Interrogations of Zaki Tuktarov, February 1, 1965, Matvijenko Proceedings, vol. 13, pp. 95–97; and Ivan Knysh, January 29, 1948, Iskaradov Proceedings, pp. 229–34.

29. Black, "Foot Soldiers of the Final Solution," 22, and 73–74, n. 162. For documentation on the unique link between Majdanek and Operation Reinhard, see Tomasz Kranz, Extermination; Barbara Schwindt, Majdanek; Elissa Koslov, Gewalt; and Tomasz Kranz, "Das KL Lublin: Zwischen Planung und Realizierung," in Herbert, Konzentrationslager, 371. For the suggestion that Auschwitz-Birkenau also played a significant role in Operation Reinhard, see Perz and Sandkuhler, Auschwitz.

30. Black, "Foot Soldiers of the Final Solution," 74, n. 163; see Witte and Tyas, New Document, 469–470; and Kranz, Extermination, 72–73, and 75, n. 171. For the figure of 24,000, see radio transmission intercept from the SSPF Lublin District (Hofle) to the commander of the Sipo and SD Krakow (Heim), "Bimonthly Report Deployment Reinhard," 13/15 OLQ de OMQ/1005/83 24 250, German Police Decodes: No. 3 Traffic, January 11, 1943, HW 16/23, PRO. For the significance of this message, see Witte, New Document. It is not 100% certain that the 24,000 were gassed on arrival. Schwidt argues in Majdanek, pp. 83–86 and 204–67, that they were not killed immediately, and that gassing Jews upon arrival at Majdanek mainly took place in 1943, when they were deported from the Warsaw Ghetto. However, Kranz, in Extermination, pp. 48–62, does believe that those arriving in fall 1942 were gassed on arrival, and Dr. Black stated that he was inclined to agree with this view.

31. Black, "Foot Soldiers of the Final Solution," 74, n. 167; see Schwindt, Majdanek, 156–71; and Kranz, Extermination, 40–48.

32. David Rich, "Reinhardt's Footsoldiers: Soviet Trophy Documents and Investigative Records as Sources," in Remembering for the Future: The Holocaust in an Age of Genocide, ed. John Roth and Elizabeth Maxwell (New York and Basingstoke, UK: Palgrave, 2001), 694.

33. Robin O'Neal, "Sources of Manpower," in Belzec: Stepping Stone to Genocide (online book, no page number) (New York: JewishGen, 2008), www.jewishgen.org/Yizkor/Belzec1/bel040.html.

34. Ibid.

35. Ibid.

36. Black, "Foot Soldiers of the Final Solution," 41.

37. Ibid., 5.

38. Ibid., 72, n. 155.

39. Ibid., 93, n. 285. These figures are based on a report submitted by Hofle in 1943 to the RSHA and the HSSPF Krakow, Kruger. See radio transmission of January 11, 1943, National Archive, Kew Gardens, RG HW 16/23 13/15/OLQ de OMQ 1005 83 234 250. This source was provided to Dr. Black by Stephan Tyas.

40. Black, "Foot Soldiers of the Final Solution," 93, n. 286. The SS Garrison Administration in Lublin categorized the looted property that was confiscated: hard currency, precious metals, foreign currency, gold coins, jewels and other valuables, and textiles (e.g., clothing and bedding). See "Preliminary Concluding Report of the Cashier's Department Aktion Reinhard," Lublin, December 15, 1943, signed by Rzepa, Wippern, and Globocnik, appendix 2 to Globocnik to Himmler, January 5, 1944, Federal Archive Berlin, NS 19/2234, pp. 50–56, copy in USHMM, RG 14.015M.

41. Black, "Foot Soldiers of the Final Solution," 38.

42. Black, "Police Auxiliaries for Operation Reinhard," 362, n. 89. See Elizabeth B. White, "Majdanek Cornerstone of Himmler's SS Empire in the East," Simon Wiesenthal Center Annual 7 (1990): 3–21; and Jan Erik Schulte, Zwangsarbeit und Vernichtung: Das Wirtschaftsimperium der SS; Oswald Pohl und das SS-Wirtschafts-Verwaltungs-Hauptamt, 1933–1945 (Paderborn, Germany: F. Schöningh, 2001), 263–335.

43. Black, "Police Auxiliaries for Operation Reinhard," 362, n. 89.

44. Black, "Foot Soldiers of the Final Solution," 22.

45. Ibid., 22.

46. Ibid., 23, and 76, n. 178. Protocols of Interrogations of Georg Michalsen, January 24, 1961, and June 29/30, 1961, Streibel Proceedings, vol. 4, p. 487, and vol. 6, pp. 1,092–93. For Trawniki guards from Treblinka I, see Protoco of Interrogation of Karl Prefi, September 26, 1960, Proceedings against Ludwig Hahn et al. (Hahn Proceedings) State Archive Hamburg, 141 Js 192/60, vol. 5, pp. 920–21. The SS and police held about 10,000 Warsaw Jews at a transit facility on the outskirts of Warsaw and transferred them to Majdanek, Lipowa Street labor camp in Lublin and other labor camps. See Schwindt, Majdanek, 137–38.

47. Black, "Foot Soldiers of the Final Solution," 23–24.

48. Ibid., 77, n. 184. See Protocol of Interrogation of Georg Pankratov, November 2, 1968, Litvinenko Proceedings, vol. 2, pp. 71–74; and Dieter Pohl, *Von der "Judenpolitik" zur Judenmord: Der Distrikt Lublin des Generalgouvernements, 1939–1944* (Frankfurt: Peter Lang, 1993), 138.

49. Black, "Foot Soldiers of the Final Solution," 25, and 78, n. 187. Internal memo signed by Globocnik to the department heads on his staff as SSPF Lublin District, February 16, 1942, IPN Archive, RG SSPF Lublin, CSW 891/6, p. 46; undated memo signed by Hanelt, "SS-Mannschaftshaus Lublin," probably dated April or May 1942; Black, "Foot Soldiers of the Final Solution," 18–23.

50. Black, "Foot Soldiers of the Final Solution," 25.

51. Ibid., 25, and 79, n. 190. On Himmler's order, see Himmler to Pohl (SS-WVHA), Kruger (HSSPF Ost), and Globocnik (SSPF Lublin), October 9, 1942, NARA, RG 238, NO-1611; and Black, "Foot Soldiers of the Final Solution," 75–76, n. 175. On the responsibility of the SS and police commanders for Jewish ghetto-clearing operations, for the Galicia District, see SSPF Galicia, signed Fritz Katzmann, to HSSPF Krakow, Friedrich Wilhelm Kruger, "Solution of the Jewish Question in Galicia," June 30, 1943, IMT XXXVII L-18 (Katzmann Report), pp. 391–431. For Radom District, see Judgment in the Proceedings against Paul Degenhardt, Commander of the Municipal Police in Czestochowa, 1942–1944, May 24, 1966 (Judgment against Degenhardt), BA-ZSt, II 206 AR-Z 224/59, vol. 5, pp. 791–93. For the role of the security police and SD Lublin in the Lublin Ghetto in spring 1942, see Judgment in the Proceedings against Lothar Hoffmann et al., March 1, 1973, Hoffmann Proceedings, vol. 4, pp. 103–105.

52. Black, "Foot Soldiers of the Final Solution," 79, n. 192. Letter Globocnik to Rudolf Brandt, on the personal staff of the *Reichsführer-SS*, June 21, 1943, NARA, RG 238, NO-485.

53. Black, "Foot Soldiers of the Final Solution," 25.

54. Ibid., 26.

55. Ibid., 26.

56. Ibid., 26, and 80, n. 205. Most of the Trawniki guards who deployed to help suppress the Warsaw Ghetto uprising and were then assigned to Poniatowa labor camp can be identified from the following wartime documents: Warsaw Detachment Roster, April 17, 1943, FSB Archive Moscow, RG K-779, 16/312 "e"/ 411, pp. 127–30; Poniatowa Detachment Roster, October 3, 1943, FSB Archive Moscow, RG K-779, 16/312 "e"/ 411, pp. 102–103; Poniatowa Detachment Roster, November 17, 1943, FSB Archive Moscow, RG K-779, 16/312 "e"/ 411, pp. 135–37; and Poniatowa Detachment Roster, March 31, 1944, FSB Archive Moscow, RG K-779, 16/312 "e"/410, pp. 332–33.

57. Black, "Foot Soldiers of the Final Solution," 27.

58. Ibid., 28.

59. Black, "Police Auxiliaries for Operation Reinhard," 344; and Black, "Foot Soldiers of the Final Solution," 83, n. 216. During Operation Harvest Festival, the Jews assigned to work at the TWL in Lublin were marched to Majdanek and presumably shot. See Protocol of Interrogation of Alois Rzepa, August 19, 1974, Streibel Proceedings, pp. 21, 245–21, 246. The importance of the regional troop supply depots to the SS and police bases is discussed in Schulte, *Zwangsarbeit*, 202–203, 278–279, 316–320.

60. Black, "Foot Soldiers of the Final Solution," 28, and 82, n. 212. For unclear reasons, but probably regarding their value as aircraft-part manufacturers, the Jewish workers at Budzyn labor camp were not eliminated during Operation Harvest Festival like most of the rest of the Jews in Lublin District in late 1943. Budzyn was closed down on July 22, 1944, and the SS evacuated the remaining prisoners there westward. Many of these prisoners survived the war and, in addition to a few surviving ghetto fighters, are among the richest sources of information on the destruction of the Warsaw Ghetto.

61. Ibid., 29.

62. Ibid., 82–83, n. 213. For the planning and execution of Operation Harvest Festival, see Grabitz and Scheffler, *Letzte Spuren*, 328–29; and Protocol of Interrogation of SS-Gruppenführer Jakob Sporrenberg, SSPF Lublin, February 25, 1946, IPN Archive, RG Sad Apelacyjny Lublin (SAL), file no. 193, pp. 125–128. For the mass shootings at Poniatowa, see Protocols of Interrogations of Rudolf B., May 17, 1961, Streibel Proceedings, vol. 5, pp. 929–40, and October 26, 1961, Hoffmann Proceedings, vol. 19, pp. 2,940–49; Martin D., October 28, 1963, Streibel Proceedings, vol. 5, pp. 1,611–13; and Heinrich Gley, November 23–24, 1961, Michalsen Proceedings, vol. 13, pp. 2,446–48. For the mass shootings at Trawniki, see Protocols of Interrogations of Kurt Z., May 25, 1963, Hahn Proceedings, vol. 48, pp. 9,155–64; and Franz Skubinin, May 30, 1963, reproduced in Grabitz and Scheffler, *Letzte Spuren*, 267–68. For unclear reasons, the SS and police spared the Jewish laborers at Krasnik labor camp just as they had spared them at Budzyn. For statements re Trawniki guards guarding the camp perimeter at Poniatowa during the mass shootings, see Protocols of Interrogations of Stephan B., April 14, 1970, Streibel Proceedings, vol. 85, p. 16,114; Ivan Lukanyuk, April 12, 1948, Lukanyuk Proceedings, SBU Archive Ivano-Frankivsk/Stanislavov, 5072/2123, p. 15; and Vasili Shkarpovich, April 28, 1948, and May 25, 1948, Shkarpovich Proceedings, pp. 16 and 34. For the names of the Trawniki guards assigned to Poniatowa at the time of the mass shootings there, see Poniatowa Detachment Roster (being transferred back to Trawniki), November 17, 1943, FSB Archive Moscow, RG K-779, 16/312 "e"/411, pp. 135–37.

63. Black, "Foot Soldiers of the Final Solution," 84, n. 219. For Trawniki guards who served there, see Protocol of Interrogation of Ivan Mistyuk, January 23, 1950, Litvinenko Proceedings, vol. 9, pp. 114–22; *Dienstausweis* #415 of Alexander Kirelacha, Kirelacha Proceedings, 18114/2041, vol. 1, pp. 16–17; and *Personalbogen* #838 of Jakob Zechmeister, Tsekhmistro Proceedings, Zechmeister TPF, p. 81.

64. Black, "Foot Soldiers of the Final Solution," 29.

65. Ibid., 84, n. 220; Lublin Detachment to SSPF Lvov (Janowska Roster), May 17, 1943, FSB Archive Moscow, RG K-779, 16/312 "e"/410, pp. 270–72; Lublin Detachment to SSPF Lvov (Janowska Roster), May 19, 1943, FSB Archive Moscow, RG K-779, 16/312 "e"/410, p. 274; and SS Training Camp Trawniki to Lvov Labor Camp (Janowska Roster), September 25, 1943, FSB Archive Moscow, RG K-779, 16/312 "e"/411, p. 141.

66. Black, "Foot Soldiers of the Final Solution," 30; David Rich, "The Trawniki Kommando of the Janowska Labor Camp," 8 (according to Dr. Rich, it was a three-day operation); Interrogation of Egor Lobyntsev, 1968, Litvinenko Trial, Case #158, Archive file #57252, vol. 1, pp. 183–88, SBU Archive Lvov: most of the former guards in postwar interrogations estimated that 10,000–15,000 Jews were shot; Black, "Foot Soldiers of the Final Solution," 84, n. 221; Protocol of interrogation of Nikolaj Gordejew, December 18, 1964, Matvijenko Proceedings, vol. 7, pp. 199–200; Rich, "The Trawniki Kommando," 9, n. 17: "The escort and shooting details changed multiple times during the course of each day, probably on two-hour rotations"; Interrogation of Vasili Litvinenko, 1969, Litvinenko Trial, Case #158, Archive file #57252, vol. 1 p. 126–28, SBU Archive Lvov; and Interrogation of Egor Lobyntsev, 1968, Litvinenko Trial, Case #158, Archive file #57252, vol. 1, pp. 183–88, SBU Archive Lvov.

67. Black, "Foot Soldiers of the Final Solution," 30, and 84, n. 222; and Protocol of interrogation of Nikolaj Skorokhod, November 24, 1947, Skorokhod Proceedings, 34–42.

68. Rich, "The Trawniki Kommando," 9, n. 19; and Interrogation of Alexander Minochkin, 1965, Matwijenko Trial, Case #4, Archive file #100366, vol. 6, p. 53–55 ob., FSB Archive Krasnodar.

69. Black, "Foot Soldiers of the Final Solution," 30; Thomas Sandkuhler had described the final massacre and liquidation of Jews in Galicia, including Janowska, as part of Operation Erntefest. Rich, "The Trawniki Kommando," 11, n. 23; 5,000–6,000 Jews were reportedly shot over a two-day period. Interrogation of Ivan Tarasov, 1964, Matwijenko Trial, Case #4, Archive file #100366, vol. 6, FSB Archive Krasnodar; and Black, "Foot Soldiers of the Final Solution," 84, n. 223. For further descriptions of the mass shootings, see Protocols of Interrogations of Vasili Litvinenko, October 9, 1968, Litvinenko Proceedings, vol. 1, pp. 183–88. For the number of Jews murdered, see Dieter Pohl, *Judenverfolgung*, 338 and 359–60.

70. Rich, "The Trawniki Kommando," 12: Rich believes that the SSPF Lvov's *SS-Gruppenführer*, Katzmann, ordered the camp liquidated on his own initiative, rather than the initiative coming from the SSPF Lublin if it had been part of Operation Erntefest."

71. Ibid., 13, n. 25; and Interrogation of Egor Lobyntsev, 1968, Litvinenko Trial, Case #158, Archive file #57252, SBU Archive Lvov.

72. Black, "Foot Soldiers of the Final Solution," 30, and 85, n. 225. For the names of the Trawniki guards assigned to the camp at the time it was liquidated due to the advance of the Red Army, see Treblinka I Roster, April 6, 1944, FSB Archive Moscow, RG K-779, 16/312 "e"/410, p. 343–345; Black, "Foot Soldiers of the Final Solution," 85, n. 226. On the mass shootings, see Protocols of Interrogations of Alexander Moskalenko, May 6, 1969, Kurt Franz Proceedings, vol. 21, pp. 5,680–86; Alexander Moskalenko, November 17, 1947, Moskalenko Proceedings, 45–61; Nikolaj Belous, March 15 and 31, 1949, Belous Proceedings, 15–19 and 26–35; Semen Kharkovskij, May 11, 1973, Streibel Proceedings, vol. 4, pp. 670–79; and Alexander Kolgushkin, May 17, 1973, Streibel Proceedings, vol. 4, pp. 649–56.

73. Chris Webb and Michel Chocholaty, *The Treblinka Death Camp: History, Biographies, Remembrance* (Stuttgart: Ibidem Verlag, 2014).

74. Black, "Foot Soldiers of the Final Solution," 30.

75. Ibid., 30, and 86, n. 230; Protocol of Interrogation of Peter Klemeshov, July 18, 1951, Matvijenko Proceedings, vol. 4, pp. 104–11; and Black, "Foot Soldiers of the Final Solution," 95, n. 299. Most of the Trawniki guards assigned to Plaszow were transferred to Sachsenhausen in late May 1944. Plaszow HQ to Sachsenhausen HQ, July 4, 1944, RGVA, 1367/1/143, pp. 21–22.

76. Black, "Foot Soldiers of the Final Solution," 31, and 86, n. 231; Protocols of Interrogations of Fedor Gorun, May 20, 1966, Zuev Proceedings, vol. 14, pp. 25–26, and March 7, 1951, Gorun Proceedings, SBU Archive Kiev, 6035/4277, pp. 55–64; and Evdokim Parfinyuk, October 24, 1961, Schultz Proceedings, vol. 24, pp. 145–51.

77. Black, "Foot Soldiers of the Final Solution," 87, n. 236; Trawniki guards assigned to the SS Garrison Administration in Lublin guarded this storage room. Globocnik and other SS officers sometimes visited the death camps and then returned to the SSPF Headquarters in Lublin with sealed packages, which probably contained valuables.

78. Black, "Foot Soldiers of the Final Solution," 31, and 88, n. 240; Protocol of Trial Testimony of Georg Wippern, May 6, 1974, Streibel Proceedings, vol. 131, pp. 26,766–81; and Protocols of Interrogations of Georg Wippern, April 17, 1962, Hoffmann Proceedings, vol. 36, pp. 3,425–36, and December 6, 1962, Bolender Proceedings, vol. 9, pp. 1,715–23. See also Schulte, *Zwangsarbeit*, 416–18.

79. Black, "Foot Soldiers of the Final Solution," 88, n. 241; and SSPF Lublin, signed Globocnik, to the Personal Staff of the *Reichsführer-SS*, Grothmann, March 3, 1943, with attached report signed by Wippern, "Accounting Ledger for the Estimated Value of the Jewish Possessions Received Here up to February 3, 1943, for Transport," February 27, 1943, Federal Archive Berlin, NS 19/2234, pp. 1–7, copy in USHMM, RG 14.015M.

80. Black, "Foot Soldiers of the Final Solution," 31, and 87, n. 239; and SS-WVHA / Office Group A, signed by August Frank, to the SS Garrison Administration Lublin and Head of the Administration Department at Auschwitz, September 26, 1942, NARA, RG 238, NO-724. Perz and Sandkuhler, in *Auschwitz*, provides an analysis of the coordination between Lublin and Auschwitz on storing, processing, and shipping the confiscated goods. For an explanation of the sorting and evaluating of the goods at the storage depots in Lublin, both the one on Chopin Street and the one at the Old Airfield Camp, see Protocol of Interrogation of Georg Wippern, December 6, 1962, Bolender Proceedings, vol. 9, pp. 1,718–23.

81. Black, "Foot Soldiers of the Final Solution," 38.

82. Ibid., 94, n. 296; and Head of the SS-WVHA, "Memo on the Takeover of Jewish Labor Camps of the SSPFs of the General Government," signed Pohl, September 7, 1943, NARA, RG 238, NO-599. In addition to labor camps in Lublin District, Pohl also took over other camps where Trawniki guards were assigned, including the Warsaw concentration camp and Plaszow in Krakow. The SS-WVHA, however, did not take over Janowska in Lvov District or Treblinka I.

83. Black, "Foot Soldiers of the Final Solution," 40.

84. Black, "Police Auxiliaries for Operation Reinhard," 344.

85. Black, "Foot Soldiers of the Final Solution," 40.

86. Ibid., 41–42, and 97, n. 311; and Protocol of Interrogation of Ivan Bogdanov, December 2, 1947, FSB Archive Moscow, RG 20869, vol. 13, pp. 286–301.

87. Black, "Foot Soldiers of the Final Solution," 98, n. 312; Protocol of Interrogation of former *SS-Gruppenführer* Jakob Sporrenberg, February 25, 1946, with appendix, Report of US Army War Crimes Investigation Unit No. 1030, titled "Extracts From Consolidated Report No. PWIS Dat (n) 22," September 6, 1945, on Interrogation of SS-Obersturmführer Johann Offermann and SS-Unterscharführer Karl Klein by PWIS Det (Norway) at Akershus Prison, Oslo, no date; and Black, "Foot Soldiers of the Final Solution," 62, n. 92. SS-Untersturmführer Willi Franz, one of the Trawniki battalion commanders, went missing in action while on a reconnaissance mission for the Streibel Battalion as it withdrew through central Poland in summer 1944.

88. Black, "Foot Soldiers of the Final Solution," 42.

89. Ibid., 44–45.

90. David Rich, "The Third Reich Enlists the New Soviet Man: Eastern Auxiliary Guards at Auschwitz-Birkenau in Spring 1943," *Russian History* 41, no. 2 (2014): 275.

91. Danuta Czech, *Auschwitz Chronicle, 1939-1945: From the Archives of the Auschwitz Memorial and the German Federal Archives* (New York: Henry Holt, 1989), 365.

92. Rich, "The Third Reich Enlists the New Soviet Man," 276.

93. Ibid., 276, n. 18; and Interrogation of Vasili Shuller, July 9, 1965, SBU Archive Dnepropetrovsk, Zuev Trial, Case #44, Archive file #32132, vol. 1, pp. 124–27.

94. Rich, "The Third Reich Enlists the New Soviet Man," 276, n. 18; and Interrogation of Akim Zuev, August 13, 1966, SBU Archive Dnepropetrovsk, Zuev Trial, Case #44, Archive file #32132, vol. 12, pp. 67–70.

95. Rich, "The Third Reich Enlists the New Soviet Man," 277.

96. Ibid., 277, n. 20; Akim Zuev described his guard duties at Birkenau in this format. Interrogation of Akim Zuev, August 13, 1966, SBU Archive Dnepropetrovsk, Zuev Trial, Case #44, Archive file #32132, vol. 12, pp. 67–70.

97. Rich, "The Third Reich Enlists the New Soviet Man," 277.

98. Ibid., 278.

99. Ibid., 278, n. 22; Interrogation of Taras Olejnik, September 29, 1965, SBU Archive Dnepropetrovsk, Zuev Trial, Case #44, Archive file #32132, vol. 1, pp. 54–58; and Interrogation of Vasili Shuller, July 9, 1965, SBU Archive Dnepropetrovsk, Zuev Trial, Case #44, Archive file #32132, vol. 1, pp. 124–27.

100. Rich, "The Third Reich Enlists the New Soviet Man," 279, n. 26; and Auschwitz concentration camp, signed Hoss, to SS-WVHA / Office Group D Berlin, "Desertion of Ukrainian Guard Force at Auschwitz," July 5, 1943, FSB Archive Moscow, File K-779, f. 16, op. 312e, d. 410, pp. 231–34.

101. Rich, "The Third Reich Enlists the New Soviet Man," 280, n. 29; and SS-WVHA / Office Group D Directive, "Ukrainian SS-Men," July 10, 1943, Federal Archive Berlin, NS-3, folder 426, p. 101.

102. Black, "Foot Soldiers of the Final Solution," 39.

103. Tadeusz Piotrowski, *Poland's Holocaust* (Jefferson, NC: McFarland, 1998), 22 and 299–300, n. 10; also see Maria Wardzyńska, *Formacja Wachmannschaften des SS- und Polizeiführer im Distrikt Lublin* (Warsaw: Główna Komisja Badania Zbrodni przeciwko Narodowi Polskiemu, 1992). The SS Ukrainian Guard Force (SS-Ukrainische Wachmannschaften), trained in Trawniki, participated in these actions.

104. Agnieszka Jaczyńska, *Sonderlaboratorium SS Zamojszczyzna, Pierwszy Obszar Osiedlenczy w Generalnym Gubernatorstwie* (Lublin, Poland: Instytut Pamieci Narodowej, 2012), 20.
105. Ibid., 20.
106. Ibid., 21.
107. Ibid.
108. Ibid.
109. Ibid.
110. Ibid.
111. Ibid., 73.
112. Ibid.
113. Ibid.
114. Ibid., 94.
115. Ibid.
116. Ibid., 121.
117. Ibid.
118. Ibid., 135.
119. Ibid., 160.
120. Ibid., 242.
121. Ibid., 283.
122. Webb and Chocholaty, *Treblinka Death Camp*, statement of Sergei Vasilenko, 1961, Kiev, Schultz Trial.
123. Statement of Franciszek Zabecki, Treblinka Railway station master, undated.
124. Webb and Chocholaty, *Treblinka Death Camp*.
125. Ibid., statement of Nikolaj Malagon, March 18, 1978.
126. Tregenza, *"Disappearance" of SS-Hauptscharführer Lorenz Hackenholt*, 16.
127. Webb and Chocholaty, *Treblinka Death Camp*, statement of Pavel Leleko, February 20, 1945.
128. Ibid., statement of Pavel Leleko, 1950.
129. Ibid., statement of Eliahu Rosenberg.
130. Ibid., statement of Pinchas Epstein. Coincidentally, Epstein worked as an engine mechanic after the war.
131. Ibid., statement of former *SS-Unterscharführer* Otto Horn.
132. Ibid., 224: statement of Pavel Leleko, February 20, 1945.
133. Ibid., 225: statement of Prokofij Ryabtsev, 1961, Kiev, Schultz Trial.
134. Ibid., statement of Pavel Leleko, February 20, 1945, Leleko Proceedings.
135. David Rich, "'Reinhard' and Operation 1005? Corpse Disposal in Generalgouvernement Killing Centers, 1942–1944," 14, n. 36; and Interrogation of Dimitri Borodin, July 19, 1961, Schultz Trial, vol. 3, pp. 76–87, USHMM, RG-31.018M, reel 63.
136. Rich, "'Reinhard' and Operation 1005?," 6, n. 11; and Interrogation of Alexei Govorov, September 7, 1961, Schultz Trial, vol. 27, pp. 36–48, USHMM, RG-31.018M, reel 63.
137. Rich, "'Reinhard' and Operation 1005?," 6, n. 12; and Interrogation of Emanuel Schultz, March 13, 1961, Schultz Trial, vol. 2, pp. 130–36, USHMM, RG-31.018M, reel 62. Shultz was assigned to Treblinka II starting in mid-1942 and worked in the camp's administrative office. He stated during his postwar interrogation to Soviet authorities that "I was a witness when the chief of staff, SS-Scharführer Willi Metzig, gave a telephone report in July 1943 on the number of people exterminated in the camp. I believe he was providing the information to Lublin. He cited the number of 1.3 million people." What is known is that the number killed in the camp as of December 31, 1942 was 714,000.
138. Rich, "'Reinhard' and Operation 1005?," 7, n. 13; and Interrogation of Evdokim Parfinyuk, September 1, 1961, Schultz Trial, vol. 24, pp. 60–73, USHMM, RG-31.018M, reel 63.
139. Rich, "'Reinhard' and Operation 1005?," 5, n. 8; and Interrogation of Ivan Shevchenko, September 8, 1944, SBU Archive Donetsk/Stalino, Archive #37834, Iskaradov Trial, pp. 196–206. Shevchenko estimated that he may have shot up to fifty such survivors of the gassing process during his eleven months of service at Treblinka II, August 1942–July 1943. Other former guards also reported that sometimes Jews survived the gassing process.
140. Rich, "'Reinhard' and Operation 1005?," 9, n. 18; and Interrogation of Ivan Shevchenko, September 8, 1944, SBU Archive Donetsk/Stalino, Archive file #37834, Iskaradov Trial.
141. Rich, "'Reinhard' and Operation 1005?," 12, n. 30; and Interrogation of Piotr Goncharov, February 27, 1951, Schultz Trial, vol. 33, pp. 206–15, USHMM, RG-31.018M, reel 63. Goncharov served at Treblinka II, October 1942–October 25, 1943.
142. Rich, "'Reinhard' and Operation 1005?," 13, n. 34; and Interrogation of Ivan Safonov, April 20, 1961, Schultz Trial, vol. 32, pp. 22–26, USHMM, RG-31.018M, reel 63. "The heavy use of alcohol by everyone at Treblinka was a consequence of the foul smell" of the burning bodies. Interrogation of Fedor Ryabeka, April 25, 1961, Schultz Trial, vol. 11, pp. 4–10, USHMM, RG-31.018M, reel 62.

143. Rich, "'Reinhard' and Operation 1005?," 13–14, n. 35; and Interrogation of Pavel Leleko, November 18, 1944, SBU Archive Nikolayev?, Archive file #14054, Leleko Trial, pp. 28–39.

144. Rich, "'Reinhard' and Operation 1005?," 19, n. 43; and Interrogation of Alexej Govorov, September 12, 1961, Schultz Trial, vol. 27, pp. 89–96, USHMM, RG-31.018M, reel 63. Govorov served at Treblinka II, June 1942–March 1943.

145. Webb and Chocholaty, *Treblinka Death Camp*, 221.

146. Ibid.

147. Yoram Sheftel, *Defending Ivan the Terrible: The Conspiracy to Convict John Demjanjuk* (Washington DC: Regnery, 1996), 374; and Marchenko TPF, submitted into evidence at Demjanjuk Appeal, Israel, 1992.

148. Webb and Chocholaty, *Treblinka Death Camp*: statement of Nikolai Shalayev, 1951, Shalayev Trial, Voronezh; and statement of Samuel Pritsch, 1961, Kiev, Schultz Trial.

149. Ibid., statement of Nikolaj Malagon, March 1978.

150. Ibid., statement of Fedor Ryabeka, 1961; and statement of Ivan Terekhov, 1961, Kiev, Schultz Trial.

151. Ibid., statement of Grigorij Skydan, 1950, Baranovichi, Skydan Trial.

152. Ibid., statement of Fedor Ryabeka, 1961, Kiev, Schultz Trial.

153. Ibid.

154. Ibid.

155. Ibid., statement of Nikolai Shalayev, 1950, Voronezh, Shalayev Proceedings.

156. Ibid., statement of Sergei Vasilenko, 1961, Kiev, Schultz Trial.

157. Ibid., statement of Nikolai Shalayev, 1951; and statement of Filip Levchishin, 1962, Kiev, Schultz Trial.

158. Ibid., statement of Grigorij Skydan, 1950; and statement of Samuel Pritsch, 1961, Kiev, Schultz Trial.

159. Ibid., statement of Grigorij Skydan, 1950.

160. Ibid., statement of Grigorij Skydan, 1950.

161. Ibid., statement of Sergei Vasilenko, 1961.

162. Ibid., statement of Pavel Leleko, February 20, 1945; and statement of Nikolaj Kulak, 1947.

163. Ibid., statement of Pavel Leleko, February 20, 1945.

164. Ibid., statement of Pavel Leleko, February 20, 1945.

165. Ibid., statement of Sergei Vasilenko, 1961.

166. Ibid., statement of Fedor Ryabeka, 1961.

167. Ibid., statement of Pavel Leleko, February 20, 1945; and statement of Prokofij Ryabtsev, 1961.

168. Ibid., statement of Nikolaj Kulak, 1947.

169. Ibid., statement of Pavel Leleko, February 20, 1945.

170. Ibid., statement of former *SS-Scharführer* Heinrich Matthes.

171. Ibid., statement of former *SS-Unterscharführer* Otto Horn.

172. Ibid., statement of Nikolai Shalayev, May 1951.

173. Ibid., statement of Nikolai Shalayev, December 1951.

174. Ibid., statement of Nikolai Shalayev, 1951. Shalayev's participation in running the gas chambers certainly extended well beyond the three weeks that he claimed.

175. Ibid., statement of Nikolai Shalayev, 1950.

176. Ibid., statement of Grigorij Skydan, 1950.

177. Ibid., statement of Ananij Kuzminsky, 1965.

178. Ibid., statement of Grigorij Skydan, 1950.

179. Ibid., statement of Ivan Terekhov, 1961; statement of Fedor Ryabeka, 1961; and statement of Alexandra Kirpa, 1951.

180. Ibid., statement of Fedor Ryabeka, 1961.

181. Ibid., 228.

182. Ibid., statement of Nikolai Shalayev, 1950.

183. Ibid.

184. Ibid.

185. Statement of Larry D., Axis History Forum, *https://forum.axishistory.com*. Larry had been a researcher for the Demjanjuk defense team in 1990.

186. Ibid., statements of September 1, 2004, and March 17, 2012.

187. Sheftel, *Defending Ivan the Terrible*, 374.

188. Ibid., 375.

189. Yitzhak Arad, *Belzec, Sobibor, Treblinka: The Operation Reinhard Death Camps* (Bloomington: Indiana University Press, 1987), 283 and 285.

190. Ibid., 272.

191. Ibid.

192. Webb and Chocholaty, *Treblinka Death Camp*, statement of Fedor Fedorenko, Fort Lauderdale, Florida, 1978.

193. Arad, *Belzec, Sobibor, Treblinka*, 294.

194. Webb and Chocholaty, *Treblinka Death Camp*.

195. Black, "Foot Soldiers of the Final Solution," 21.

196. Webb and Chocholaty, *Treblinka Death Camp*.

197. Ibid.; see Martyna Rusiniak-Karwat, *Oboz zaglady Treblinka II w pamieci spolecznej, 1943–1989* (Warsaw: Wydawnictwo Neriton, 2008). This work focuses on the functioning of the postcamp terrain in the context of human awareness and to create a memory of Treblinka in the context of social awareness.

198. Webb and Chocholaty, *Treblinka Death Camp*; see Rusiniak, *Oboz zaglady Treblinka II*.

199. Webb and Chocholaty, *Treblinka Death Camp*; see IPN Archive Warsaw.

200. Webb and Chocholaty, *Treblinka Death Camp*.

201. Ibid.

202. Ibid.; and Alexander Donat, ed., *The Death Camp Treblinka: A Documentary* (New York: Holocaust Library, 1979).

203. O'Neal, "Sources of Manpower," in *Belzec: Stepping Stone to Genocide*, n. 47, www.jewishgen.org/Yizkor/belzec1/bel040.html.

204. Ibid.

205. Ibid.

206. Statement of Krystyna Natyna, Belzec, 1966, IPN Archive Lublin, IPN Lu-08/298.

207. Interrogation of Robert Juhrs, 1961, Oberhauser Proceedings.

208. Dieter Pohl, "Die Trawniki-Männer im Vernichtungslager Belzec, 1941–1943," in *NS-Gewaltherrschaft: Beitrage zur historischen Forschung und juristischen Aufarbeitung*, vol. 11, ed. Alfred Gottwaldt, Norbert Kampe, and Peter Klein (Berlin: Edition Hentrich, 2005), 283.

209. Robert Kuwalek, *Das Vernichtungslager Belzec* (Berlin: Metropol Verlag, 2013), 126, n. 48.

210. Ibid., 126, n. 50.

211. Statement of Michael Kusmierczak, Belzec, 1966, IPN Archive Lublin, IPN Lu-08/298.

212. Statement of former *SS-Unterscharführer* Gustav Munzberger.

213. Statement of former *SS-Scharführer* Werner Dubois.

214. Statement of former *SS-Scharführer* Karl Schluch.

215. Statement of former *SS-Oberscharführer* Heinrich Gley.

216. O'Neal, "Belzec: Second Phase," in *Belzec: Stepping Stone to Genocide*, www.jewishgen.org/Yizkor/belzec1/bel100.html; statement of former prisoner Rudolf Reder, December 1945, Krakow, before the Main Commission for the Investigation of Nazi Crimes in Poland, no. R 102/46.

217. Ibid., statement of former prisoner Rudolf Reder.

218. Pohl, "Die Trawniki-Männer," 283–84; Interrogation of Andrej Kuchma, September 6, 1965; Interrogation of Grigorij Nesmejan, September 28, 1965; Interrogation of Alexander Semigodow, July 7, 1965; Zuev Proceedings, vol. 2, pp. 217, 233–41, 254–64; and Vasili Bronov, 1950, FSB Archive Omsk. Kunz testified in war crime trials decades after the war. Siebert and Schneider have never been accounted for.

219. Rich, "'Reinhard' and Operation 1005?," 4, n. 7; and Interrogation of Vasili Shuller, Krasnodar, December 14, 1964, SBU Archive Dnepropetrovsk, Archive file #32132, Zuev Trial, vol. 1, pp. 104–12, USHMM RG-31.018M, reel 75.

220. Rich, "'Reinhard' and Operation 1005?," 6, n. 10; and Interrogation of Piotr Brovtsev, March 6, 1965, FSB Archive Krasnodar, Archive file #100366, Matvienko Trial, vol. 10, pp. 113–16.

221. Rich, "'Reinhard' and Operation 1005?," 7, n. 14; and Interrogation of Alexander Zakharov, January 9, 1965, SBU Archive Dnepropetrovsk, Archive file #32132, Zuev Trial, vol. 1, pp. 82–85, USHMM, RG-31.018M, reel 75.

222. Rich, "'Reinhard' and Operation 1005?," 8, n. 17; and Interrogation of Yuri Danilov, October 11, 1948, SBU Archive Lvov, Archive file #10085, Danilov Trial, pp. 23–24.

223. O'Neal, *Belzec: Stepping Stone to Genocide*.

224. Rich, "'Reinhard' and Operation 1005?," 9, n. 20; and Interrogation of Vladimir Emelyanov, September 23, 1947, SBU Archive Kiev, Archive file #57636, Vasilenko Trial, pp. 66–73: this interrogation statement made by Emelyanov was widely circulated among MGB/KGB offices investigating former Trawniki guards who had been assigned to the Reinhard death camps. Interrogation of Vasili Orlowskij, August 22, 1975, ZSt-Ludwigsburg, Streibel Proceedings, AR 643/71, pp. 513–59.

225. Rich, "'Reinhard and Operation 1005?," 9, n. 20; Interrogation of Nikolai Leontev, June 30, 1964, FSB Archive Krasnodar, Archive file #100366, Matvienko Trial, vol. 1, pp. 37–43; Interrogation of Yuri Danilov, October 11, 1948, SBU Archive Lvov, Archive file #10085, Danilov Trial, p. 25; and Interrogation of Fedor Gorun, November 16, 1964, FSB Archive Krasnodar, Archive file #100366, Matvienko Trial, vol. 9, pp. 66–73.

226. Rich, "'Reinhard and Operation 1005?," 10, n. 21; and Interrogation of Ivan Kozlovskij, September 29, 1964, FSB Archive Krasnodar, Archive file #100366, Matvienko Trial, vol. 9, pp. 22–29. Kozlovskij served at Belzec from March to December 1942, and at Sobibor from January to March 1943.

227. Rich, "'Reinhard and Operation 1005?," 10, n. 22; and Interrogation of Vladimir Emelyanov, September 23, 1947, SBU Archive Kiev, Archive file #57636, Vasilenko Trial, pp. 66–73.

228. Rich, "'Reinhard and Operation 1005?," 10, n. 23; and Interrogation of Nikolai Leontev, June 30, 1964, FSB Archive Krasnodar, Archive file #100366, Matvienko Trial, vol. 1, pp. 37–43.

229. Rich, "'Reinhard and Operation 1005?," 10, n. 24; and Interrogation of Vasili Orlowskij, August 22, 1975, ZSt-Ludwigsburg, Streibel Proceedings, AR 643/71, pp. 513–59.

230. Kuwalek, *Das Vernichtungslager Belzec*, 233, n. 12; statement of Stanislaw Kozak.

231. Black, "Foot Soldiers of the Final Solution," 21.

232. Statement of Maria Warzocha, Belzec, 1965, IPN Archive Lublin, IPN Lu-08/298.

233. Statement of Maria Warzocha, Belzec, 1966, IPN Archive Lublin, IPN Lu-08/298.

234. Statement of Edward Luczynski (uncle of Maria Warzocha).

235. IPN Archive Lublin, Lu 1/15/105: investigation records regarding the crimes committed at Belzec death camp, 1945–49; statement of Edward Luczynski, October 15, 1945, p. 26; and statement of Maria Wlasiuk, February 21, 1946, p. 69.

236. Kuwalek, *Das Vernichtungslager Belzec*, 115–116, n. 19.

237. Statement of Maria Warzocha, Belzec, 1966, IPN Archive Lublin, IPN Lu08/298.

238. SS Training Camp Trawniki, List of men detailed to the Warsaw Detachment, April 17, 1943, Zuev Proceedings, Case #44, Archive #32132, vol. 3, pp. 276–84, SBU Archive Dnepropetrovsk; also located in RG K-779, fund 16, opis 312 "e," delo 411, pp. 115–30, FSB Archive Moscow.

239. Commander of Trawniki training camp, signed Heinze, to Lublin Detachment, May 17, 1943, RG K-779, f. 16, op. 312 "e," d. 411, pp. 257–59, FSB Archive Moscow.

240. O'Neal, "Sources of Manpower," in *Belzec: Stepping Stone to Genocide*, n. 65 (Robin O'Neal told the author that he had gotten the information from the Operation Reinhard historian Michael Tregenza, who lives in Lublin).

241. Philip Bialowitz and Joseph Bialowitz, *A Promise at Sobibor: A Jewish Boy's Story of Revolt and Survival in Nazi-Occupied Poland* (Madison: University of Wisconsin Press, 2013).

242. Ibid.

243. Marek Bem, *Sobibor Extermination Camp, 1942–1943* (Amsterdam: Stichting Sobibor / Sobibor Foundation, 2015), 97–98, n. 81; Arad, *Belzec, Sobibor, Treblinka*, 76 and 410, n. 3; and statement of former *SS-Oberscharführer* Kurt Bolender, Criminal Police Court, Munich, June 5, 1962, Oberhauser Proceedings, vol. 7, pp. 1320–21.

244. Arad, *Belzec, Sobibor, Treblinka*, 77 and 410, n. 7; and statement of former *SS-Oberscharführer* Erich Bauer, Bolender Proceedings, vol. 4, p. 787.

245. Rich, "Reinhard and Operation 1005?," 11.

246. Ibid., 11, n. 25; and Interrogation of Nikolaj Goncharenko, May 5, 1949, SBU Archive Zaporozhe, Archive file #2362, Goncharenko Trial, pp. 21–32. Goncharenko served at Sobibor starting on March 26, 1943, and claims to have been assigned there for only around two months.

247. Rich, "Reinhard and Operation 1005?," 11, n. 26; and Interrogation of Wolodymyr Sharan, July 5, 1947, SBU Archive Lvov, Archive file #29805, Kopytyuk Trial, pp. 115–18.

248. Rich, "Reinhard and Operation 1005?," 11, n. 27; and Interrogation of Wasyl Kartashev, May 4, 1949, SBU Archive Ternopil, Archive file #10230, Kartashev Trial, pp. 20–33. Kartashev's service at Sobibor began in August 1942.

249. Rich, "Reinhard and Operation 1005?," 11, n. 28; and Interrogation of Nikolaj Pavli, November 17, 1949, SBU Archive Donetsk/Stalino, Archive file #6442, Pavli Trial, pp. 22–25.

250. Statement of Ignat Danilchenko, 1985, Lisakowsk, Kazakhstan.

251. http://deathcamps.org/sobibor/trawnikis.html.

252. Stefano Di Giusto and Tommaso Chiussi, *Globocnik's Men in Italy, 1943–1945: Abteilung R and the SS-Wachmannschaften of the Operationszone Adriatisches Kustenland* (Atglen, PA: Schiffer, 2017), 225, n. 34.

253. http://deathcamps.org/sobibor/trawnikis.html.

254. Bem, *Sobibor Extermination Camp, 1942–1943*, 97–98, n. 81; Arad, *Belzec, Sobibor, Treblinka*, 76 and 410, n. 3; statement of former *SS-Oberscharführer* Kurt Bolender, Criminal Police Court, Munich, June 5, 1962, Oberhauser Proceedings, vol. 7, pp. 1, 320–21; and Interrogation of Nikolai Shalayev, 1950, Shalayev Proceedings, Voronezh.

255. Bialowitz and Bialowitz, *A Promise at Sobibor*.

256. Statement of Leon Feldhendler's wife, Yad Vashem; Adam Rutkowski, Tomasz Blatt, and Zelda Metz.

257. Bialowitz and Bialowitz, *A Promise at Sobibor*.

258. Ibid.

259. Di Giusto and Chiussi, *Globocnik's Men in Italy*, 114, and 222, n. 8; Letter from Globocnik to von Herff, October 27, 1943, Schwarzenbacher personnel file, Bundesarchiv Berlin; Di Giusto and Chiussi, *Globocnik's Men in Italy*, 222–23, n. 9; and Depositions of Oberhauser, May 3, 1971, IRSML-FVG, Risiera collection, box 88 (published in Adolfo Scalpelli, *San Sabba*, vol. 2, pp. 31–35), and September 24, 1973, HHStA, Wiesbaden, Abt. 631a, #1330. In the first deposition, Oberhauser claimed to have been assigned to this Trawniki company when it arrived in

Trieste; however, in the second deposition he said he had not been assigned to it. He had been a Trawniki platoon commander back in Lublin in 1941 and at Belzec. He was also Christian Wirth's assistant and escort, a role that he also retained when assigned to the Adriatic coast region.

260. Di Giusto and Chiussi, *Globocnik's Men in Italy*, 114.

261. Ibid., 115, and 224, n. 21; and Deposition of Alexej Mihalic, January 16, 1976, during investigations for the Risiera San Sabba trial.

262. Di Giusto and Chiussi, *Globocnik's Men in Italy*, 115.

263. Ibid., 119.

264. Ibid., 36–37.

265. Ibid., 37.

266. Ibid., 223, n. 19.

267. Ibid., 223, n. 20; and Oberhauser deposition, September 24, 1973, HHStA, Wiesbaden, Abt. 631a, #1330.

268. Di Giusto and Chiussi, *Globocnik's Men in Italy*, 223, n. 20; and Prasch deposition, November 23, 1963, HHStA, Wiesbaden, Abt. 631a, #1330.

269. Di Giusto and Chiussi, *Globocnik's Men in Italy*, 223–24, n. 20; see Jerzy Grzybowski, "An Outline History of the 13th Belorussian Battalion of the SD Auxiliary Police (Schuma Battalion der SD 13)," *Journal of Slavic Military Studies* 23, no. 3 (2010): 461–76.

270. Di Giusto and Chiussi, *Globocnik's Men in Italy*, 225, n. 34.

271. Ibid., 124.

272. Ibid., 146, and 230, n. 81; for a time, Bolender had commanded the Trawniki guard contingent in Sobibor.

273. Ibid., 146–47.

274. Ibid., 150.

275. Ibid., 40.

276. Ibid., 212, n. 43.

277. Ibid., 21.

278. Ibid., 21–24.

279. Ibid., 211, n. 26; on the incident, see Tone Ferenc, *Satan, njegovo delo in smrt* (Ljubljana, Slovenia: Borec, 1979). A description of the incident is also included in the history of the partisan unit that carried out the attack, in Maks Zadnik, *Istrski odred* (Nova Gorica, Slovenia: Odbor Istrskega odreda, 1975), 317–23. It is not known how reliable the reconstruction of the event was, including the claim that a Ukrainian named Nikolai died with Wirth in the attack. Hauptwachtmeister der Schupo Konrad Geng, who was Wirth's driver, was lightly wounded, according to his own postwar deposition on September 1, 1970, not badly wounded as was claimed in the reconstruction. See IRSML-FVG, Risiera Collection, box 88, also published in Adolfo Scalpelli, *San Sabba: Istruttoria e processo per il Lager della Risiera*, vol. 2 (Trieste, Italy: Aned-Lint, 1995), 97.

280. Di Giusto and Chiussi, *Globocnik's Men in Italy*, 27.

281. Ibid., 28.

282. Ibid., 31.

283. Ibid., 32.

284. Ibid.

285. Ibid.

286. Ibid.

287. Ibid., 34.

288. Ibid., 211, n. 35; and Deposition of Oberhauser, May 3, 1971, IRSML-FVG, Risiera Collection, box 88, published in Scalpelli, *San Sabba*, vol. 2, pp. 31–35.

289. Di Giusto and Chiussi, *Globocnik's Men in Italy*, 34.

290. Ibid., 35.

291. Ibid.

292. Ibid., 211, n. 37.

293. Ibid., 36.

294. Ibid., 222, n. 8.

295. Ibid., 119–20, and 224, n. 25; a report by the partisan unit, "Juznoprimorski odred," dated June 3, 1944, published in *Zbornik dokumentov in podatkov o narodnoosvobodilni vojni jugoslovanskih narodov*, vol. VI, part 14, document #18.

296. Di Giusto and Chiussi, *Globocnik's Men in Italy*, 120.

297. Ibid., 120, and 224, n. 27; and *Befehlsblatt des Befehlshabers der Sipo und des SD* in Trieste, #23, July 5, 1944. According to Tone Ferenc, in "La polizia tedesca nella Zona d'Operazioni "Litorale Adriatico" 1943–1945," *Storia Contemporanea in Friuli* 10 (1979): 24–25, prior to Hornof, temporary command of the battalion had been given to SS-Hauptsturmführer Gustav Hanelt, who was on Globocnik's staff and was tasked with personnel matters. No confirmation that Hanelt had led the battalion could be found.

298. Di Giusto and Chiussi, *Globocnik's Men in Italy*, 120.

299. Ibid., 121, and 224, n. 31; Deposition of Kurt Franz, August 9, 1967, IRSML-FVG, Risiera Collection, box 88; Depositions of Kurt Franz, December 3 and 30, 1959, LA NRW, Duisburg, Rep. 388, #743; Deposition of Dietrich Allers, April 19, 1960, LA NRW, Duisburg, Rep. 388, #747; Kurt Franz personnel file, Bundesarchiv Berlin; and Tone Ferenc, "Kurt Franz," in Siegfried J. Pucher, *Il nazista di Trieste: Vita e crimini di Odilo Globocnik, l'uomo che inventò Treblinka* (Trieste, Italy: Beit, 2011), 229–42.

300. Di Giusto and Chiussi, *Globocnik's Men in Italy*, 122.

301. Ibid., 122, and 224, n. 32. His burial report contained the following information: identity tag #262, SS-FHA, Staff company, unit: Einsatz R: SS-Wachmannschaft Battalion. The place of his death is confirmed by a report from the *prefettura* of Udine on partisan activity, according to which, "the German SS lieutenant commander of the SS in Gemona" was killed in a firefight in San Pietro di Ragogna on June 19, 1944 (Archivio di Stato in Udine, Prefettura-Archivio di Gabinetto, box 044, folder 156). According to a report by the *Carabinieri*, the firefight started when a car carrying a German officer, a woman, and a driver stopped near a truck parked at the side of the road to try to identify the people in it. The officer was killed and the woman was wounded, and among the truck passengers, there was one dead and two wounded. On the incident, there was also a partisan account, according to Ermes Brezzaro, *Ragogna nella Resistenza* (Rodeano, Italy: Editrice Lito Immagine, 1997), 259–60: on June 19, a pickup truck carrying some partisans driving toward the Pinzano bridge crossed paths with a German car near the San Pietro turnabout. In a resulting firefight, a German officer was killed, and a woman traveling with him was wounded by gunshot wounds and died. Three partisans were wounded, one of whom died shortly thereafter.

302. Di Giusto and Chiussi, *Globocnik's Men in Italy*, 152.

303. Ibid., 54.

304. Ibid., 54–55.

305. Ibid., 214, n. 72.

306. Ibid., 55, and 214, n. 73; and Serbian Military Archives, box K-32 A/II, folder 17.

307. Di Giusto and Chiussi, *Globocnik's Men in Italy*, 55.

308. Ibid.

309. Ibid.

310. Ibid., 214, n. 74.

311. Ibid., 103.

312. Ibid., 220, n. 144; on the military operations of the last weeks of the war in the Adriatic coast region, see Stefano Di Giusto, *Operationszone Adriatisches Küstenland* (Udine, Italy: Istituto friulano per la storia del movimento di liberazione, 2005), 641–715.

313. Di Giusto and Chiussi, *Globocnik's Men in Italy*, 103.

314. Ibid.

315. Ibid., 105.

316. Ibid., 106.

317. Ibid.

318. Ibid., 220, n. 148.

319. Ibid., 153.

320. Ibid., 232, n. 10.

Chapter 2

1. Rich, "The Third Reich Enlists the New Soviet Man," 275.

2. Email between author and Dr. David Rich, August 18, 2016.

3. Angelika Benz, *Handlanger der SS: Die Rolle der Trawniki-Männer im Holocaust* (Berlin: Metropol Verlag, 2015), 48–49.

4. Black, "Police Auxiliaries for Operation Reinhard," 356.

5. Ibid.

6. Ibid., 357.

7. Ibid., 357–58.

8. Ibid., 358.

9. Ibid.

10. Black, "Foot Soldiers of the Final Solution," 6.

11. Ibid.

12. Memo of the SSPF Lublin / SS Training Camp Trawniki, signed Streibel and Sporrenberg, List of Recommendations for Awarding of the Eastern Peoples Bravery Medal 2nd Class in Bronze with Swords, June 7, 1944, Archive of the GKBZPWP.

13. Letter of SS Special Staff Sporrenberg / SS Streibel Battalion, signed Streibel, to HSSPF East in Krakow, List of Recommendations for awarding of the War Merit Medal, September 26, 1944, File, Poland Documents, Zentrale Stelle, Ludwigsburg, Germany.

14. Memo from Streibel Battalion, signed Streibel, List of Recommendations for Awarding of the Brave Conduct Award, 2nd Class in Bronze, September 26, 1944, Archive of the Main Commission for the Investigation of Nazi Crimes in Poland, IPN Archive Warsaw, sygn. WO, VII/12/9; Demjanjuk Investigation.

15. Black, "Foot Soldiers of the Final Solution," 33.

16. Roster of Streibel Battalion, 1944, Central State Archive Prague, Czech Republic.

17. Black, "Foot Soldiers of the Final Solution," 66, n. 109; Commander of Feldgendarmerie Troop 942 to the SS and Police Court Krakow and the court of the Wehrmacht Administration HQ Lublin, August 26, 1943, Denkiewicz TPF, RG 20869, FSB Archive Moscow; Dr. Peter Black, correspondence with the author.

18. Black, "Foot Soldiers of the Final Solution," 33.

19. Ibid.

20. Haage TPF, RG 20869, FSB Archive Moscow.

21. Black, "Foot Soldiers of the Final Solution," 66, n. 109; Hryb TPF, Central State Archive Kiev.

22. Roster of Streibel Battalion, 1945, Central State Archive Prague.

23. Ibid.

24. Black, "Foot Soldiers of the Final Solution," 11.

25. Flossenbürg Roster, undated, Bundesarchiv Berlin-Lichterfelde, NS 4F1, vol. 20, Demjanjuk Trial, Israel.

26. Black, "Foot Soldiers of the Final Solution," 34; Ostaficzuk TPF, Central State Archive Kiev.

27. Flossenbürg Roster, October 1, 1943.

28. Black, "Foot Soldiers of the Final Solution," 33; Potschinok TPF, Central State Archive Kiev.

29. Black, "Foot Soldiers of the Final Solution," 34; Pronin, TPF, Central State Archive Kiev.

30. Pudenoks TPF, Central State Archive Kiev.

31. Black, "Foot Soldiers of the Final Solution," 33; Shalamow TPF, Central State Archive Kiev.

32. Flossenbürg Roster, undated, Bundesarchiv Berlin-Lichterfelde, NS 4F1, vol. 20, Demjanjuk Trial, Israel.

33. Black, "Foot Soldiers of the Final Solution," 33; Soljanin TPF, RG 20869, FSB Archive Moscow.

34. Black, "Foot Soldiers of the Final Solution," 33; Wisgunow TPF, FSB Archive Moscow.

35. Dr. David Rich, correspondence with the author; Interrogation of Alexei Zhukov, 1965, Matwijenko Trial, Case #4, Archive file #100366, vol. 8, pp. 212–15, FSB Archive Krasnodar.

36. Black, "Foot Soldiers of the Final Solution," 41, and 97, n. 307; Report of SS and Police Base 15 to 3rd Company / 5th Regiment of the Galician-SS Volunteers, March 26, 1944, FSB Archive Moscow, RG K-779, 16/312 "e"/409, p. 294.

37. Black, "Foot Soldiers of the Final Solution," 33.

38. Dr. David Rich, correspondence with the author; and Interrogation of Vasili Litvinenko, 1965, Matwijenko Trial, Case #4, Archive file #100366, vol. 8, pp. 212–15, FSB Archive Krasnodar.

39. Black, "Foot Soldiers of the Final Solution," 33.

40. Ibid., 34.

41. Ibid., 35, and 90, n. 267; and Protocol of interrogation of Erich Lachmann, March 3, 1969, Streibel Proceedings, vol. 81, p. 15,465.

42. Black, "Foot Soldiers of the Final Solution," 36, and 90, n. 268; Streibel wanted to get rid of some of the eastern Ukrainians and replace them gradually with western Ukrainians.

43. Ibid., 86, n. 232; Trawniki training camp, signed Grimm, to Ernst Heinkel Aircraft Works Inc. / Plant Security Directorate, Rostock, January 13, 1943, FSB Archive Moscow, RG K-779; and Plant Security Directorate, Ernst Heinkel Aircraft Works to SS Garrison Administration Lublin / Branch Office Trawniki, October 26, 1943, IPN Archive, RG SSPF Lublin, Central Archive file 891/18.

44. Black, "Foot Soldiers of the Final Solution," p. 88, n. 244; and Commander of SS Training Camp Trawniki, signed by Majowski, "Battalion Order No. 178/43," December 31, 1943, FSB Archive Moscow, RG K-779 16/312 "e" 409, p. 334.

45. Kuwalek, *Das Vernichtungslager Belzec*, 125, n. 47; and Testimony of Heinrich Unverhau, June 21, 1960, Oberhauser Proceedings, vol. 6, p. 965, Bundesarchiv Munich, 208 AR-Z 252/59.

46. Interrogation of Heinrich Gley, November 23–24, 1961, Michalsen Proceedings, 141 Js, 573/60, vol. 13, pp. 2,441–65, State Prosecutor's Office, Hamburg.

47. Statement of former *SS-Oberscharführer* Erich Bauer.

48. Statement of former *SS-Unterscharführer* Otto Horn.

49. Report from Commander of Trawniki training camp, POW Camp Detachment of the Waffen-SS, Lublin, signed Erlinger, to the Commandant's HQ, POW Camp of the Waffen-SS, January 20, 1943, fond 1173, opis 4, delo 6, p. 3, Central State Archive, Vilnius, Lithuania.

50. Report from the Commander of the SS-Totenkopf battalion, Lublin POW Camp of the Waffen-SS, initialed Langleist, to the Commandant's HQ, POW Camp of the Waffen-SS, January 24, 1943, fond 1173, opis 4, delo 6, p. 1, Central State Archive, Vilnius, Lithuania.

51. Ibid., 2; and Amanaviczius TPF, fond 1173, opis 4, pp. 3–5, Central State Archive, Vilnius, Lithuania. For leaving Majdanek without permission, Amanaviczius would be punished with one week under strict arrest and one week in a punishment platoon. After the war, this Lithuanian moved to Flanders/Belgium.

52. Black, "Foot Soldiers of the Final Solution," 14; and Bogomolow Trawniki Personnel File (TPF), SBU Archive Stalino/Donetsk.

53. French MacLean, *The Ghetto Men: The SS Destruction of the Jewish Warsaw Ghetto, April–May 1943*, (Atglen, PA: Schiffer, 2001), 167.

54. Hawriluk TPF, RG 20869, FSB Archive Moscow.

55. MacLean, *The Ghetto Men*, 167; Black, "Foot Soldiers of the Final Solution," 14; and Huculjak TPF, Record Group 20869, FSB Archive Moscow.

56. MacLean, *The Ghetto Men*, 168.

57. Ibid., 167.

58. Black, "Foot Soldiers of the Final Solution," 15; and Kobilezkj TPF, RG 20869, FSB Archive Moscow.

59. MacLean, *The Ghetto Men*, 168.

60. Maximiw TPF, SBU Archive Stanislavov/Ivano-Frankivsk.

61. MacLean, *The Ghetto Men*, 167.

62. Ibid.

63. Ibid.

64. O'Neal, "Sources of Manpower," in *Belzec: Stepping Stone to Genocide*, n. 56; statement of Georgij Skydan, February 16, 1950, and Ananij Kuzminsky, March 20, 1965; and Rich, "Reinhard's Footsoldiers," 694.

65. MacLean, *The Ghetto Men*, 167.

66. Black, "Foot Soldiers of the Final Solution," 67, n. 118; Rosgonjajew TPF, SBU Archive Dnepropetrovsk; Interrogation of Mikhail Rosgonjajew, August 24, 1948, Rosgonjajew Proceedings, SBU Archive Dnepropetrovsk; and Matwijenko Proceedings, January 19, 1965, FSB Archive Krasnodar.

67. MacLean, *The Ghetto Men*, 168.

68. Casualty Report of May 21, 1943, from Commander of Orpo Lublin District to Trawniki training camp, included in Mogilo TPF, RG 20869, FSB Archive Moscow.

69. Dr. Peter Black, correspondence with the author.

70. O'Neal, "Sources of Manpower," in *Belzec: Stepping Stone to Genocide*, nn. 56 and 57; statement of Georgij Skydan, February 16, 1950, and statement of Ananij Kuzminsky, March 20, 1965; Rich, "Reinhard's Footsoldiers," 694; and Tscherniawsky TPF, IPN Warsaw, Central Archive #903.

71. MacLean, *The Ghetto Men*, 168.

72. Roster of Streibel Battalion, 1945, Archive of the Ministry of Interior, Czech Republic, Prague.

73. Dr. David Rich, correspondence with the author; and Interrogation of Alexei Zhukov, 1965, Matwijenko Trial, Case #4, Archive file #100366, vol. 8, pp. 212–15, FSB Archive Krasnodar.

74. Rich, "'Reinhard and Operation 1005?,'" 15, n. 38; and Interrogation of Ivan Safonov, April 20, 1961, Schultz Trial, vol. 32, pp. 22–26, USHMM, RG-31.018M, reel 63. Safonov served at Treblinka II until about March 1943. The guard who had his hand shot off was Vladimir Chernyavskij.

75. Rich, "'Reinhard and Operation 1005?,'" 16, n. 39; Interrogation of Dimitri Borodin, April 20, 1961, Schultz Trial, vol. 3, pp. 39–41, USHMM, RG-31.018M, reel 62; and Interrogation of Emanuel Schultz, September 22, 1961, Schultz Trial, vol. 1, pp. 161–66, USHMM, RG-31.018M, reel 62. Other former Trawniki guards also mentioned these incidents, and KGB investigators often asked them about these events.

76. Black, "Foot Soldiers of the Final Solution," 37; and Babijtschuk Trawniki Personnel File (TPF), Central State Archive Kiev.

77. Dr. Peter Black, correspondence with the author.

78. WASt card for Ilja Baidin, undated, WASt Berlin.

79. Black, "Foot Soldiers of the Final Solution," 37; and Boschko TPF, Record Group 20869, FSB Archive Moscow.

80. Dr. Peter Black, correspondence with the author.

81. Black, "Foot Soldiers of the Final Solution," 43; and Burljajew TPF, RG 20869, FSB Archive Moscow.

82. Black, "Foot Soldiers of the Final Solution," 37.

83. Roster of Streibel Battalion, 1944, Archive of the Ministry of Interior, Czech Republic, Prague.

84. Black, "Foot Soldiers of the Final Solution," 36–37; and Flunt TPF, RG 20869, FSB Archive Moscow.

85. Black, "Police Auxiliaries for Operation Reinhard," 364, n. 95; and Glista TPF, Central State Archive Kiev.

86. Black, "Police Auxiliaries for Operation Reinhard," 364, n. 95; and Gubrijenko TPF, RG 20869, FSB Archive Moscow.

87. Hermaniuk TPF, RG 20869, FSB Archive Moscow.

88. Isatshenko TPF, RG 20869, FSB Archive Moscow.

89. Jules Schelvis, *Sobibor: A History of a Nazi Death Camp* (New York: Berg, 2007), 163; and Arad, *Belzec, Sobibor, Treblinka*, 327.

90. Di Giusto and Chiussi, *Globocnik's Men in Italy*, 225, n. 34.

91. Dr. Peter Black, correspondence with the author.

92. Ibid.

93. Ibid.; and Loch TPF, RG 20869, FSB Archive Moscow.

94. Black, "Foot Soldiers of the Final Solution," 84, n. 222; Report of SSPF Galicia District to HSSPF Krakow, October 15, 1943; and Malov TPF, RG 20869, FSB Archive Moscow.

95. Black, "Foot Soldiers of the Final Solution," 23, and 77, n. 181; Police Department Piotrkow to the Commander of Orpo Radom District, November 28, 1942; and Mandrikow TPF, RG 20869, FSB Archive Moscow.

96. Dr. Peter Black, correspondence with the author.

97. Mogilo TPF, RG 20869, FSB Archive Moscow.

98. Di Giusto and Chiussi, *Globocnik's Men in Italy*, 225, n. 34; and Nahorniak *Dienstausweis*, Nogornyak Trial, Case #5647, Archive #2656, SBU Archive Stanislavov/Ivano-Frankivsk.

99. Odartschenko TPF, RG 20869, FSB Archive Moscow.

100. Dr. Peter Black, correspondence with the author.

101. Black, "Police Auxiliaries for Operation Reinhard," 364, n. 95; and Petriuk TPF, RG 20869, FSB Archive Moscow.

102. Pidlentenschuk TPF, RG 20869, FSB Archive Moscow.

103. O'Neal, "Sources of Manpower," in *Belzec: Stepping Stone to Genocide*, and Rige TPF, RG 20869, FSB Archive Moscow.

104. Di Giusto and Chiussi, *Globocnik's Men in Italy*, 203.

105. Rubanov TPF, RG 20869, FSB Archive Moscow.

106. Saitow TPF, RG 20869, FSB Archive Moscow.

107. Dr. Peter Black, correspondence with the author; and Saplawny TPF, RG 20869, FSB Archive Moscow.

108. Di Giusto and Chiussi, *Globocnik's Men in Italy*, 225, n. 34.

109. Scheftschuk TPF, FSB Archive Moscow.

110. Di Giusto and Chiussi, *Globocnik's Men in Italy*, 225, n. 34.

111. Sokur TPF, FSB Archive Moscow.

112. Stark TPF, FSB Archive Moscow.

113. Tomasczuk TPF, FSB Archive Moscow.

114. Black, "Foot Soldiers of the Final Solution," 37; and Uchatsch TPF, FSB Archive Moscow.

115. Black, "Police Auxiliaries for Operation Reinhard," 364.

116. O'Neal, "Sources of Manpower," in *Belzec: Stepping Stone to Genocide*, n. 65 (Robin O'Neal told the author that this information was given to him by the Operation Reinhard historian Michael Tregenza, who lives in Lublin); and statement of Maria Warzocha, 1965, IPN Archive Lublin, IPN Lu-08/298.

Chapter 3

1. Dr. Peter Black, correspondence with the author.

2. Black, "Police Auxiliaries for Operation Reinhard," 359.

3. Sergej Kudryashov, "Ordinary Collaborators: The Case of the Trawniki Guards," in *Russia: War, Peace, and Diplomacy*, ed. Ljubica Erickson and Mark Erickson (London: Orion, 2005), 233.

4. Black, "Foot Soldiers of the Final Solution," 56–57, n. 58.

5. Ibid., 36, and 91, n. 270.

6. Email from Dr. Peter Black to the author, October 17, 2010.

7. Ibid.

8. Ibid., October 25, 2010.

9. Alexander Statiev, *The Soviet Counterinsurgency in the Western Borderlands* (Cambridge, UK: Cambridge University Press, 2010), 197.

10. Ibid.

11. Ibid., 198; see Yanushko, head of 1st Department, Kalinin Partisan HQ, RGASPI.

12. Statiev, *The Soviet Counterinsurgency in the Western Borderlands*, 198.

13. Kuwalek, *Das Vernichtungslager Belzec*, 120; statement of Kiril Prochorenko, Oberhauser Trial, Munich, 1965, p. 153; and statement of Anastasij Mawrodij, Oberhauser Trial, 1965, p. 168. (*Author's note*: All statements made by former Trawniki guards that were admitted into evidence during the Oberhauser Trial in Munich in 1965 had previously been given in the Zuev Trial in Dnepropetrovsk around the same time period. Those statements were simply forwarded to Munich for the Oberhauser Trial.)

14. Kuwalek, *Das Vernichtungslager Belzec*, 120; and Interrogation of Taras Olejnik, Oberhauser Trial, July 28, 1966, p. 238.

15. Pohl, "Die Trawniki-Männer im Vernichtungslager Belzec," 286, n. 29; Interrogation of Werner Dubois, September 16–18, 1961, Oberhauser Trial, vol. 6, p. 1,042; Interrogation Vasili Gulyj, July 7, 1965; and Interrogation of P. Lukjanchuk, undated, Zuev Trial, vol. 3, pp. 12–18, 105. Apparently, some guards were also arrested: KGB Archive Khmelnitsky, N. Martyniuk. Former *SS-Oberscharführer* Werner Dubois stated that the Trawniki guards had attempted to convince the Jewish prisoners in the camp to revolt. The Jewish prisoners then betrayed the guards, leading to their execution. According to Dubois's statement, other Trawniki guards carried out the execution. Cf. Janusz Peter, *W Belzcu podczas okupacji* (Tomaszów Lubelski, Poland: Tomaszowskie Towarzystwo Regionalne, 1991), 191.

16. Zuev Proceedings, Case #44, Archive #32132, vol. 6, pp. 62–71: In a document titled "Memo re: RG 20869 and RG K-779," the KGB in the mid-1960s made notations about the following Trawniki guards at Belzec:
July 8, 1942: Shot during mutiny, S. Popravka and M. Gorbachev.
November 18, 1942: Shot in flight, I. Maximenko (#454).
December 12, 1942: Shot in flight, G. Kuchichidze (#769).
January 16, 1943: Shot during mutiny, N. Tsukanov (#1126).
March 3, 1943: Shot in attempted flight, V. Kutikhin (#1260).
April 10, 1943: Shot during mutiny, Sivochenko, Puzanov, Kudryavtsev, P. Ivanov, I. Bondar, G. Ezhov.
May 16, 1943: Shot, Markusenko.

17. Mikhail Korshikow Trawniki Personnel File (TPF), Record Group (RG) 20869, FSB Archive Moscow 18; Pohl, "Die Trawniki-Männer," 287; Interrogation of Kiril Prochorenko, 1965, Oberhauser Trial, pp. 150–61; Mikhail Korshikow TPF, RG 20869, FSB Archive Moscow; and Ivan Baskakov TPF, FSB Archive Yaroslavl.

19. Kuwalek, *Das Vernichtungslager Belzec*, 122, n. 35; and interview with Marian Surowiec, 2004 (*Author's note*: although this doesn't explain why the other guards went with him).

20. Statement of Krystyna Natyna, Belzec, IPN Archive Lublin 08/298, 1966.

21. Statement of Maria Warzocha, Belzec, IPN Archive Lublin 08/298, 1966.

22. Statement of Josef Lewko, Belzec, IPN Archive Lublin 08/298, undated.

23. Statement of Mieczyslaw Kudyba, Belzec, IPN Archive Lublin 08/298, 1966.

24. Statement of Maria Misiewicz, Belzec, IPN Archive Lublin 08/298, 1966, 1965.

25. Kuwalek, *Das Vernichtungslager Belzec*, 225, nn. 36 and 37; and IPN Archive Lublin, 08/298, trial records regarding the criminal activities of SS personnel in Lublin District, 1965–1966, vol. 1, statement of Maria Misiewicz, January 28, 1965. Misiewicz is the only witness who said that Jews escaped with Woloshin and the other guards who deserted in March 1943. With regard to prisoner escapes, Pola Hirszman, wife of Belzec prisoner-escapee Chaim Hirszman, stated to have heard from her husband that an attempt had been made to organize resistance in the camp. The entire prisoner population of the camp planned to flee during a revolt; however, the plot was betrayed and the attempt failed. AiiH, Reports and Testimony of survivors, 301/1476, Report of Chaim Hirszman, p. 7. Pola Hirszman did not state additional details of the alleged escape or make remarks regarding who might have betrayed the planned escape.

26. Interrogation of Mikhail Korshikow, Sverdlovsk/Yekaterinburg Region, April 9,1947, Trial of Korshikow, FSB Archive Moscow.

27. Interrogation of Mikhail Korshikow, Krasnodar Region, September 9, 1964, Trial of Matwijenko et al., FSB Archive Krasnodar.

28. Interrogation of Piotr Browzew, Leningrad, August 1975, Trial of Streibel et al.

29. Kuwalek, *Das Vernichtungslager Belzec*, 122–23, n. 37; see Trial of Matwijenko et al., Krasnodar, 1964; statement of Piotr Brovzev, Oberhauser Trial, 1966, p. 68; and statement of Grigorij Nesmejan, Oberhauser Trial, September 28, 1965, p. 119. Nesmejan himself did not desert Belzec but did desert the post he had after Belzec-Tarnawatka, which was near Belzec.

30. Roster of Trawniki Guards sent to Belzec, March 27, 1943, RG K-779, FSB Archive Moscow.

31. Dr. Dieter Pohl, correspondence with author; Zuev Trial, FSB Archive Krasnodar, 1965; Eugen Binder TPF, RG 20869, FSB Archive Moscow; Grigorij Jeschow/Yezhov TPF, RG 20869, FSB Archive Moscow; Black, "Foot Soldiers of the Final Solution," 90, n. 263; and Interrogation of Boris Babin, January 8, 1965, Matwijenko Proceedings, vol. 13, pp. 83–94.

32. Pohl, "Die Trawniki-Männer," 287, n. 33; Interrogation of Dimitri Pundik, Oberhauser Trial, September 22, 1965, pp. 44–56 (Pundik spoke of as many as sixteen or seventeen guards being shot); statement of Mieczyslaw Kudyba, October 14, 1945, Polish War Crimes Commission of the Zamosc District Court, IPN Lublin, File #Ds. 1604/45; statement of Robert Juhrs, Oberhauser Trial, File #AR-Z 252/59, January 7, 1963; and Summary of Trawniki personnel files in the FSB Archive Moscow, Zuev Trial, vol. 6, pp. 62–71, which includes the personnel files for Eugen Binder and many other Trawniki guards shot in Belzec up until the time that the camp closed down completely in July 1943.

33. Roster of Trawniki Guards sent to Belzec, April 12, 1943, RG K-779, FSB Archive Moscow.

34. Arad, *Belzec, Sobibor, Treblinka*, 266; Angelika Benz, *Handlanger der SS: Die Rolle der Trawniki-Männer im Holocaust* (Berlin: Metropol Verlag, 2015), 243, nn. 144–146; statement of Chaim Engel, Sobibor Proceedings, Bundes Archive B 162/4429, Bl. 885ff; Report from Police Chief in Chelm, Tischer, to Police Chief in Lublin, July 1, 1943, Archive ZIH-Warsaw, Sobibor files, AMSW, Police Lublin, vol. 77, p. 58; Tomasz Blatt, *Sobibor*, 58, 87; and statement of Karl Frenzel, in Schelvis, *Sobibor: A History of a Nazi Death Camp*, 94.

35. Schelvis, *Sobibor: A History of a Nazi Death Camp*, 136–37; Bem, *Sobibor Extermination Camp*, 256 nn. 34 and 35; and letter of January 7, 1943 from the gendarmerie in Chelm to the commander of the police in Lublin, file ref. No. 804/23, NIOD Archive.

36. Bem, *Sobibor Extermination Camp*, 256, n. 36; and statement of Hersz Cukierman, ZIH Archive, File Ref. #301/14, Sept. 17, 1944.

37. Solonina TPF; Solonina Trial, SBU Archive Kiev.

38. Demida TPF, RG 20869, FSB Archive Moscow.

39. Report of SS-Sonderkommando Sobibor to SSPF Lublin District / Einsatz Reinhard / Inspector of SS-Sonderkommandos, July 1, 1943, signed Niemann, 16/312 "e"/409, p. 42, RG K-779, FSB Archive Moscow.

40. Bem, *Sobibor Extermination Camp*, 76, nn. 68, 77, 132 and 133; and Zachar Poplawski's memo to an official of the Communist Party of Belorussia, Brest Region, re: Report of Ivan Karakach on the Sobibor Death Camp, October 7, 1943 (copy in Marek Bem's private collection).

41. Ivschenko TPF; Ivchenko Trial, SBU Archive Kharkov.

42. Bem, *Sobibor Extermination Camp*, 253 and 255.

43. Ibid., 250–51, and 258: In an instance that may or may not have been related to this, one night a group of partisans had approached the camp area. The Germans raised the alarm as a result. All camp prisoners were herded out of their barracks to the roll-call yard to be counted. It is likely that this event was connected to an operation carried out on the orders of the AK commander of the Wlodawa District, Romuald Kompf. On a night in August 1943, a four-man AK squad broke into an office near the Sobibor camp, where they destroyed documents and set the building on fire. In his memoirs, Kompf stated that his unit was making plans to launch an attack and liquidate the Sobibor camp; however, it was canceled due to the camp uprising in October 1943. See *Pamięci poległym oddziału AK "Nadbużanka"* ("The AK 'Nadbuzanka' mobile unit") by Stanisław Pasikowski (Łódź, Poland, 2003), 70–71. The building the partisans destroyed was probably a private German construction company facility that was building the Sobibor-Wytyczno section of the railway line. The building was approximately 700 meters south of the Sobibor camp, along the railway tracks. The railway section the company was constructing was to connect the main railway line with a planned potato-processing plant in Wytyczno.

44. Bem, *Sobibor Extermination Camp*, 258–60, n. 42; Romuald Kompf, "The Uprising in the Bug River Region: The Memoirs of Major Romuald Kompf, Former Commander, 3rd Battalion, AK 7th Infantry Regiment, during the German Occupation of Poland," *Notebooks of the Museum of the Leczynsko-Wlodawa Lake District* 15 (2008): 27–54.

45. Bem, *Sobibor Extermination Camp*, 252–53.

46. Ibid., 253.

47. Dr. Peter Black, correspondence with author.

48. Arad, *Belzec, Sobibor, Treblinka*; statement of Leon Feldhendler's wife, Yad Vashem Archive; statement of Tomasz Blatt; and Adam Rutkowski, *B.Z.I.H. (Biuletyn Zydowskiego Instytutu Historycznego)*.

49. Arad, *Belzec, Sobibor, Treblinka*, 300 and 422, n. 3, statement of Ada Lichtman.

50. Bem, *Sobibor Extermination Camp*, 268.

51. Arad, *Belzec, Sobibor, Treblinka*, 312.

52. Bem, *Sobibor Extermination Camp*, 281.

53. Report on the Interrogation of Jakob Sporrenberg, February 25, 1946, Main Commission for the Investigation of Crimes against the Polish Nation, IPN Warsaw, Lublin Court of Appeals, file no. 193, pp. 109–30. (*Author's note:* The reliability of this statement is questionable, since most of the guards appeared to have remained loyal to the Germans during the uprising.)

54. www.sobibor.net/dragnet.html; the author has found no supporting documentary evidence other than this report to confirm this information.

55. Shur TPF, Central State Archive Kiev; Archive of the USHMM; and Dr. Peter Black, correspondence with author.

56. Piotrowski, *Poland's Holocaust*, 102 and 332, n. 141; *Powstanie w Ghetcie Warszawskim 1943 roku: Zbior dokumentow*, Warszawa, 1945; Marek Chodakiewicz and Piotr Gontarczyk, eds., *Tajne oblicze GL-AL i PPR*, vol. 1 (Warsaw: Burchard Edition, 1997).

57. Dr. Peter Black, correspondence with author; Black, "Foot Soldiers of the Final Solution," 73, n. 159; and Interrogation of Josef Loch, October 23, 1943, Loch TPF, RG 20869, FSB Archive Moscow. See *Trial of Kurt Bolender et al.*, Bundesarchive-ZSt, 208 AR-Z 251/59, vol. 3, p. 466.

58. Schelvis, *Sobibor: A History of a Nazi Death Camp*, 181 and 195, n. 32; and Report to the Commander of the Order Police in Krakow, October 24, 1943, *APL: Komendantura Placu w Lublinie-18-105*.

59. Loch TPF, RG 20869, FSB Archive Moscow.

60. Rich, "Reinhard and Operation 1005?," 17, n. 40. On the killing of SS-Unterscharführer Floss, see Interrogation of Zugwachmann Joseph Loch, October 23, 1943, J. Loch TPF #168, FSB Archive Moscow, File 20869, vol. 13, pp. 123–48; and Report of SS Court Officer / SS Garrison Administration Lublin, November 2, 1943, FSB Archive Moscow, File 20869, vol. 23, p. 539, which lists the three Trawniki guards who deserted from the train following the shooting of Floss-Vasili Hetmenets, Grigorij Derevyanko, and Ivan Shevchenko. The incident is also described in Leszek Siemion, *Lubelszczyzna w latach okupacji hitlerowskiej* (Lublin, Poland: Wydawnictwo Lubelskie, 1977), 187. Benz, *Handlanger der SS*, 243, n. 143; statement of Franz Rum, an *SS-Scharführer* in Treblinka and Sobibor, Sobibor Proceedings, Bundes Archive B, 162/4429, Bl. 921; and statement of Josef Oberhauser, July 18, 1961, State Archive Munich, Oberhauser Proceedings, Staanw. 33033/4, Bl. 1488ff.

61. Black, "Foot Soldiers of the Final Solution," 99, n. 318; and Interrogation of Ivan Tkachuk, 1950.

62. Interrogation of Ivan Tkachuk, March 25, 1965, FSB Archive Krasnodar, Matvijenko Trial.

63. Black, "Foot Soldiers of the Final Solution," 34 and 89, n. 257; and Report from SS-Zugwachmann Oswald Strebel, Obermaydan Estate to Commander of Treblinka I, Theodor van Eupen, February 4, 1944, RG K-779, FSB Archive Moscow.

64. Auschwitz concentration camp, WVHA/D, July 5, 1943, Zuev Trial, vol. 6, pp. 37–38.

65. Dr. Peter Black, correspondence with author.

66. Black, "Foot Soldiers of the Final Solution,"35.

67. Rich, "The Third Reich Enlists the New Soviet Man," 278.

68. Ibid., 278–79.

69. Franciszek Piper, ed., *Auschwitz, 1940–1945*, vol. 3 (Oświęcim, Poland: Auschwitz-Birkenau State Museum, 2000), 133, n. 420. At least two of the killed men were Philip Wergun and Alexander Chrushchev; a notation stating that they were shot while fleeing Auschwitz was put in their Trawniki personnel files. See Philip Wergun TPF and Alexander Chrushchev TPF, both from RG 20869, FSB Archive Moscow.

70. See Kon Piekarski, *Escape Hell: The Story of a Polish Underground Officer in Auschwitz and Buchenwald* (Toronto: Dundurn, 1996), Report of Kon Piekarski to AK HQ, July 10, 1943; and Report of the Polish Underground, undated?

71. Rich, "The Third Reich Enlists the New Soviet Man," 279.

72. Ibid., 278–79, n. 23; and Gordijenko Trial, Archive file #66437, SBU Archive Kiev.

73. Rich, "The Third Reich Enlists the New Soviet Man," 279, n. 24; Interrogation of Ivan Kozlovskij, September 29, 1964, Matwijenko Trial, Krasnodar; and Interrogation of Fedor Gorun, May 11, 1951, Criminal Case #6035, Archive file #4277, Gorun Trial, SBU Archive Kiev.

74. Memo from Lublin POW Camp Detachment to Trawniki training camp, November 28, 1942, RG K-779, FSB Archive Moscow.

75. Interrogation of Fedor Tartynskij, SBU Archive Stalino/Donetsk, 1948.

76. Report of the Commander of the SS-Totenkopf battalion, Lublin POW Camp, signed Langleist, to the Commandant's Staff, Lublin POW Camp, January 24, 1943, file I. f. 5, "SS-Totenkopf Battalion Correspondence, Lists of SS Men, 1941–1944," p. 37, Archive of the Majdanek Museum.

77. Report from the commander of the SS-Totenkopf battalion, Lublin POW Camp of the Waffen-SS, initialed Langleist, to the Commandant's HQ, POW Camp of the Waffen-SS, January 24, 1943, Central State Archive, Vilnius, Lithuania.

78. Dr. Peter Black, correspondence with the author; and Koslow TPF, Timin TPF, and Stoilow TPF, all in RG 20869, FSB Archive Moscow.

79. Roster for Warsaw concentration camp, March 1944, RG K-779, FSB Archive Moscow.

80. Trawniki training camp, signed Franz, to SS and Police Court VI in Krakow, October 1, 1943, FSB Archive Moscow, RG K-779, fond 16, opis 312 "e," delo 409, folio 120.

81. Interrogation of Ignat Danilchenko, SBU Archive Dnepropetrovsk, 1949.

82. Tymczuk TPF, RG 20869, FSB Archive Moscow; and Report of Desertion of SS-Wachmann Eugen Tymczuk, SS-WVHA, Trawniki Training Camp, signed Streibel, December 9, 1943, FSB Archive Moscow.

83. Tschaplinski TPF, Central State Archive Kiev; and Archive of the USHMM.

84. Dr. Peter Black, correspondence with author.

85. Interrogation of Andrej Kuchma, SBU Archive Kiev, February 8, 1950.

86. Dr. Peter Black, correspondence with author.

87. Rich, "The Third Reich Enlists the New Soviet Man," 282, n. 32; and Interrogation of Josef Masyuk, Criminal Case #4501, Archive file #891, SBU Archive Ivano-Frankivsk/Stanislavov, August 20, 1947.

88. Testimony of Rudolf Reiss, Hamburg, 1988, Demjanjuk Trial in Jerusalem.

89. Interrogation of Nikolaj Chernyshev, SBU Archive Stalino/Donetsk, 1948.

90. Interrogation of Andrej Vasilega, SBU Archive Stalino/Donetsk, July 12, 1948.

91. Bojczuk TPF, Central State Archive Kiev.

92. Black, "Foot Soldiers of the Final Solution," 88, n. 249; and Hul TPF, Central State Archive Kiev.

93. Djomin TPF, RG 20869, FSB Archive Moscow.

94. Schpak TPF, Central State Archive Kiev; and Archive of the USHMM.

95. Bachulski TPF, Central State Archive Kiev.

96. Tolotschko TPF, Central State Archive Kiev.

97. Zezulka TPF, Central State Archive Kiev.

98. Interrogation of Ivan Knysch, Trial of Ivan Knysch, SBU Archive Stalino/Donetsk, 1948.

99. Saniuk TPF, Central State Archive Kiev; Archive of the USHMM.

100. www.deathcamps.org/reinhard/maytchenko.html; Archive of the Majdanek State Museum; Documents of the Regional Commission for the Investigation of Nazi Crimes, Warsaw; and Investigation of the Trawniki camp, 1966–1967.

101. Interrogation of Ivan Grigorchuk, Kolomiya, 1947.

102. Interrogation of Mikhail Moskalik, SBU Archive Stanislavov/Ivano-Frankivsk region, 1949.

103. Interrogation of Hermann Reese, Proceedings against Streibel, Hamburg, 1962.

104. Interrogation of Hermann Reese, Proceedings against Streibel, Hamburg, 1962.

105. Interrogation of Mikhail Laptev, Matwijenko Trial, February 27, 1965, FSB Archive Krasnodar.

106. Interrogation of Ivan Lukanyuk, SBU Archive Stanislavov/Ivano-Frankivsk, 1948.

107. Black, "Foot Soldiers of the Final Solution," 80, n. 202; and Trawniki Training Camp, signed Streibel, to commander of Sipo Lublin, March 2, 1943, FSB Archive Moscow, RG K-779, 16/312 "e"/410, pp. 65–69.

108. Interrogation of Petro Kuschnir, SBU Archive Stanislavov/Ivano-Frankivsk, 1946.

109. Interrogation of Vladimir Terletskij, SBU Archive Stanislavov/Ivano-Frankivsk, 1948.

110. Trial Proceedings of Vladimir Terletskij, SBU Archive Stanislavov/Ivano-Frankivsk, June 29, 1948.

111. Interrogation of Wasyl Shyndykevskj, SBU Archive Stanislavov/Ivano-Frankivsk, 1949.

112. Investigation of Kostinow, Keliwnik, and Prigoditsch, RG 20869, vol. 24, pp. 231–39, 245–51, 258–63, 269–86, FSB Archive Moscow; Kostinow TPF, RG 20869, FSB Archive Moscow; and Yevgenij Prigoditsch TPF, RG 20869, FSB Archive Moscow.

113. Black, "Foot Soldiers of the Final Solution," 35 and 90, n. 266; and SS and Police Commander Krakow / Plaszow Labor Camp report to Commander of Security Police Krakow, August 31, 1943, RG K-779, FSB Archive Moscow, 16/312, "e"/410, p. 7.

114. Shmuel Krukowski, *The War of the Doomed: Jewish Armed Resistance in Poland, 1942–1944* (New York: Holmes and Meier, 1984), 250.

115. Interrogation of Mikhail Laptev, Matwijenko Trial, February 27, 1965, FSB Archive Krasnodar.

116. Dr. Peter Black, correspondence with the author.

117. Ibid.

118. Interrogation of Vladimir Emelyanov, September 23, 1947, Iskaradov Trial, SBU Archive Stalino/Donetsk.

119. Examination of Archive File (Record Group) K-779, signed Lieutenant Boechko, July 8, 1966, Prikhodko Trial, Case #113, Archive #56911, vol. 21, pp. 42–47, SBU Archive Lvov.

120. Report from SSPF Galicia to SS Training Camp Trawniki, August 9, 1943, RG K-779, fund 16, opis 312 "e," delo 409, p. 29, FSB Archive Moscow.

121. Interrogation of Andrej Sergienko, 1948, Knysh Trial, Case #5336, Archive file #37099, pp. 184–90, SBU Archive Stalino/Donetsk; Interrogation of Nikolaj Skorokhod, 1968, Litvinenko Trial, Case #158, Archive file # 57252, vol. 7, pp. 119–22, SBU Archive Lvov; and Interrogation of Nikolaj Sherstnev-Butenko, 1965, Pankratov and Zhukov Trial, Case #113, Archive file #56911, vol. 8, pp. 114–17, SBU Archive Lvov.

122. Dr. Peter Black, correspondence with the author.

123. Ibid.

124. Gordejew TPF, Gordejew Proceedings, FSB Archive Kalinin/Tver.

125. Black, "Foot Soldiers of the Final Solution," 34 and 89, n. 255; and Interrogation of Nikolaj Skorokhod, Trial of Nikolaj Skorokhod, 1947.

126. Dr. Peter Black, correspondence with the author.

127. Ibid.

128. Ibid.; and Bukowjan TPF, RG 20869, FSB Archive Moscow.

129. Dr. Peter Black, correspondence with the author; and Interrogation of Andrej Sergienko, Trial of Ivan Knysch, 1948, SBU Archive Stalino/Donetsk.

130. Rjaboschapka TPF, RG 20869, FSB Archive Moscow.

131. Chapayev TPF, RG 20869, FSB Archive Moscow; Filipow TPF, RG 20869, FSB Archive Moscow; and Safronow TPF, RG 20869, FSB Archive Moscow.

132. Interrogation of Vladas Amanaviczius, Flanders, June 26, 1971, Swidersky Proceedings, file 8 Ks 4/70, Dusseldorf District Court.

133. Interrogation of Fedor Vilshun, Moscow, September 12, 1971, FSB Archive Moscow.

134. Black, "Foot Soldiers of the Final Solution," 85, n. 226.

135. Kuwalek, *Das Vernichtungslager Belzec*, 122–23, n. 37.

136. Dr. Peter Black, correspondence with the author.

137. Memo from SS-Hauptsturmführer Michalsen to Trawniki Training Camp, May 3, 1943, RG K-779, FSB Archive Moscow; Black, "Foot Soldiers of the Final Solution," 90, n. 264; and Report of Trawniki Training Camp to the Commander of the Sipo Lublin, May 6, 1943, RG K-779, FSB Archive Moscow.

138. Black, "Foot Soldiers of the Final Solution," 90, n. 264; special thanks to Dr. Peter Black for pointing out the ethnic diversity of this particular group of deserters.

139. Dr. David Rich, correspondence with the author on January 16, 2018; and memo from Lublin Detachment to SS Training Camp Trawniki, June 5, 1943, RG K-779, fund 16, opis 312 "e," delo 411, p. 61, FSB Archive Moscow.

140. Pilipiuk TPF, RG 20869, FSB Archive Moscow.

141. Jurtschenko TPF, RG 20869, FSB Archive Moscow.

142. Black, "Foot Soldiers of the Final Solution," 91, n. 271; SS and Police Court Lublin, Judgment in the Proceedings against Wachmann Vladimir Bruchaki, May 4, 1944; and Bruchaki TPF, Central State Archive Kiev.

143. Personnel Status Report from the Lublin Detachment, signed Basener, to Trawniki Training Camp, signed for by Majowski, April 6, 1944, RG K-779, FSB Archive Moscow.

144. Ibid., 33; and Interrogation of Vladimir Pronin, Trial of Pronin, 1947, SBU Archive Zaporozhe.

145. Tscherkasow TPF, RG 20869, FSB Archive Moscow.

146. Ciuki TPF, Central State Archive, Kiev; Archive of the USHMM.

147. Jankowsky TPF, RG 20869, FSB Archive Moscow.

148. Choruk TPF, Central State Archive Kiev; and Archive of the USHMM.

149. Szczerbacz TPF, Central State Archive Kiev.

150. Schewtschuk TPF, Central State Archive Kiev.

151. Tschup TPF, Central State Archive Kiev.

152. Interrogation of Fedor Vyshivanyuk, SBU Archive Stanislavov/Ivano-Frankivsk, 1946.

153. Interrogation of Petr Koval, SBU Archive Zaporozhe, February 8, 1949, Koval Trial.

154. Black, "Foot Soldiers of the Final Solution," 33; and Garin TPF, RG K-779, FSB Archive Moscow.

155. Interrogation of Nikolai Shalayev, 1950, Shalayev Proceedings, Voronezh.

156. Ibid.

157. Bem, *Sobibor Extermination Camp*, 97–98, n. 81; Arad, *Belzec, Sobibor, Treblinka*, 76 and 410, n. 3; and statement of former *SS-Oberscharführer* Kurt Bolender, Criminal Police Court, Munich, June 5, 1962, Oberhauser Proceedings, vol. 7, pp. 1,320–21.

158. Dr. Peter Black, correspondence with the author.

159. Di Giusto and Chiussi, *Globocnik's Men in Italy*, 117.

160. Interrogation of Vasili Bronov, Blagoveshchensk, Amur region, October 11, 1950, Bronov Trial, FSB Archive Omsk.

161. Interrogation of Nikolaj Akhtimijchuk, September 20, 1948, FSB Archive Krasnoyarsk.

162. Interrogation of Vasili Litvinenko, Litvinenko Trial, January 19, 1968, SBU Archive Lvov.

Chapter 4

1. For statements to this effect, see Testimony of Rudolf Reiss, June 1973, Trial of Streibel et al.; Testimony of Heinrich Schaefer, June 1973, Trial of Streibel et al.; Interrogation of Nikolaj Malagon, Zaporozhe, 1978; and Interrogation of Semen Kharkovskij, Kharkov, December 1980. It is the opinion of this author that this is evident in several of the photographs on the Trawniki *Personalbogens*. Some of the recruits must have been photographed for their personnel files before they were even issued their new uniforms, since some of them can clearly be seen wearing what appear to be their Red Army overcoats in the photos.

2. Bem, *Sobibor Extermination Camp*, 253; statement of Irena Sujko, speaking of the guard Volodia Kaszewadzki in Sobibor; and statement of Eugen Turovsky, speaking of the guard Fedor Federenko in Treblinka II.

3. Testimony of Josef Czarny, Demjanjuk Trial, Jerusalem, 1987.

4. Testimony of Chil Rajchman, Demjanjuk Trial, Jerusalem, 1987.

5. Interrogation of Ivan Knysch, Stalino/Donetsk, 1948; Interrogation of Fedor Vilshun, Moscow, 1971; and Testimony of Gustav Boraks, Demjanjuk Trial, Jerusalem, 1987.

6. Statement of Stanislaw Smajzner, at Sobibor.

7. Interrogation of Nikolaj Chernyshev, SBU Archive Stalino/Donetsk, 1948.

8. Interrogation of Ivan Chornobaj, SBU Archive Lvov, April 1949; Interrogation of Piotr Browzew, Leningrad,

August 1975, Streibel Trial; Interrogation of Jakob Engelhardt, August 1975, Streibel Trial; and Interrogation of Semen Kharkovskij, Kharkov, December 1980, Kairys Proceedings.

9. Testimony of Abram Thiessen, Hoffmann Trial, 1971.

10. Circular to all deployed detachments of Trawniki Training Camp, signed Streibel, October 19, 1942, IPN Warsaw, Central Archive 156, KdG Lublin, sygn. 77, pp. 82–83.

11. Order, signed Globocnik, May 10, 1943, IPN Warsaw, RG 891 (SSPF Lublin), sygn. 5, fols. 149–50.

12. Testimony of Karl Streibel, Hamburg, January 1973, Trial of Streibel et al.

13. Testimony of Heinrich Schaefer, June 1973, Trial of Streibel et al.

14. Some Jews even referred to the Trawniki guards in this color uniform as *karalochies*—cockroaches. See Schelvis, *Sobibor: A History of a Nazi Death Camp*, 34.

15. For examples of testimony on the wearing of the black uniform, see Interrogations of: Filip Babenko, Kiev, 1948, Babenko Trial; Ivan Shvidkij, Stalino/Donetsk, 1952, Shvidkij Trial; Mikhail Laptev, Krasnodar, 1965, Matwijenko Trial; Alexander Fedchenko, Lvov, 1968, Litvinenko Trial; Yakov Savenko, Simferopol, 1978; Nikolaj Malagon, Zaporozhe, 1978; and Ignat Danilchenko, Tyumen, 1979, Demjanjuk Investigation. For examples of documentary evidence on the wearing of the black uniform, see "Report of Desertion" on the following persons—Petro Kuschnir, August 1943; Vasili Djomin, September 1943; Vladimir Terletskij, October 1943; and Wolodymyr Shur, November 1943, from RG K-779, FSB Archive Moscow and Central State Archive Kiev.

16. Testimony of Rudolf Reiss, Trial of Streibel et al., June 1973. For examples of documentary evidence on the wearing of the earth-brown uniform, see "Report of Desertion" on the following persons: Wasyl Shyndykevskij, January 1944; Ivan Tolotschko, February 1944; Boris Safronow, April 1944; Ivan Chapayev, April 1944; Ivan Filipow, April 1944; and Vasilij Rjaboschapka, March or May 1944.

17. For examples of documentary evidence on the wearing of this uniform, see "Reports of Desertion" on the following persons: Ivan Sczerbacz, March 1944; Ivan Knysch, June 1944; Ivan Saniuk, June 1944; and Eugen Tymchuk, July 1944.

18. For examples of guards who had the black uniform but also an earth-gray overcoat, see "Reports of Desertion" on the following persons: Mychajlo Pankiv, October 1943; Jaroslau Lohyn, October 1943; Jaroslau Kosak, November 1943; Stanislau Swidrak, November 1943; and Wolodymyr Stryhun, March 1944.

19. For an example of documentary evidence of this, see "Report of Desertion" of O. Fedorowicz, 1944; for an example of a former guard who didn't state the color of the entire uniform but did state that the overcoat was gray, see Testimony of Georgij Skydan, Baranovichi, Skydan Trial, May 1950.

20. Interrogation of Heinrich Schaefer, June 1973, Trial of Streibel et al.

21. Di Giusto and Chiussi, *Globocnik's Men in Italy*, 158, n. 12.

22. Ibid., 233, n. 12; and *Urteil der 1. Strafkammer des Landgerichts Munchen II als Schwurgericht in der Strafsache gegen Demjanjuk Iwan Nikolai*, Lfd. #924 LG Munchen II, May 12, 2011, JuNSV Bd. XLIX, p. 237.

23. Di Giusto and Chiussi, *Globocnik's Men in Italy*, 233, n. 12.

24. Ibid., 160; and Deposition of Oberhauser, June 12, 1973, HHSta, Wiesbaden, Abt. 461, #36346/12, p. 234, n. 15.

25. Di Giusto and Chiussi, *Globocnik's Men in Italy*, 160.

26. Ibid.

27. Ibid., 234, n. 17.

28. Ibid., 160.

29. Ibid., 234, n. 19.

30. Ibid., 160 and 234, n. 20.

31. Ibid., 161.

32. Ibid., 162.

33. Ibid., 168.

34. Ibid., 236, n. 32.

Appendix
Assignment Locations

1. Black, "Foot Soldiers of the Final Solution," 29, and 83, n. 214; and Commander of Orpo Lublin, "List of the SS and Police Bases in Lublin District, July 27, 1942, IPN Archive, RG KdG Lublin, Central Archive 156/275, p. 34, copy in Archive of the USHMM, RG 15.011M, reel 20. For Globocnik and Pohl collaborating on the establishment of the SS and Police Bases, see Schulte, *Zwangsarbeit*, 259–96.

Rosters

1. This is not an official roster. It was compiled by the author on the basis of various sources.

2. Letter from the deputy of the *Reichsfuhrer-SS* and chief of the German police for the establishment of SS

and police bases in the New Eastern Territories / Trawniki training camp, to the commander of the security police and SD Warsaw, April 8, 1942, Office of the Governor of Warsaw District, folder 61, p. 12, Provincial State Archive, Warsaw.

3. This is not an official roster. No known rosters for the Trawniki guards at Treblinka II are known to have survived the war. This was compiled by the author from various sources.

4. This is not an official roster. Rosters for Trawniki guards serving at Belzec prior to March 27, 1943, are not known to have survived the war. The author compiled this list from various sources.

5. This is not an official roster. No known rosters for the Trawniki guards serving at Sobibor prior to March 26, 1943, are known to have survived the war. This list was compiled by the author from various sources.

6. This is not an official roster. No known rosters for Trawniki guards serving at Janowska in 1942 are known to have survived the war. Three rosters for 1943, two in May and one in September, are known to exist; however, the author did not have access to them for this study. This list was compiled by the author from various sources.

7. Commander of Trawniki Training Camp, signed Grimm, to POW Camp Detachment Lublin, received by Heinsch, February 15, 1943, RG K-779, fund 16, inventory 312 "e," serial #410, p. 286, FSB Archive Moscow.

8. Trawniki Training Camp, signed von Heinze, to SSPF Krakow, March 18, 1943, RG K-779, fund 16, opis 312 "e," delo 411, pp. 53–54, FSB Archive Moscow.

9. Memo from SS Training Camp Trawniki to SS Concentration Camp Sobibor, March 26, 1943, Prikhodko Trial, Case #113, Archive #56911, vol. 21, pp. 64–68, SBU Archive Lvov; *US v. Demjanjuk*; Demjanjuk prosecution, Israel.

10. Commander of Trawniki Training Camp, signed Schwarzenbacher, to SS Labor Camp Belzec, March 27, 1943, RG K-779, fund 16, opis 312 "e," delo 411, pp. 280–81, FSB Archive Moscow.

11. Deployment from Trawniki Training Camp to Auschwitz concentration camp, March 29, 1943, Zuev Proceedings, Case #44, Archive #32132, vol. 3, pp. 259–66, SBU Archive Dnepropetrovsk; and RG K-779, fund 16, inventory 312 "e," serial #410, pp. 179–82, FSB Archive Moscow.

12. Memo from commander of Trawniki Training Camp, signed Schwarzenbacher, to SS-Sonderkommando Belzec, April 12, 1943, RG K-779, fund 16, opis 312 "e," delo 410, p. 242, FSB Archive Moscow.

13. SS Training Camp Trawniki, List of men detailed to the Warsaw Detachment, April 17, 1943, Zuev Proceedings, Case #44, Archive #32132, vol. 3, pp. 276–84, SBU Archive Dnepropetrovsk; and RG K-779, fund 16, opis 312 "e," delo 411, pp. 115–30, FSB Archive Moscow.

14. Commander of Lublin Detachment, signed Basener, to SS Labor Camp Sobibor, September 16, 1943, RG K-779, fund 16, opis 312 "e," delo 411, pp. 112–14, FSB Archive Moscow.

15. Roster, Treblinka Labor Camp, received by Majowski, April 6, 1944, RG K-779, fund 16, opis 312 "e," delo 410, pp. 343–45, FSB Archive Moscow.

16. This is not an official roster. It is not certain whether any rosters for the Trawniki guards assigned to the HSSPF Adriatic Coast survived the war. This list was compiled by the author from various sources.

17. SS Streibel Battalion Roster of NCOs, SS Enlistees, and *Wachmänner* reported missing since January 12, 1945, folder 114-242-7, pp. 29–30, Archive of the Ministry of Interior, Prague, Czech Republic.

SOURCES

BOOKS

Arad, Yitzchak. *Belzec, Sobibor, Treblinka: The Operation Reinhard Death Camps.* Bloomington: Indiana University Press, 1987.

Bem, Marek. *Sobibor Extermination Camp, 1942–1943.* Amsterdam: Stichting Sobibor / Sobibor Foundation, 2015.

Benz, Angelika. *Handlanger der SS: Die Rolle der Trawniki-Männer im Holocaust.* Berlin: Metropol Verlag, 2015.

Bialowitz, Philip, and Joseph Bialowitz. *A Promise at Sobibor: A Jewish Boy's Story of Revolt and Survival in Nazi-Occupied Poland.* Madison: University of Wisconsin Press, 2013.

Czech, Danuta. *Auschwitz Chronicle, 1939–1945: From The Archives of the Auschwitz Memorial and the German Federal Archives.* New York: Henry Holt, 1989.

Di Giusto, Stefano, and Tommaso Chiussi. *Globocnik's Men in Italy, 1943–1945: Abteilung R and the SS-Wachmannschaften of the Operationszone Adriatisches Kustenland.* Atglen, PA: Schiffer, 2017.

Jaczynska, Agniezska. *Sonderlaboratorium SS Zamojszczyzna: Pierwszy Obszar Osiedlenczy w Generalnym Gubernatorstwie.* Lublin, Poland: Instytut Pamieci Narodowej, 2012.

Krukowski, Shmuel. *The War of the Doomed: Jewish Armed Resistance in Poland, 1942–1944.* New York: Holmes and Meier, 1984.

Kuwalek, Robert. *Das Vernichtungslager Belzec.* Berlin: Metropol Verlag, 2013.

MacLean, French. *The Ghetto Men: The SS Destruction of the Jewish Warsaw Ghetto, April–May 1943.* Atglen, PA: Schiffer, 2001.

O'Neal, Robin. *Belzec: Stepping Stone to Genocide.* New York: JewishGen, 2008. www.jewishgen. org.

Piekarski, Kon. *Escape Hell: The Story of a Polish Underground Officer in Auschwitz and Buchenwald.* Toronto: Dundurn, 1996.

Piotrowski, Tadeusz. *Poland's Holocaust.* Jefferson, NC: McFarland, 1998.

Piper, Franciszek, ed. *Auschwitz, 1940–1945.* Vol. 3. Oświęcim, Poland: Auschwitz-Birkenau State Museum, 2000.

Schelvis, Jules. *Sobibor: A History of a Nazi Death Camp.* New York: Berg, 2007.

Sheftel, Yoram. *Defending Ivan the Terrible: The Conspiracy to Convict John Demjanjuk.* Washington DC: Regnery, 1996.

Statiev, Alexander. *The Soviet Counterinsurgency in the Western Borderlands.* Cambridge, UK: Cambridge University Press, 2010.

Webb, Chris, and Michel Chocholaty. *The Treblinka Death Camp: History, Biographies, Remembrance.* Stuttgart: Ibidem Verlag, 2014.

ARTICLES

Black, Peter R. "Foot Soldiers of the Final Solution: The Trawniki Training Camp and Operation Reinhard." *Holocaust and Genocide Studies* 25, no. 1 (Spring 2011): 1–99.

Black, Peter R. "Police Auxiliaries for Operation Reinhard: Shedding Light on the Trawniki Training Camp through Documents from behind the Iron Curtain." In *Secret Intelligence and the Holocaust.* Edited by David Bankier, 327–66. New York: Enigma Books, 2006.

Kudryashov, Sergej. "Ordinary Collaborators: The Case of the Travniki Guards." In *Russia: War, Peace, and Diplomacy.* Edited by Ljubica Erickson and Mark Erickson, 226–39. London: Orion, 2005.

Pohl, Dieter. "Die Trawniki-Männer im Vernichtungslager Belzec, 1941–1943." In *NS-Gewaltherrschaft: Beitrage zur historischen Forschung und juristischen Aufarbeitung.* Vol. 11. Edited by Alfred Gottwaldt, Norbert Kampe, and Peter Klein, 278–89. Berlin: Edition Hentrich, 2005.

Rich, David A. "'Reinhard' and Operation 1005? Corpse Disposal in Generalgouvernement Killing Centers, 1942–1944." Paper presented at the conference "Operation 1005: Nazi Attempts to Erase the Evidence of Mass Murder in Eastern and Central Europe, 1942–1944," held in 2009 at College des Bernardins Paris.

Rich, David A. "Reinhard's Footsoldiers: Soviet Trophy Documents and Investigative Records as Sources." In *Remembering for the Future: The Holocaust in an Age of Genocide.* Vol. 1, *History.* Edited by John Roth and Elizabeth Maxwell, 687–701. New York and Basingstoke, UK: Palgrave, 2001.

Rich, David A. "The Third Reich Enlists the New Soviet Man: Eastern Auxiliary Guards at Auschwitz-Birkenau in Spring 1943." *Russian History* 41, no. 2 (2014): 269–82.

Rich, David A. "The Trawniki Kommando of the Janowska Labor Camp." Paper presented at the "Against Our Will" conference, held in 2015 at the University of Jena, Germany.

Tregenza, Michael. "The 'Disappearance' of SS-Hauptscharführer Lorenz Hackenholt: A Report on the 1959–1963 West German Police Search for Lorenz Hackenholt, the Gas Chamber Expert of the Aktion Reinhard Extermination Camps." https://phdn.org/archives/holocaust-history.org/Tregenza/Tregenza00.shtml.

INTERNET

http://deathcamps.org
https://forum.axishistory.com
http://holocaustresearchproject.org
www.jewishgen.org/Yizkor/belzec
http://sobibor.net/dragnet.html

ARCHIVES

Former Soviet Union
Central State Archive, Kiev, Ukraine
Central State Archive, Vilnius, Lithuania
Federal Security Service (FSB) Central Archive, Moscow, Russian Federation

Europe
Archive of the Ministry of Interior / Central State Archive, Prague, Czech Republic
Bundesarchiv Ludwigsburg, Germany (ZStL), Central Judicial Office for the Investigation
    of Nazi Crimes
Institute of National Remembrance (IPN) Archive, Lublin, Poland
IPN Archive, Warsaw, Poland
State Archive, Munich, Germany

US
Archive of the US Holocaust Memorial Museum, Washington, DC
US Department of Justice, Criminal Division, Human Rights and Special Prosecutions Section
    (formerly known as the Office of Special Investigations, OSI), Washington, DC, courtesy
    of the Freedom of Information Act (FOIA)

INDEX